VOLUME 667

SEPTEMBER 2016

THE ANNALS

of The American Academy of Political
and Social Science

Elections in America

Special Editor:
LARRY M. BARTELS
Vanderbilt University

Los Angeles | London | New Delhi
Singapore | Washington DC | Melbourne

Origin and Purpose. The Academy was organized December 14, 1889, to promote the progress of political and social science, especially through publications and meetings. The Academy does not take sides in controverted questions, but seeks to gather and present reliable information to assist the public in forming an intelligent and accurate judgment.

Meetings. The Academy occasionally holds a meeting in the spring extending over two days.

Publications. THE ANNALS of The American Academy of Political and Social Science is the bimonthly publication of the Academy. Each issue contains articles on some prominent social or political problem, written at the invitation of the editors. These volumes constitute important reference works on the topics with which they deal, and they are extensively cited by authorities throughout the United States and abroad.

Subscriptions. THE ANNALS of The American Academy of Political and Social Science (ISSN 0002-7162) (J295) is published bimonthly—in January, March, May, July, September, and November—by SAGE Publications, 2455 Teller Road, Thousand Oaks, CA 91320. Periodicals postage paid at Thousand Oaks, California, and at additional mailing offices. POSTMASTER: Send address changes to The Annals of The American Academy of Political and Social Science, c/o SAGE Publications, 2455 Teller Road, Thousand Oaks, CA 91320. Institutions may subscribe to THE ANNALS at the annual rate: $1014 (clothbound, $1146). Individuals may subscribe to the ANNALS at the annual rate: $118 (clothbound, $175). Single issues of THE ANNALS may be obtained by individuals for $37 each (clothbound, $50). Single issues of THE ANNALS have proven to be excellent supplementary texts for classroom use. Direct inquiries regarding adoptions to THE ANNALS c/o SAGE Publications (address below).

All correspondence concerning membership in the Academy, dues renewals, inquiries about membership status, and/or purchase of single issues of THE ANNALS should be sent to THE ANNALS c/o SAGE Publications, 2455 Teller Road, Thousand Oaks, CA 91320. Telephone: (800) 818-SAGE (7243) and (805) 499-0721; Fax/Order line: (805) 375-1700; e-mail: journals@sagepub.com. *Please note that orders under $30 must be prepaid.* For all customers outside the Americas, please visit http://www.sagepub.co.uk/customerCare.nav for information.

Printed on acid-free paper

THE ANNALS

© 2016 by The American Academy of Political and Social Science

Editorial Office: 202 S. 36th Street, Philadelphia, PA 19104-3806
For information about individual and institutional subscriptions address:
SAGE Publications
2455 Teller Road
Thousand Oaks, CA 91320

For SAGE Publications: Peter Geraghty (Production) and Mimi Nguyen (Marketing)

From India and South Asia,
write to:
SAGE PUBLICATIONS INDIA Pvt Ltd
B-42 Panchsheel Enclave, P.O. Box 4109
New Delhi 110 017
INDIA

From Europe, the Middle East,
and Africa, write to:
SAGE PUBLICATIONS LTD
1 Oliver's Yard, 55 City Road
London EC1Y 1SP
UNITED KINGDOM

International Standard Serial Number ISSN 0002-7162
ISBN 978-1-5063-7375-1 (Vol. 667, 2016) paper
ISBN 978-1-5063-7374-4 (Vol. 667, 2016) cloth
Manufactured in the United States of America. First printing, September 2016

Please visit http://ann.sagepub.com and under the "More about this journal" menu on the right-hand side, click on the Abstracting/Indexing link to view a full list of databases in which this journal is indexed.

Information about membership rates, institutional subscriptions, and back issue prices may be found on the facing page.

Advertising. Current rates and specifications may be obtained by writing to The Annals Advertising and Promotion Manager at the Thousand Oaks office (address above). Acceptance of advertising in this journal in no way implies endorsement of the advertised product or service by SAGE or the journal's affiliated society(ies) or the journal editor(s). No endorsement is intended or implied. SAGE reserves the right to reject any advertising it deems as inappropriate for this journal.

Claims. Claims for undelivered copies must be made no later than six months following month of publication. The publisher will supply replacement issues when losses have been sustained in transit and when the reserve stock will permit.

Change of Address. Six weeks' advance notice must be given when notifying of change of address. Please send the old address label along with the new address to the SAGE office address above to ensure proper identification. Please specify the name of the journal.

THE ANNALS

OF THE AMERICAN ACADEMY OF POLITICAL AND SOCIAL SCIENCE

Volume 667   September 2016

IN THIS ISSUE:

2016 Daniel Patrick Moynihan Lecture

The Decline of the American Family: Can Anything Be
Done to Stop the Damage? . . . . *Ron Haskins and Isabel V. Sawhill*   8

Elections in America

Special Editor: LARRY M. BARTELS

Elections in America . . . . *Larry M. Bartels*   36

The Electoral Landscape of 2016 . . . . *John Sides, Michael Tesler,*
and Lynn Vavreck   50

The Obama Legacy and the Future of Partisan Conflict: Demographic Change
and Generational Imprinting . . . . *Gary C. Jacobson*   72

Back to the Future? What the Politics of the Late Nineteenth Century Can
Tell Us about the 2016 Election . . . . *Julia Azari and Marc J. Hetherington*   92

What The Heck Are We Doing in Ottumwa, Anyway? Presidential Candidate
Visits and Their Political Consequence . . . . *Thomas Wood*   110

Ideologically Extreme Candidates in U.S. Presidential Elections,
1948–2012 . . . . *Marty Cohen, Mary C. McGrath,*
Peter Aronow, and John Zaller   126

Failure to Converge: Presidential Candidates, Core Partisans, and the Missing
Middle in American Electoral Politics . . . . *Larry M. Bartels*   143

Ideological Factions in the Republican and Democratic
Parties . . . . *Hans Noel*   166

Rise of the *Trumpenvolk*: Populism in the 2016 Election . . . . *J. Eric Oliver and Wendy M. Rahn*   189

National Forces in State Legislative Elections . . . . *Steven Rogers*   207

Polarization, Gridlock, and Presidential Campaign Politics in 2016. . . . . *Gary C. Jacobson*   226

FORTHCOMING

Briefing to the President: Failed Middle Eastern States and Countering Violent Extremism
Special Editors: RICHARD A. CLARKE, RAND BEERS,
EMILIAN PAPADOPOULOS, and PAUL SALEM

New Data for the Social and Behavioral Sciences: Social Observatories and Data Linkages
Special Editors: SANDRA HOEFERTH and EMILIO MORAN

2016 Daniel Patrick Moynihan Lecture

Keywords: Moynihan; family; marriage; nonmarital births; race; child development; poverty

The Decline of the American Family: Can Anything Be Done to Stop the Damage?

By
RON HASKINS
and
ISABEL V. SAWHILL

We have spent many years studying what has been happening to the American family. Haskins first addressed the issue when he was with the House Ways and Means Committee, which has jurisdiction over several social programs, especially the programs for adoption and foster care and the Aid to Families with Dependent Children program, which required knowledge of research on family well-being. He began writing about family issues shortly after he joined the Brookings Institution in 2001 (Haskins and Sawhill 2003). Sawhill's first book, coauthored with Heather Ross, and published in 1975, was about the growth of single-parent families and their consequences for children (Ross and Sawhill 1975).

Ron Haskins holds the Cabot Family Chair in Economic Studies at the Brookings Institution, where he codirects the Center on Children and Families. He is also a senior consultant at the Annie E. Casey Foundation. He is the president of the Association for Public Policy Analysis and Management.

Isabel V. Sawhill is a senior fellow in Economic Studies at the Brookings Institution, where she has also been a vice president and center director. She served in the Bill Clinton administration as an associate director of the Office of Management and Budget.

NOTE: Ron Haskins and Isabel Sawhill were the winners of the 2016 Daniel Patrick Moynihan Prize, awarded annually by the American Academy of Political and Social Science to recognize individuals who are champions of social science in the public realm—women and men whose careers demonstrate how public policy can be more effective when it is informed by sound science. Each year, we invite the Moynihan Prize recipients to deliver a public lecture on a topic of their choosing. This is the third year that the lecture has been published as a stand-alone piece in *The ANNALS.*

Correspondence: rhaskins@brookings.edu

DOI: 10.1177/0002716216663129

Like so many others in the scholarly and political worlds, we have been greatly influenced by the ideas of Daniel Patrick Moynihan. Now as the fortunate recipients of a prize given in his name, we happily acknowledge our indebtedness to his thinking, and we dedicate this article to his memory without in any way implying that he would have agreed with everything we say.

The history of his writing on the topic is well known. In 1965, as an assistant secretary in the Department of Labor, he wrote an internal report for members of the Johnson administration on his insights about the major impediment to continuing black progress (Moynihan 1965a). No paper written by a federal official has ever had as much influence as the Moynihan Report, as it was famously dubbed. The primary barrier to black progress in his view was weaknesses in the black family. He spoke of a "tangle of pathology" in the ghetto and was later ostracized both for his use of such language and for singling out the large proportion of single-parent families within the black community as an impediment to progress and thereby appearing to "blame the victim."

In their excellent review of this period and its aftermath in an earlier issue of *The ANNALS*, Douglas S. Massey and Robert J. Sampson (2009), as well as William Julius Wilson (2009), all note the unfairness of these attacks on Moynihan. In particular, his critics at the time often ignored the fact that he believed the ultimate cause of the breakdown of black families was centuries of oppression and persecution, and that he argued for an affirmative effort to compensate for the consequences of that oppression, including a federal jobs program.

Nonetheless, fierce criticism of the Moynihan Report took its toll, not just on Moynihan personally but also on social science research and debate for decades (Rainwater and Yancey 1967). It would be a long time before any scholar or public intellectual would dare to address the sensitive issue of how differences in family structure affect school performance, employment, crime, and the related differences between blacks and whites. A few courageous souls broke the impasse by researching the way in which family structure affected both black communities and the lives of children, whether black or white, growing up in fatherless families. William Julius Wilson (1987), Sara McLanahan (McLanahan and Sandefur 1997), and those who contributed to the earlier issue of *The ANNALS* come to mind as first-rate examples of some of this newer scholarship.

Contributing to a more open discussion of these questions were data showing that the growth of single-parent families was increasingly affecting not just black communities but white and Latino communities as well. Charles Murray, in his book *Coming Apart* (2012), for example, focuses only on white families, placing declines in marriage at the center of his story of communities beleaguered by low levels of education, male joblessness, crime, and single-parent families. Other researchers, such as Andrew Cherlin (2014), note that as technological change and globalization have dried up high-paying jobs for those with little education, the white working class family has also begun to disintegrate. By 2000, the fraction (22 percent) of white single parents was as high as the fraction of black families that had so alarmed Moynihan in 1965 (Sawhill 2013). As Moynihan wrote in *Family and Nation* (based on his Godkin lectures at Harvard in 1985): "Certain jobs simply are no longer there, while the people who once held them are" (Moynihan 1986).

In his later writing, Moynihan evinced considerable humility about how much public policy alone could change this trajectory and the corresponding need for a more limited government than many of his liberal contemporaries thought desirable. He believed in the Catholic doctrine of subsidiarity and in the power of the smallest unit, the family, to shape lives. Although this view is often associated with conservative thinkers, Moynihan was no conservative (Weiner 2016). Not only did he support many liberal policies, from welfare to jobs programs, but he was the architect of the Family Assistance Plan, introduced by President Nixon shortly after his reelection in 1969. That plan would have replaced most other antipoverty programs, encouraged work, and provided a guaranteed income to low-income Americans. Its defeat in the Senate Finance Committee was due, in part, to the opposition of progressive advocates who believed that it was insufficiently generous despite the fact that by today's standards it seems almost utopian. It would have provided a basic income of $1,600 to every American family with dependent children, or the equivalent of almost $10,000 in today's dollars (Hess 2014).

Our conclusions on the family will be at least somewhat Moynihanesque. Like him, we think families are important and that marriage is beneficial to children. Our book, *Creating an Opportunity Society* (2009), and several issues of the *Future of Children* that we have coedited (McLanahan and Sawhill 2015; McLanahan, Donahue, and Haskins 2005) lay out a plethora of evidence that two parents are better than one. Indeed, we think there is now a consensus within the social science community about the adverse consequences for children of the breakdown of the family. And like Moynihan, we think a little humility is in order about what we really know about the causes of this breakdown and what, if anything, might work to restore the family. Finally, Moynihan believed that culture and other influences, such as economics and politics, were intertwined in a complex causal web, and we agree. As he noted, "the central conservative truth is that it is culture, not politics, that determines the success of a society. The central liberal truth is that it is politics that can change a culture and save it from itself" (Moynihan 1986).[1]

Although much is owed to Moynihan, we address many developments that he could not have foreseen in 1965. One development is a growing class divide in marriage rates. In the 1950s and 1960s, marriage was not only widespread but varied little by education or other measures of socioeconomic status. Now marriage rates are linked much more strongly to measures of class, especially women's education level. This raises the issue of the relative importance of class versus race in creating these trends.

A second development is the much greater prevalence of cohabitation—the new "marriage-lite"—and the challenges this creates for data analysis on living arrangements and for public policy, which is still based primarily on more traditional definitions of who shares living expenses with whom. Given that about 40 percent of American children spend some time in families headed by cohabiting parents by the age of 12, a new field of study focused on cohabiting parents has been established (Manning 2015).

A third development is new research suggesting that boys are more adversely affected than girls by growing up without a father, raising the specter of a vicious circle in which growing up in a single-parent family leads to diminished prospects for boys and young men, which then leads to even further declines in marriage.

A fourth development is the reform of welfare, something that Moynihan worked on during his long Senate career, even though he strongly opposed both the Clinton administration's welfare reform bill and the bill that eventually passed in the mid-1990s. He condemned both in very strong language.[2] Cash welfare has been partially replaced by the Earned Income Tax Credit and other work supports that have fewer putative adverse effects on marriage and work than the old welfare system. But government taxes and benefits still penalize marriage in some instances, leading to calls for their reform.

A fifth development is the sharply rising educational attainment, especially of women, along with the associated tendency to delay marriage to later ages. A corollary to collapsing marriage rates is a rise in pregnancies and births among unmarried young adults in their twenties over the past three or four decades. Young people in their twenties may be delaying marriage, or foregoing it altogether, but they are not refraining from sex. Although teen pregnancy rates have declined sharply, the problem has moved up the age scale. Most of these pregnancies among the unmarried result from young single adults (under 30) drifting into unstable relationships. A report from the Guttmacher Institute found that 73 percent of pregnancies to unmarried women aged 20–24 were unplanned (Zolna and Lindberg 2012). These births also make women less marriageable, since most men they might later meet are at least somewhat reluctant to take responsibility for someone else's child (Lichter and Graefe 2001).

In the remainder of this article, we briefly review the most recent evidence of trends in the family—as Moynihan famously said, we are all entitled to our own opinions but not to our own facts (Hess 2014)—and then explore two more complicated questions: the causes and consequences of these trends. And finally, we examine the various ways in which either government or nongovernmental institutions might slow or reverse these trends. In each case, we focus especially on recent research that has opened up new ways of thinking about these family issues and what as a society we ought to do in response.

Everyone's Entitled to Their Own Opinions but Not to Their Own Facts

As shown in Figure 1, the growth of single-parent families has been dramatic (Cancian and Haskins 2014). From 7 percent of all families with children in 1950, the share of single-parent families increased sharply to 31 percent in 2015. Most of these single parents are mothers, but a moderate and growing proportion are fathers (22 percent in 2015).

Another way of looking at the same trends is from the perspective of children. What proportion of children is born outside marriage? Again, the trends have been dramatic, although they have leveled off for most groups in recent years (see Figure 2). By 2014, about 29 percent of non-Hispanic white children, 53

FIGURE 1
Living Arrangements for Families with Children Under 18, 1950–2015

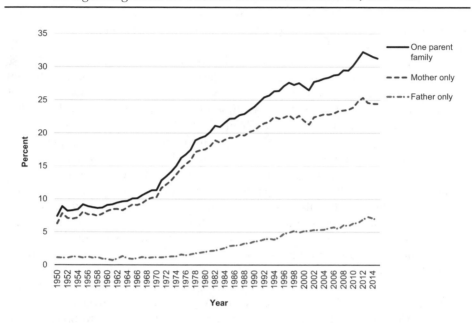

SOURCE: U.S. Census Bureau (2016).

percent of Hispanic children, 71 percent of black children, and 40 percent of all children in the United States were born outside marriage. It is the growth of unwed childbearing that has been the driver of increasing single parenthood since the 1980s. Divorce rates have actually declined slightly, especially among the well-educated.

Children born outside marriage are not necessarily living in a single-parent family. An increasing number live with two cohabiting adults (see Figure 3).[3] In some cases, this includes both of their biological parents, but in just as many cases it includes a biological parent (usually the mother) and an unrelated boy-friend (Manning 2015). Children who live with two stable, committed biological parents appear to fare as well as those in married-parent families, but such dura-ble relationships are relatively rare. Cohabitations tend to be fragile, especially those that occur as the result of an unplanned pregnancy. Nearly 40 percent of cohabiting couples who have a baby are no longer together by the time the child reaches age five, about three times the breakup rate for married couples over the same period (Hymowitz et al. 2013). This instability is not good for children (Manning 2015). Further, those in cohabiting relationships do not have the same legal rights as those in married-parent families.[4] If the couple were to marry, "marriage bonuses" or "marriage penalties" in tax or benefit programs would be created, often both. For example, eligibility for health benefits under Medicaid

FIGURE 2
Births to Unmarried Women by Race, 1970–2014

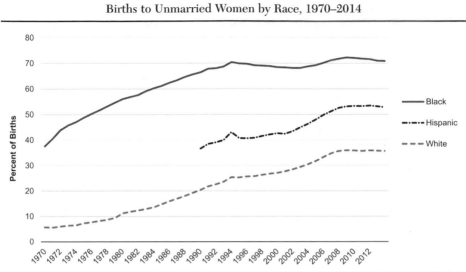

SOURCE: National Center for Health Statistics for years 1970–2003; subsequent years from National Vital Statistics Reports.

or the Affordable Care Act depends on the tax filing unit and thus excludes the income of an unmarried partner. By contrast, in the Food Stamp program (Supplemental Nutrition Assistance Program), the income of everyone in the household is counted. (We will say more about these marriage penalties and bonuses in the policy section.)

Despite the growth of single parents and unwed births among whites, the racial gaps are still wide and cannot be entirely explained by differences in socioeconomic status as measured by, say, educational attainment (see Figure 4). Of course, educational attainment is not a sufficient indicator of class, and a more robust analysis that included measures of wealth, employment, incarceration, and early death among black men, not to mention the adverse effects of residential and social segregation, would undoubtedly explain more of the racial gap in marriage rates. Still, most analysts have not been able to fully account for the differences (Raley, Sweeney, and Wondra 2015). While many people assume that slavery, which often broke up families, is at least partly to blame, the large black-white gap did not emerge until about the 1960s.[5] It is quite possible that the initial divergence in the 1960s was driven by some combination of limited job prospects for men and the availability of welfare for women, enabling them to support their children outside marriage. We say "enabling" rather than "causing" because evidence that welfare benefits caused the breakdown of the family is quite limited (Ellwood and Jencks 2004). But whatever factors caused a gap to emerge, culture and history are likely to play a role in sustaining it. For example, marriage rates are higher among Hispanics than among non-Hispanic blacks even though the former are economically just as disadvantaged (Raley, Sweeney, and Wondra 2015).

FIGURE 3
Families with Children Under 18 in Cohabiting Households

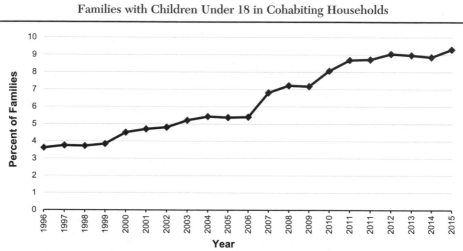

SOURCE: United States Census Bureau Table UC-1. Unmarried Couples of the Opposite Sex/1, by Presence of Children/2: 1960 to Present and Table FM-1. Families by Presence of Own Children Under 18: 1950 to Present.

Causes of the Trends

Most of the research that has attempted to explain these trends in family composition and living arrangements has focused on three primary drivers: increased opportunities for women; declining economic prospects among men, especially the least skilled; and changes in social norms or cultural attitudes. Although there is little consensus on the relative importance of each driver, most experts have concluded that both economics and culture have played a role (Sawhill 2014; Cherlin 2014).

The traditional model of marriage was based on the advantages of specialization within the household. Men, it was argued, had a comparative advantage in being the breadwinners while women were more suited to being homemakers (Becker 1974). But with the large-scale entry of women into the labor force, this model has become increasingly obsolete. The economic foundation of marriage is rapidly crumbling. Instead, marriage is now a symbol of commitment to another adult and facilitates joint parenting when children are involved. It also serves as a vehicle for the pooling of resources and for the mutual enjoyment of the lifestyle those resources make possible (Stevenson and Wolfers 2007; Lundberg and Pollak 1996; Reeves 2014).

Although the traditional model is on the wane, the perception that men should be breadwinners has not disappeared (Wang and Parker 2014). Women and men both still expect men to bring home a paycheck, and stagnant or falling real earnings for less educated men are widely hypothesized to have had an adverse effect on marriage. The empirical research on the size of this effect is quite mixed but

FIGURE 4
Births to Unmarried Women by Race and Education Level, 2014

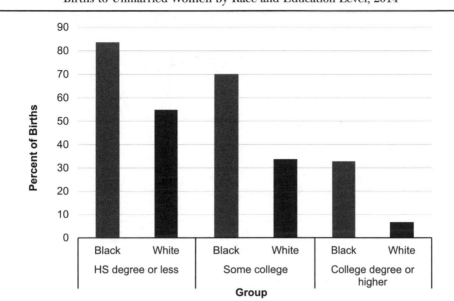

SOURCE: Authors' calculations from CDC WONDER, Natality online database. Available from http://wonder.cdc.gov/natality.html

tends to show that declines in men's earnings have had modest effects overall (Sawhill and Venator 2015). A recent paper by David Autor, David Dorn, and Gordon Hanson (2016), using a sophisticated methodology to tease out the exogenous effects of trade-induced declines in employment opportunities among men, finds that the declines have had a significant but small effect on marriage rates. Several other studies have found that the effects of male employment on marriage are larger for blacks than for whites, and this can be traced to high rates of incarceration and very high rates of joblessness among young black men. In short, the evidence that marriage is disappearing among less-skilled whites is limited, but there is a shortage of marriageable men within the black community (Wilson and Neckerman 1986; Thomas and Sawhill 2002; Sawhill and Venator 2015). One promising response to this shortage is criminal justice reform.

The literature on the causes of the retreat from marriage tends to make two assumptions that are unlikely to hold true in the future. The first is the assumption that men will continue to be the primary breadwinners in most families. Although this remains true for now—and is a clear motivation for marriage—its influence is likely to erode over time. Even now, 40 percent of all primary breadwinners are women; and Edin and Nelson (2013) note that many men in low-income communities expect the mother of their children to support the family. A second assumption is that marriages will continue to take place within same-race groups. Currently, a very small fraction of all marriages are interracial, but this is changing rapidly (Frey 2014).

FIGURE 5
Attitudes toward Sex, Marriage, and Childbearing

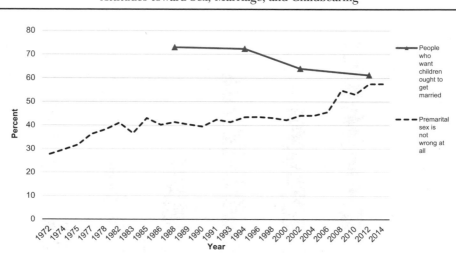

SOURCE: Authors' calculations from General Social Survey.

Accompanying these changes in the economic prospects of women and men, and interacting with them, has been a radical shift in cultural norms. Although most Americans still think that single parenting is a problem, they increasingly see marriage and childbearing as separate events and no longer disapprove of premarital sex, cohabitation, or births outside of marriage. The data in Figure 5 show how much more permissive attitudes toward premarital sex have become over the past four decades. An even more compelling illustration of shifting norms may be the way in which language has evolved. Forty or fifty years ago, a woman who had had sex before marriage was called "loose" or worse, children born outside marriage were termed "illegitimate," and couples who cohabited were said to be "living in sin." In most circles, these terms have now been abandoned and even condemned—a manifestation of how much attitudes have changed.

Consequences

Many researchers have attempted to examine the effects of single parenthood on children. The major challenge has been how to separate the effects of single parenthood from all of the other factors associated with being a single parent, such as being less educated, younger, or from a disadvantaged background or neighborhood as compared to being part of a married couple. Put differently, if it is these disadvantages that lead to single parenthood in the first place, then we could be wrongly attributing deficits in child development to family structure when it is really the result of a whole set of disadvantages associated with being a single parent.

Nevertheless, there are by now countless studies that have attempted to adjust for such differences, and they still find some negative effects for children, at least on average. These negative effects include dropping out of high school or college, a higher rate of crime and teen pregnancy, more behavioral or mental health problems, and lower levels of employment as an adult.[6] As Sara McLanahan and Christopher Jencks (2015) have written: "when taken together these studies are beginning to tell a consistent story. A recent review of 45 studies using quasi-experimental methods concluded that growing up apart from one's father does reduce a child's life chances in many domains."

Changes in the family have also had economic consequences, such as higher rates of poverty, more income inequality, and less social mobility. Again, there is a chicken and egg problem here, but strong research clearly implicates family structure as one reason for each of these economic outcomes.

For example, McLanahan and Percheski (2008) find that family structure has become an important mechanism for the reproduction of class, race, and gender inequalities. In an analysis of trends between 1977 and 2012, Wilcox, Price, and Lerman (2015) find that state-level economic outcomes are significantly influenced by various measures of family structure even after controlling for a variety of other likely influences. States with more married parents have higher gross domestic product per capita, more mobility, lower child poverty, and higher median incomes.

In still another study, Sawhill uses a simple shift share analysis and then adjusts the results for selection bias to examine the impact of the growth of single-parent families on poverty rates. She finds that child poverty rates have risen by 5 percentage points or by 23 percent as a result of the growth of single-parent families between 1970 and 2013 (Sawhill 2014).[7] She argues that as social programs have reduced child poverty, family fragmentation has pushed rates in the opposite direction.

Finally, the breakdown of the family—by adding to the number of low-income households at the bottom of the distribution—has contributed to rising income inequality, explaining anywhere from 15 to 40 percent of increased inequality in recent decades (M. Martin 2006; Burtless 1999).[8]

All of the above findings on the effects of family structure on children's development and on economic outcomes need some interpretation. It is possible that what matters most is not just the structure of the family but its stability. As we noted, cohabiting relationships are usually short-lived, and just under half of these unmarried parents go on to form new relationships and have additional children with a new person or in some cases several new people. According to the Fragile Families study, 80 percent of the children born to unmarried parents experienced either family instability or their parent having a child with a new partner before they were age five (McLanahan 2011).

A second interpretation of the above findings is very simple. Two parents have twice as much time as one and can devote that extra time either to working or providing care to their children. It is worth remembering that a second income, even a low one, is likely to bring more resources into the household than the most generous social assistance program. This is one reason the poverty rate among single parents is four or five times as high as the rate among two-parent families (Moynihan 1996; Haskins 2015). Most of the latter have two paychecks, not just one. Some analysts control for income when looking at the effects of single parenting on children, but income is largely if not entirely endogenous (that is, a consequence of having two adults in the household). The same is true of parental time spent with children (Kalil, Ryan, and Chor 2014).

A third possibility is that individuals who make good partners also make good parents. They may simply have the maturity, the commitment, or the relationship skills that facilitate both. These kinds of personal attributes are not easily measured and controlled for in social science research and thus could explain some of the observed differences.

How one interprets this evidence is important. It does not mean that all single parents are doing a bad job or that all of the children growing up in such families are adversely affected. Nor does it mean that marriage is always the solution. Many of the fathers of these children are in prison, and are violent, addicts, or unable to play a positive role in their children's lives (Edin and Nelson 2013; Wildeman and Western 2010). Finally, as emphasized in our discussion of the causes of the retreat from marriage, the relationship between changes in the economy, such as the disappearance of well-paid jobs for less skilled men, and the limited prospects of young women from low-income neighborhoods are part of this story. We cannot completely sort out the chicken from the egg and should recognize that more single parents means more poverty or related disadvantages—and more poverty and lack of opportunity, in turn, causes more single-parent families to form.

Although we have known for some time that children who grow up in single-parent families do not fare as well as those with two parents, some scholars are now finding that the consequences are especially serious for boys. Not only do boys need fathers, presumably to learn how to become men and how to control their impulses, but less obviously, and almost counterintuitively, it turns out that boys are more sensitive or less resilient than girls (Bertrand and Pan 2011). The kind of parenting they receive affects their development, including their behavior and their performance in school, more than parenting affects the development of girls.

Until now, these speculations about the disproportionate consequences of single parenthood for boys have been based on limited evidence. But new research from Stanford professor Raj Chetty and a team of colleagues (2016) shows that the effects on boys are clearly larger than for girls. They occur regardless of family income but are especially pronounced for boys living in high-poverty, largely minority neighborhoods. According to this research, when they become adults, boys from low-income, single-parent families are less likely to work, to earn a decent income, and to go to college not just compared with other boys but also compared with their sisters or girls who grew up in similar circumstances. These effects are largest when the families live in metropolitan areas ("commuting zones"[9]) with a high fraction of black residents, high levels of racial and income segregation, and lots of single-parent families. In short, it is not just the boy's own family situation that matters but also the kind of neighborhood in which he grows up. Exposure to high rates of crime and other potentially toxic peer influences without the constraining influence of adult males within their families seems to set these boys on a very different course than other boys, and perhaps more surprisingly, a different course from their sisters.

If single parenting affects boys more than girls, and an increasing number of boys are growing up in such families, the implications for the socialization of boys are troubling (Autor and Wasserman 2013). Moynihan was especially concerned about the lack of male authority in many inner-city families and communities. He (1965b) argued that "a community that allows a large number of young men to grow up in broken families, dominated by women, never acquiring any stable relationship to male authority, never acquiring any set of rational expectations about the future—that community asks for and gets chaos." But Moynihan could not have predicted how, in combination with a criminal justice system that locked up a large proportion of young black men with little education, often for nonviolent offenses, so many children would be deprived of having a father in the home. In addition, when these men return to the community with a prison record, it becomes almost impossible for them to find work (Western and Wildeman 2009). Joblessness then starts the entire cycle over again, discouraging marriage, necessitating illicit activity, and potentially producing a new generation of boys without fathers.

Although the research to date has focused on boys, we should remember that most single-parent families begin with an unwed and unplanned pregnancy and that these are more likely to occur when a girl grows up in a single-parent family in a distressed neighborhood. So providing the girls in such communities with both the motivation (access to education, decent jobs, and alternative sources of identity beyond motherhood) and the means (access to the most effective forms of contraception) to avoid an early unwed birth needs to be part of the response as well.

Before we discuss evidence on ways to increase marriage rates and reduce the negative impacts of single parenting, though, we think it useful to provide a brief summary of what research on marriage suggests is the reason living in a married-couple family is best for children's development. The extensive literature on marriage has found evidence from one or more studies that supports each of a large number of mechanisms that contribute to the relationship between a stable, two-parent family structure and child well-being. A recent masterful review by marriage scholar David Ribar (2015) reports evidence on a host of household and parent attributes that are important to improving child outcomes, including total household income, parents' ability to "specialize" in certain aspects of household productivity, father involvement in childrearing, parents' physical and mental health, parenting quality, social supports, health insurance, home ownership, and family stability. All of these favor married-couple families. Ribar argues that "the likely advantages of marriage for children's wellbeing are hard to replicate through policy interventions other than those that bolster marriages themselves" (p. 23). Ribar's conclusion is that, as in so many other issues of child development, there is no single mechanism that exhaustively explains any given child outcome. Explaining the advantages of marriage for child development requires appeal to a host of mechanisms.

What to Do

Increasing the share of children and adults in married-couple or stable cohabiting families would have three likely impacts (American Enterprise Institute and Brookings 2015). Given the very high poverty rates that characterize mother-headed families, the first impact would be a decline in poverty rates, especially for children. A decline in poverty rates would also necessarily mean a decline in income inequality. Second, child development would improve because children in families headed by women experience more problems than children in married-couple families, as we noted. Third, increased marriage rates would likely contribute to the well-being of adults, especially men (Waite and Gallagher 2000).

But the policy solutions for which we have evidence suggest that even well-financed and implemented policies would not reverse the trends in family composition or fully ameliorate their consequences. On the other hand, we do have evidence that some policies produce modest impacts and others might be called promising.

We consider five types of policies or programs that could increase marriage rates or the stability of cohabitation. These include policies to reduce nonmarital births, make tax and transfer policies more profamily, improve couple relationships, use media campaigns to emphasize the importance of family stability for children, and help young men to become better partners. Even if these policies were successful, we would still have millions of children being reared in female-headed families who need support, so we should also help them to avoid poverty and achieve a reasonable level of financial well-being.

Birth control to reduce unplanned pregnancies and nonmarital births

More or better use of birth control could reduce teen pregnancy rates, unintended pregnancies at older ages, and abortion rates. In addition, by reducing the number of single-parent families, it could reduce poverty and income inequality and promote children's development. On top of all of these benefits, birth control saves the government money. In fact, it already produces this entire range of benefits, but more effective use of birth control would expand them.

In recent years, there have been several large-scale studies of efforts to increase the voluntary use of birth control, especially the use of long-acting, reversible contraception (LARC) by low-income mothers. These prospective studies involved making contraception free, training medical personnel, conducting social marketing campaigns to encourage the use of birth control, and using better counseling to explain the advantages and disadvantages of various types of contraceptives.

One of these studies, conducted in the St. Louis area and called the Contraceptive CHOICE Project, enrolled more than 9,000 low-income mothers and gave them the option of choosing their own method of birth control at no cost (Winner et al. 2012). Participants were 14 to 45 years old; were either not using any contraception or were willing to consider switching to a different method; did not want to become pregnant for at least the next 12 months; and were either sexually active or planning to be sexually active with a male partner during the next six months. At the end of three years, the pregnancy rate for those who used the pill, patch, or ring was 9.4 percent; the rate for those who used LARCs (IUDs and implants) was 0.9 percent; and the rate for those who received injections was 0.7 percent. Similar large-scale studies have been conducted in Iowa and Colorado with similar results (Biggs et al. 2015; Ricketts, Klingler, and Schwalberg 2014).

None of these studies used random assignment. Although the size of the effects (compared with what was happening in other cities or states) makes it unlikely that such effects are due to other factors operating at the same time, we cannot know this for sure. Another study involving fifteen states, led by the Bixby Center at the University of California, San Francisco, did involve a randomized control trial of forty clinics (Harper et al. 2015). The Bixby study found that provider training alone (with no reduction in the cost of birth control) caused the unplanned pregnancy rate to drop by almost half in one year's time for women who came to the clinic seeking family planning. Another group of women in the study came to the clinics seeking an abortion and were offered a LARC afterward. In these cases, there were no significant differences between the pregnancy rates of women in the treatment and control clinics. The authors believe the lack of effect in these abortion-related cases was primarily because women who wanted a LARC were not easily able to obtain one due to greater cost barriers (the cost is less likely to be covered by a government program when a woman gets an abortion) and the need to return to the clinic for a second visit to obtain the LARC.

There have also been effective efforts to reduce teen pregnancy rates. Since the early 1990s, teen birth rates have declined almost every year and have fallen by over 50 percent, from 59.9 per 1,000 teen females in 1990 to 26.5 per 1,000 in 2013 (J. Martin et al. 2015). Even so, American teenagers still have much higher birth rates than teens in many other nations with advanced economies. Japan, Denmark, and the Netherlands, for example, all have rates under 5 per 1,000 (Ventura, Hamilton, and Matthews 2014).

To further drive down the teen pregnancy rates, the Obama administration has launched a major initiative. Working with the research firm Mathematica Policy Research and Child Trends, the administration reviewed all published and unpublished evaluations of teen pregnancy prevention programs that they could find (Mathematica Policy Research and Child Trends 2010). After reviewing nearly 1,000 studies in accord with detailed procedures developed by the Department of Health and Human Services, the team identified thirty-one model teen pregnancy prevention programs (more were identified later) with rigorous evidence of impacts on sexual activity, use of contraceptives, sexually transmitted infections, or pregnancy rates. The administration is now funding and evaluating 75 initiatives that replicate one of these model programs, enrolling more than 100,000 teens annually in 37 states. The administration hopes to identify the most effective programs and encourage expansion of those programs.

One of the most impressive findings from research on family planning is the number of studies that have shown net savings from subsidized payments for birth control, as a recent review on the website the Incidental Economist demonstrates (Liebman 2014). Here's the basic math: the average insurance payment for a vaginal delivery is around $18,000; the cost of a C-section is $28,000. If there are complications, these costs can skyrocket. By comparison, the average cost of contraception is between $100 and $600 annually (Klein 2014). Combine these numbers on cost data with the facts that nearly 70 percent of births to unmarried women ages 20–29 are unplanned and that, when given a choice between types of birth control provided without charge, as many as 70 percent of low-income women select the most effective form of birth control (LARCs), it is clear that there are serious savings to be had by expanding the availability of subsidized birth control to low-income women. Although these women may go on to have children later, they often gain more education, get experience in the labor market, and form more stable relationships by delaying parenthood. At least four studies have produced estimates of the benefit-cost ratios of expanded use of effective contraception; the estimates range from savings of $3.74 to $7.00 for every $1 spent on birth control (Sawhill, Thomas, and Monea 2010; Frost, Finer, and Tapales 2008; Frost, Henshaw, and Sonfield 2010; Thomas 2012).

There is little doubt that birth control initiatives, especially the increased use of LARCs, will reduce nonmarital and unplanned births. Reductions in these births will in turn save money. In addition, avoiding nonmarital births at an early age can increase the chance that women will marry later in life (Lichter and Graefe 2001).

Reduce marriage penalties in tax and transfer programs

The tax code and means-tested programs can present disincentives for marriage, because single people who marry and combine their incomes could see higher taxes and fewer means-tested benefits. The earned income tax credit (EITC), which is intended primarily to increase work incentive and augment the income of low-income workers, especially parents, is designed so that qualified workers receive more money as they earn more up to a certain amount; then their EITC payment is flat for several thousand dollars of additional earnings; then the EITC payment phases out over a broad income range. But if a mother with two children and $18,000 in earnings marries a man earning $32,000, her EITC falls from the maximum of $5,548 to zero. The amount of the EITC marriage penalty or incentive hangs on the combined income of the husband and wife.

One of the few studies to estimate the impact of marriage on the size of the EITC and cash welfare based on a sample representative of the population was conducted by Greg Acs and Elain Maag (2005)[10] of the Urban Institute. The authors identified 744 cohabiting couples with children in the Survey of American Families who had a combined income under 200 percent of poverty. They calculated the impact that marriage would have on their EITC benefit as it existed in 2008 as well as the couples' Temporary Assistance for Needy Families (TANF) welfare benefit, if the mother received one.

A major finding was that 75 percent of the cohabiting low-income couples would receive a marriage bonus from the EITC, while only 10 percent would receive a penalty (the remaining 15 percent would experience little to no change). The average increase in the EITC for the 75 percent who received it would be about $1,400. Other tax code exemptions, deductions, and credits that these couples could qualify for if married increased the marriage bonus to a total of around $2,400. For the 10 percent who were hit with a marriage penalty from the EITC, the average total penalty was around $1,750.

Turning to the TANF program, because TANF benefits phase out rapidly as earnings increase, almost all the cohabiting couples who received TANF would have their benefit reduced if they married. But only 14 percent of the couples were receiving TANF benefits. For this small minority of couples, the reduction in the TANF benefit was between $1,800 and $2,100. Of the 14 percent of couples who received TANF, fewer than 4 percent got both a tax penalty and a TANF reduction; for these families, the combined loss was substantial, about $3,300. But 70 percent of the 14 percent who received a TANF reduction also received an EITC bonus. The combined tax bonus and TANF reduction for these couples still left them with a net marriage bonus that averaged $1,300.

Two conclusions are justified. First, a small minority of cohabiting couples with combined income under 200 percent of poverty who marry would be subjected to an EITC marriage penalty. Second, the marriage penalty for the relatively small group of mothers and fathers who receive TANF seems likely to be substantial. Moreover, the study considered only the EITC and related tax credits and the TANF cash benefit, but other welfare benefits such as Medicaid, food stamps, housing, school lunch, and child care also have phase-out rules. A recent study by researchers at the Urban Institute found that nearly 80 percent of a representative sample of families with children with incomes below 200 percent of the poverty line received at least one welfare benefit, and 45 percent received two or more (Edelstein, Pergamit, and Ratcliffe 2014). In many cases, there would be marriage penalties from these programs. An especially serious disincentive occurs in the Medicaid program, where eligibility ends abruptly at a given income level, which varies widely across states (Centers for Medicare and Medicaid Services 2014; Garfield and Damico 2014).

It follows from these considerations about means-tested benefits that we should worry more about the marriage penalty that low-income couples encounter from means-tested programs than about the EITC and other tax credits, especially because the Tax Relief Act of 2010 extended the bottom 15 percent tax bracket for married couples filing jointly, increased the standard deduction, and extended the EITC phase-out range for married couples, all of which reduce the tax penalty associated with marriage.

Extending the phase-out range for tax benefits to reduce the disincentive to work for married couples would be expensive. As one moves up the income scale into the range where many married couples are likely to be located, many households become eligible for the reduced tax bill, leading to big revenue losses. In addition, there is not good evidence that these changes in taxes or benefits have strong effects on people's propensity to marry. Thus, the benefit-cost ratio of such policies is likely to be small.

Improving the relationships of married and cohabiting couples

Based on the view that marriage and even improved relationships among unmarried couples would be good for the adults and children involved, the George W. Bush administration launched a marriage initiative in 2001 to determine whether marriage education and associated services for couples might improve relationship quality and help couples either to get married or to prolong their relationship and, if so, whether these impacts would in turn have a positive impact on children's development and behavior.

A major part of the Bush initiative was the Building Strong Families (BSF) program, evaluated by the research firm Mathematica. The program aimed to strengthen the relationships and parenting skills of young couples who had a baby together outside of marriage. The program was implemented with more than 5,000 couples randomly assigned to an experimental or a control group at eight sites. Parents in the experimental group were offered marriage education classes in groups, using a formal curriculum, as well as advice and support from a family-services coordinator.

The evaluation measured the quality of the couples' relationships, their coparenting relationships, family stability, children's social-emotional development, and other outcomes. These measures were collected both at 15 months and 36 months after participants had enrolled in the program. At 15 months, the BSF program produced few significant effects, including no effects on whether the couples stayed together or got married (Wood et al. 2010). However, the Oklahoma program produced a pattern of positive effects, while the Baltimore program saw some negative impacts, including a slight increase in physical assaults by the father. The positive effects in Oklahoma included relationship happiness, parenting skills, support and affection, use of constructive behaviors to resolve conflicts, avoidance of destructive conflict behaviors, marital fidelity, quality of coparenting, whether the father lived with the child, and whether the father provided substantial financial support.

Mathematica's 36-month follow-up again showed few impacts across the eight sites (Wood et al. 2012). Although most of the Oklahoma impacts had disappeared by 36 months, one important remaining difference was that children in the treatment group were about 20 percent more likely to still be living with both of their parents as compared with children in the control group.

The second Bush marriage initiative, called Supporting Healthy Marriage, was similar to BSF, but attempted to increase the relationship skills of couples who were already married rather than unmarried couples. Results from Supporting

Healthy Marriage are somewhat more encouraging than those obtained from BSF, but most of the effects were not statistically significant, and even the significant effects were modest. More importantly, program couples were no more likely to stay together, and there were no effects on measures of their children's behavior or development (Lundquist et al. 2014).

The Bush administration initiative was the first large-scale effort to develop marriage programs for poor couples and to test their effectiveness. The fact that the initial effort to conduct such large and complex programs produced disappointing results should not be too surprising. It is not inconceivable that the programs could be improved over time. This is especially the case because other high-quality studies have shown that marriage education can have a positive effect on couples' relationships and breakup rates, although these studies did not focus exclusively on low-income couples (Hawkins 2013; Schulz, Cowan, and Cowan 2006; Stanley et al. 2010).

Moreover, Philip and Carolyn Cowan, two of the most experienced researchers and designers of couple relationship programs, recently reviewed the evidence on education programs for couples and reached three conclusions: first, without intervention, "average couple relationship satisfaction declines"; second, including fathers in the programs "results in value-added contributions to family functioning"; and third, eight of nine studies of couple relationship programs that include child outcomes show benefits for children (Cowan and Cowan 2014). That only two of the nine studies reviewed by the Cowans focused on low-income families somewhat limits the application of their conclusions to low-income families.

Thus, it may be premature to abandon Bush's marriage education initiatives. It would be especially useful to replicate the Oklahoma program with a focus on finding ways to reduce its costs and maintain its impacts. Another issue that needs more study is participation rates. Only 61 percent of those who enrolled in the programs attended even one session, and among those who did attend, the median curriculum completion level was only 40 percent (Dion et al. 2008). It seems unlikely that any curriculum can be effective when so many participants never show up and a majority of the rest miss more than half the sessions.

Help young men

In his heralded 1987 book *The Truly Disadvantaged*, sociologist William Julius Wilson argued that unemployment among young black men was a key to explaining the decline of marriage among black couples. Wilson constructed a "black marriageable male index" based on comparing the number of employed black men to the number of black women in the same age range. He shows that in 1960, the ratio was about 70 employed black men for every 100 black women in the 20 to 24 age range. By the 1980s, the ratio had fallen to 50 employed black men for every 100 black women.

In addition to their high rates of unemployment, nearly 60 percent of black high school dropouts born between 1965 and 1969 had been in prison by the time they reached their early thirties (Pettit and Western 2004). Having a prison record makes it difficult to find work when men leave prison. Prison also disrupts their relationships with relatives—especially children—and friends. It would be hard to imagine a combination of factors that would do more to reduce marriage prospects than a lousy work history and a prison record.

One reason young men may have such difficulty with the law is that they have little or no consistent contact with their fathers. David Autor and Melanie Wasserman (2013) review evidence showing that single mothers spend less time with sons and harshly discipline them more often than daughters. Similarly, they note that although boys in general act out in school more often than girls, the gap is greater for boys and girls from female-headed families than for boys and girls from married-couple families. Boys also see their fathers much less after their parents separate, and given the high rates of single parenthood in low-income and minority communities, the bond between fathers and sons is more often disrupted in these communities (Carlson and Turner 2010).

At least two public policies could improve young men's chances of finding work and help them to develop healthy relationships with young women. The two policies are support for programs that prepare them for employment (Mead 2011) and that reduce their rates of incarceration. Among the former, several programs that have been tested by random-assignment evaluations have shown positive impacts on young men's employment (Holzer 2014). Foremost among them are the Career Academies program and apprenticeship programs that give young people a skill and a certificate, often through community colleges (Kemple and Willner 2008; Lerman 2014). The Career Academies program even led to higher marriage rates.

But Career Academies may be an outlier. Daniel Schneider (2015) reviewed sixteen experimental programs involving early childhood development, work-force training, and income support that aimed to improve the economic well-being of low-income men and women. Most of the programs produced positive effects on the economic well-being of young men, young women, or both, but only a few, including Career Academies, had strong impacts on marriage rates. Based on Schneider's review, there is only modest evidence that programs that increase economic well-being also increase marriage rates.

There is a growing consensus that states and the federal government should loosen mandatory sentencing laws and thereby reduce the number of nonviolent offenders who serve long prison sentences. Many states, sometimes forced by budget shortages, are already beginning to change their mandatory sentencing laws, although we know little about the effects of these changes. At the federal level, many politicians from both parties have proposed reforms of mandatory sentencing laws for nonviolent offenses as well as new or improved prison release programs to help former prisoners adapt to civilian life, especially by finding a job (Jalonick 2016; Wildeman, Wakefield, and Lee 2016).

In addition to Career Academies and apprenticeship programs, both evaluated by large randomized evaluations, another program for young men that shows promise based on a large randomized trial is the Becoming a Man (BAM) program developed by the Crime Lab at the University of Chicago (2012). Reflecting the principles of cognitive behavioral therapy, BAM enrolled 2,740 male students in grades 7 through 10 from 18 Chicago schools and randomly assigned approximately half of them to receive the program. Students selected for the program were considered to be at risk for behavioral problems but, based on their school records, were nonetheless likely to attend school enough to benefit from the BAM intervention. They participated in the program during school hours, during after-school hours, or both. The during-school program consisted of twenty-seven one-hour small-group sessions that met weekly during the school year. Each session aimed to develop a specific cognitive-behavioral skill such as self-regulation or interpersonal problem solving. The after-school program consisted of sports activities and emphasized conflict resolution skills and social and emotional learning.

Using school records, a composite measure was formed consisting of number of days present, grade point average, and end-of-year enrollment. Data on criminal behavior was obtained from records maintained by the Illinois Criminal Justice Information Authority. The composite school engagement outcome showed significant differences during both the program year and the next school year between program and control students, favoring students participating in the program. Similarly, arrest records showed that program students had 44 percent fewer arrests for violent crime than control students. The researchers concluded that these impacts "provide the most rigorous, large-scale evidence to date that a social-cognitive skill intervention can improve both schooling and delinquency outcomes for disadvantaged youth" (University of Chicago Crime Lab 2012, 4).

Although examination of national data on marriage, school performance, employment and earnings, and arrests does not provide much room for optimism that the nation is making progress with young, minority males, programs such as Career Academies, apprenticeships, and BAM show that knowledge of how to improve the lives of these vulnerable young men is increasing. These and similar programs should be expanded; meanwhile, program development and evaluation must continue to discover new programs that can improve the life chances of young men.

Help single mothers

We may hope that the decline in marriage rates and increase in nonmarital birth rates will turn around, but meanwhile a huge share of the nation's children will continue to live in female-headed families. For this reason, maintaining or even expanding the focus of state and federal policies on these female-headed families is warranted.

The nation has taken two broad approaches to help poor single mothers and their children. One is to provide cash and noncash support. The federal and state governments now spend about $1 trillion annually on these programs, a considerable portion of which goes to female-headed families (Congressional Research Service 2012).[11] The major programs included in this estimate are Medicaid, food and nutrition programs, Supplemental Security Income, the EITC, the Additional Child Tax Credit, and housing programs. The second approach is to encourage

poor mothers to work, usually at low-wage jobs, and then use government programs to subsidize their earnings. One of the great tensions in American social
policy centers is whether it is better to give welfare benefits to able-bodied mothers or to encourage and cajole them to work and then subsidize their earnings,
which are often below the poverty level (Mead 1986; Haskins 2006). A key event
in the work approach was passage of the 1996 welfare reform law, which greatly
strengthened work requirements and gave states an incentive to enforce them.

Although the welfare reform law had shortcomings, its passage was followed
by a substantial increase in the proportion of poor single mothers who were
employed. We can get a good idea of the course of the employment-to-population ratios after welfare reform by comparing the ratio for the average of the five
years before welfare reform (1991–95) with the average ratio of the five years
following welfare reform (1997–2001). The former average was 46.4 percent; the
latter was 62.6 percent—an increase of 35 percent. This may well be the biggest
increase in work rates over a short period for any demographic group in American
history. The recessions of 2001 and 2007–9 reduced the employment-to-population ratios of never-married mothers (and nearly every other group). For never-
married mothers, the decline was from a high of 66 percent in 2000 to a low of
57 percent in 2011. But as the economy recovered from the Great Recession of
2007–9, the employment-to-population ratio began to move up again in 2012.
The 60 percent rate for never-married mothers in 2014 is nearly 30 percent
above the comparable rate in the five years before welfare reform. A careful
analysis of the composition of income among the nation's mother-headed families
with children by the nonpartisan Congressional Research Service shows that
today federal programs reduce the poverty rate among these families by about 50
percent (Gabe 2014; Heinrich and Scholz 2011).

However, during the recessions that began in 2001 and 2007, work rates fell
and poverty rates increased among mother-headed families, showing that, like
other families, single-mother families depend on the economy to generate jobs if
they are to continue making economic progress. Another piece of bad news is
that some mothers have problems making the transition to work and often use up
their time-limited TANF benefits, are eliminated from the rolls for rule violation,
or leave the rolls voluntarily, perhaps to work at a job they later lose. This group
of mothers lacks both earnings and TANF benefits. In one study, their annual
income was $6,178, compared with $17,681 for working mothers who left TANF.
Not surprisingly, these mothers and their children have high rates of poverty
(Blank and Kovak 2007; Loprest and Nichols 2011).

Several policy changes could help poor, single working mothers increase their
income and in some cases escape poverty. First, states could do a better job of
helping the mothers prepare for and find work (Germanis 2015a, 2015b).
Second, we could do more to ensure that these mothers and children get child
support, especially by persuading states, perhaps with financial incentives, to give
all child support collections to the mothers by ending the state and federal practice of retaining part of child support payments as an offset to welfare or other
benefits. A third reform would be to help states mount work programs for non-
custodial fathers who owe child support so that they have earnings with which to

make payments. Other worthwhile improvements in the work support system would be to expand child care subsidies and to provide subsidized jobs for mothers and fathers who cannot find work. Helping more low-income parents with their child care bill would increase their incentive to work, provide an income supplement, and reduce a serious inequity in current law that allows only some low-income working families to receive a child care subsidy while similar families receive no subsidy. During the Great Recession, states used federal emergency funds to subsidize around 260,000 jobs, most of them in the private sector (Pavetti, Schott, and Lower-Basch 2011). Some analysts argue that the federal government should make subsidized employment a permanent feature of federal policy (Dutta-Gupta et al. 2016). Developing state expertise in subsidizing jobs would be especially appropriate if Congress strengthened the work requirements in the nation's food stamp and housing programs to extend the message that the able-bodied must work or prepare for work as a condition of receiving means-tested benefits.

Concluding Thoughts

The breakdown of the family has increased the nation's poverty rate, increased income inequality, adversely affected the development of millions of children, and increased spending on social programs. Some scholars believe that for these reasons we should do more to encourage marriage and not give up just because some programs have had disappointing effects so far (Haskins 2014, 2015; Wilcox and Wolfinger 2016). Other scholars question whether restoring marriage to its former status as the central feature of American family life and the culturally accepted way to raise children is possible, even if desirable (Sawhill 2014). Reversal of demographic trends that have been moving in the same direction for four decades seems unlikely, especially in low-income communities of color where marriage has virtually disappeared. In this context, it makes sense to both discourage unplanned childbearing outside of marriage and continue to provide assistance to single-parent families, ensuring that single mothers with little education gain at least a modicum of financial security. Of course, we could work simultaneously on increasing marriage rates and family stability, reducing nonmarital and unplanned births, and helping low-income single mothers care for their children. We need to do all three if one believes, as we do, that children who live with two parents and are wanted and cared for will have better lives as a result.

Notes

1. For a similar view about the interaction between structure and culture, see Wilson (2009).

2. On June 17, 1995, Moynihan referred to the Republican bill as "an act of unprecedented social vindictiveness" (Haskins 2006, 206).

3. These cohabiting couples were difficult to identify in data from the Current Population Survey until after 1995. Prior to that time, the census did track "persons of the opposite sex sharing living quarters,"

but the accuracy of these data was limited by the fact that the two people did not need consider themselves "partners."

4. See "When Unmarried Parents Split" *The Economist*. 16 January 2016, www.economist.com, for how different countries handle the legal rights of married and unmarried couples.

5. Note: Orlando Patterson (1998) believes slavery did have an effect; Raley, Sweeney, and Wondra (2015) suggest otherwise; so there is still some debate here. Based on data reviewed by Ellwood and Jencks (2004, Table 2.1, p. 39), in 1940 to 1944, by age 40, 95 percent of white women and 87 percent of black women had married. In 1960 to 1964, the figures were 89 percent for white women but only 68 percent for black women.

6. For recent reviews of this literature, see McLanahan, Tach, and Schneider (2013) and Ribar (2015). For our earlier reviews of a wider literature, see Haskins and Sawhill (2009), Haskins (2014), and Sawhill (2014).

7. Found using a shift share analysis: Shift-share poverty rate $=$ (Single Parent Child Poverty 2012) × (Proportion of Children in SPF 1970) + (Married Parent Child Poverty 2012) × (Proportion of Children in SPF 1970); then adjusted for selection using ratio from Thomas and Sawhill (2002).

8. For an excellent review, see DeParle (2012).

9. Commuting zones were developed by the Census Bureau to capture the spacial area of local labor markets without regard to political units such as counties.

10. See also Alm and Whittington (1999).

11. For an estimate that includes both federal and state spending, see Senate Committee on the Budget, Republicans, "Sessions Comments on Congressional Report Showing Welfare Is Single Largest Federal Expense," October 18, 2012, http://www.budget.senate.gov/republican/public/index.cfm/2012/10/sessions-comments-on-congressional-report-showing-welfare-is-single-largest-federal-expense.

References

Acs, Gregory, and Elaine Maag. 2005. *Irreconcilable differences? The conflict between marriage promotion initiatives for cohabiting couples with children and marriage penalties in tax and transfer programs.* Washington, DC: Urban Institute.

Alm, James, and Leslie A. Whittington. 1999. For love or money? The impact of income taxes on marriage. *Economica* 66:297–316.

American Enterprise Institute and Brookings Institution. 2015. *Opportunity, responsibility, and security: A consensus plan for reducing poverty and restoring the American dream.* Washington, DC: American Enterprise Institute and Brookings Institution.

Autor, David H., David Dorn, and Gordon H. Hanson. 2016. The China shock: Learning from labor market adjustment to large changes in trade. NBER Working Paper 21906, Cambridge, MA. Available from http://www.nber.org/papers/w21906.

Autor, David H., and Melanie Wasserman. 2013. *Wayward sons: The emerging gender gap in labor markets and education.* Washington, DC: Third Way.

Becker, Gary S. 1974. A theory of marriage. In *Economics of the family: Marriage, children, and human capital,* ed. Theodore W. Schultz, 299–351. Chicago, IL: University of Chicago Press.

Bertrand, Marianne, and Jessica Pan. 2011. The trouble with boys: Social influences and the gender gap in disruptive behavior. NBER Working Paper 17541, Cambridge, MA. Available from http://www.nber.org/papers/w17541.pdf.

Biggs, M. Antonia, Corinne H. Rocca, Claire D. Brindis, Heather Hirsch, and Daniel Grossman. 2015. Did increasing use of highly effective contraception contribute to declining abortions in Iowa? *Contraception* 91 (2): 167–73.

Blank, Rebecca, and Brian Kovak. 2007. The growing problem of disconnected single mothers. *Focus* 25 (2): 27–34.

Burtless, Gary. 1999. Effects of growing wage disparities and changing family composition on the U.S. income distribution. *European Economic Review* 43 (4–6): 853–65.

Cancian, Maria, and Ron Haskins. 2014. Changes in family composition: Implications for income, poverty, and public policy. *The ANNALS of the American Academy of Political and Social Science* 654:31–47.

Carlson, Marcia J., and Kimberly J. Turner. 2010. *Fathers' involvement and fathers' well-being over children's first five years*. Madison, WI: Institute for Research on Poverty.

Centers for Medicare and Medicaid Services. 2014. State Medicaid and CHIP income eligibility standards. Available from https://www.medicaid.gov/medicaid-chip-program-information/program-information/downloads/medicaid-and-chip-eligibility-levels-table.pdf.

Cherlin, Andrew. 2014. *Labor's love lost: The rise and fall of the working class family in America*. New York, NY: Russell Sage Foundation.

Chetty, Raj, Nathaniel Hendren, Frina Lin, Jeremy Majerovitz, and Benjamin Scuderi. 2016. Childhood environment and gender gaps in adulthood. NBER Working Paper 21936, Cambridge, MA.

Congressional Research Service. 16 October 2012. Spending for federal benefits and services for people with low income, FY2008–2011: An update of Table B-1 from CRS Report R41625, modified to remove programs for veterans. Memorandum to the Senate Budget Committee. Washington, DC: Congressional Research Service.

Cowan, Philip A., and Carolyn Pape Cowan. 2014. Controversies in couple relationship education (CRE): Overlooked evidence and implications for research and policy. *Psychology, Public Policy, and Law* 20:361–83.

DeParle, Jason. 14 July 2012. Two classes, divided by "I do." *New York Times*. Available from http://www.nytimes.com.

Dion, M. Robin, Alan M. Hershey, Heather A. Zaveri, Sarah A. Avellar, Debra A. Strong, Timothy Silman, and Ravaris Moore. 2008. *Implementation of the building strong families program*. Princeton, NJ: Mathematica Policy Research.

Dutta-Gupta, Indivar, Kali Grant, Matthew Eckel, and Peter Edelman. 2016. *Lessons learned from 40 years of subsidized employment programs*. Washington, DC: Georgetown Center on Poverty and Inequality.

Edelstein, Sara, Michael R. Pergamit, and Caroline Ratcliffe. 2014. *Characteristics of families receiving multiple public benefits*. Washington, DC: Urban Institute.

Edin, Kathryn, and Timothy J. Nelson. 2013. *Doing the best I can: Fatherhood in the inner city*. Oakland, CA: University of California Press.

Ellwood, David, T., and Christopher Jencks. 2004. The spread of single-parent families in the United States since 1960. In *The Future of the Family*, eds. Daniel Patrick Moynihan, Timothy M. Smeeding, and Lee Rainwater, 25–65. New York, NY: Russell Sage Foundation.

Frey, William H. 2014. *Diversity explosion: How new racial demographics are remaking America*. Washington, DC: Brookings Institution Press.

Frost, Jennifer J., Lawrence B. Finer, and Athena Tapales. 2008. The impact of publicly funded family planning clinic services on unintended pregnancies and government cost savings. *Journal of Health Care for the Poor and Underserved* 19:778–96.

Frost, Jennifer J., Stanley K. Henshaw, and Adam Sonfield. 2010. Contraceptive needs and services: National and state data, 2008 update. New York, NY: Guttmacher Institute.

Gabe, Tom. 2014. *Welfare, work, and poverty status of female-headed families with children, 1987–2013*. Washington, DC: Congressional Research Service.

Garfield, Rachel, and Anthony Damico. 2014. *The coverage gap: Uninsured poor adults in states that do not expand Medicaid—an update*. Menlo Park, CA: Henry J. Kaiser Family Foundation.

Germanis, Peter. 2015a. TANF is broken! It's time to reform welfare reform. Washington, DC. Unpublished manuscript.

Germanis, Peter. 2015b. TANF is broken! The Louisiana story: A response to Representative Charles Boustany. Washington, DC. Unpublished manuscript.

Harper, Cynthia C., Corinne H. Rocca, Kirsten M. Thompson, Johanna Morfesis, Suzan Goodman, Philip D. Darney, Carolyn L. Westhoff, and J. Joseph Speidel. 2015. Reductions in pregnancy rates in the USA with long-acting reversible contraception: A cluster randomized trial. *Lancet* 386 (9993): 562–68.

Haskins, Ron. 2006. *Work over welfare: The inside story of the 1996 Welfare Reform Law*. Washington, DC: Brookings Institution.

Haskins, Ron. 2014. Marriage, parenthood, and public policy. *National Affairs* 19:55–72.

Haskins, Ron. 2015. The family is here to stay—or not. *Future of Children* 25 (2): 129–53.

Haskins, Ron, and Isabel V. Sawhill. 2003. Work and marriage: The way to end poverty and welfare. Welfare Reform and Beyond Policy Brief. Washington, DC: Brookings Institution.

Haskins, Ron, and Isabel V. Sawhill. 2009. *Creating an opportunity society*. Washington, DC: Brookings Institution Press.

Hawkins, Alan J. 2013. *The forever initiative: A feasible public policy agenda to help couples form and sustain healthy marriages and relationships*. North Charleston, SC: CreateSpace.

Heinrich, Carolyn J., and John Karl Scholz, eds. 2011. *Making the work-based safety net work better: Forward-looking policies to help low-income families*. New York, NY: Russell Sage Foundation.

Hess, Stephen. 2014. *The professor and the president: Daniel Patrick Moynihan in the Nixon White House*. Washington, DC: Brookings Institution Press.

Holzer, Harry J. 2014. Improving employment outcomes for disadvantaged students. In *policies to address poverty in America*, eds. Melissa S. Kearney and Benjamin H. Harris, 87–95. Washington, DC: The Hamilton Project.

Hymowitz, Kay, Jason S. Carroll, W. Bradford Wilcox, and Kelleen Kaye. 2013. *Knot yet: The benefits and costs of delayed marriage in America*. Charlottesville, VA: National Marriage Project, University of Virginia.

Jalonick, Mary Clare.28 April 2016. Senators try to revive criminal justice overhaul. *Associated Press*. Available from http://elections.ap.org/content/senators-try-revive-criminal-justice-overhaul.

Kalil, Ariel, Rebecca Ryan, and Elise Chor. 2014. Time investments in children across family structures. *The ANNALS of the American Academy of Political and Social Science* 654:150–68.

Kemple, James J., and Cynthia J. Willner. 2008. *Career academies: Long-term impacts on labor market outcomes, educational attainment, and transitions to adulthood*. New York, NY: MDRC.

Klein, Ezra. 9 July 2014. Birth control saves money: Lots of it. *Vox*.

Lerman, Bob. 2014. Expanding apprenticeships opportunities in the United States. In *Policies to address poverty in America*, eds. Melissa S. Kearney and Benjamin H. Harris, 79–86. Washington, DC: The Hamilton Project.

Lichter, Daniel, and Deborah Reompke Graefe. 2001. Finding a mate? The marital and cohabitation histories of unwed mothers. In *Out of wedlock: Causes and consequences of nonmarital fertility*, eds. Barbara Wolfe and Lawrence L. Wu, 317–43. New York, NY: Russell Sage Foundation.

Liebman, Daniel. 9 July 2014. Does contraceptive coverage pay for itself? A review of the evidence. The Incidental Economist Blog. Available from http://theincidentaleconomist.com.

Loprest, Pamela, and Austin Nichols. 2011. *Dynamics of being disconnected from work and TANF*. Washington, DC: Urban Institute.

Lundberg, Shelly, and Robert A. Pollak. 1996. Bargaining and distribution in marriage. *Journal of Economic Perspectives* 10 (4): 139–58.

Lundquist, Erica, JoAnn Hsueh, Amy E. Lowenstein, Kristen Faucetta, Daniel Gubits, Charles Michalopoulos, and Virginia Knox. 2014. *A family-strengthening program for low-income families: Final impacts from the Supporting Healthy Marriage Evaluation*. New York, NY: MDRC.

Manning, Wendy D. 2015. Cohabitation and child wellbeing. *The Future of Children* 25 (2): 51–61.

Martin, Joyce A., Brady E. Hamilton, Michelle J. K. Osterman, Sally C. Curtin, and T. J. Matthews. 2015. Births: Final data for 2013. *National Vital Statistics Reports* 64 (1): 1–68.

Martin, Molly A. 2006. Family structure and income inequality in families with children, 1976 to 2000. *Demography* 43 (3): 421–45.

Massey, Douglas S. and Robert J. Sampson, eds. 2009. The Moynihan Report revisited: Lessons and reflections after four decades. *The ANNALS of the American Academy of Political and Social Science* 621.

Mathematica Policy Research and Child Trends. 2010. *Identifying programs that impact teen pregnancy, sexually transmitted infections, and associated sexual risk behaviors*. Princeton, NJ: Mathematica.

McLanahan, Sara. 2011. Family instability and complexity after a nonmarital birth: Outcomes for children in fragile families. In *Social class and changing families in an unequal America*, eds. Marcia J. Carlson and Paula England, 108–33. Redwood City, CA: Stanford University Press.

McLanahan, Sara, Elisabeth Donahue, and Ron Haskins. 2005. Marriage and child wellbeing. *The Future of Children* 15 (2).

McLanahan, Sara, and Christopher Jencks. 2015. Was Moynihan right? *Education Next* 15 (2): 14–20.

McLanahan, Sara, and Christine Percheski. 2008. Family structure and the reproduction of inequalities. *Annual Review of Sociology* 34:257–76.

McLanahan, Sara, and Gary Sandefur. 1997. *Growing up with a single parent: What hurts, what helps*. Cambridge, MA: Harvard University Press.

McLanahan, Sara, and Isabel V. Sawhill. 2015. Marriage and child wellbeing revisited. *The Future of Children* 25 (2).

McLanahan, Sara, Laura Tach, and Daniel Schneider. 2013. The causal effects of father absence. *Annual Review of Sociology* 39:399–427.

Mead, Lawrence M. 1986. *Beyond entitlement: The social obligations of citizenship.* New York, NY: Free Press.

Mead, Lawrence M. 2011. *Expanding work programs for poor men.* Washington, DC: American Enterprise Institute.

Moynihan, Daniel Patrick. 1965a. *The Negro family: The case for national action.* Washington, DC: United States Department of Labor.

Moynihan, Daniel Patrick. 1965b. A family policy for the nation. *America* 113 (12): 280–83.

Moynihan, Daniel Patrick. 1986. *Family and nation.* San Diego, CA: Harcourt Brace Jovanovich.

Moynihan, Daniel Patrick. 1996. *Miles to go: A personal history of social policy.* Cambridge, MA: Harvard University Press.

Murray, Charles. 2012. *Coming apart: The state of white America, 1960–2010.* New York, NY: Crown Forum.

Patterson, Orlando. 1998. *Rituals of blood: Consequences of slavery in two American centuries.* New York, NY: Basic Civitas.

Pavetti, LaDonna, Liz Schott, and Elizabeth Lower-Basch. 2011. *Creating subsidized employment opportunities for low-income parents: The legacy of the TANF emergency fund.* Washington, DC: Center on Budget and Policy Priorities and Center for Law and Social Policy.

Pettit, Becky, and Bruce Western. 2004. Mass imprisonment and the life course: Race and class inequality in U.S. incarceration. *American Sociological Review* 69:151–69.

Rainwater, Lee, and William L. Yancey. 1967. *The Moynihan Report and the politics of controversy.* Boston, MA: MIT Press.

Raley, R. Kelly, Megan M. Sweeney, and Danielle Wondra. 2015. The growing racial and ethnic divide in U.S. marriage patterns. *The Future of Children* 25 (2): 89–109.

Reeves, Richard V. 13 February 2014. How to save marriage in America. *The Atlantic.*

Ribar, David C. 2015. Why marriage matters for child wellbeing. *Future of Children* 25 (2): 11–27.

Ricketts, Sue, Greta Klingler, and Renee Schwalberg. 2014. Game change in Colorado: Widespread use of long-acting reversible contraceptives and rapid decline in births among young, low-income women. *Perspectives on Sexual and Reproductive Health* 46:125–32.

Ross, Heather L., and Isabel V. Sawhill. 1975. *Time of transition: The growth of families headed by women.* Washington, DC: The Urban Institute.

Sawhill, Isabel V. 2013. The new white Negro. *Washington Monthly,* January/February.

Sawhill, Isabel V. 2014. *Generation unbound: Drifting into sex and parenthood without marriage.* Washington, DC: Brookings Institution Press.

Sawhill, Isabel V., Adam Thomas, and Emily Monea. 2010. Ounce of prevention: Policy prescriptions to reduce the prevalence of fragile families. *Future of Children* 20 (2): 133–55.

Sawhill, Isabel V., and Joanna Venator. 2015. Is there a shortage of marriageable men? Center on Children and Families Brief No. 56. Washington, DC: Brookings.

Schneider, Daniel. 2015. Lessons learned from non-marriage experiments. *Future of Children* 25 (2): 155–78.

Schulz, Marc S., Carolyn Pape Cowan, and Philip A. Cowan. 2006. Promoting healthy beginnings: A randomized controlled trial of a preventive intervention to preserve marital quality during the transition to parenthood. *Journal of Consulting and Clinical Psychology* 74:20–31.

Stanley, Scott M., Elizabeth S. Allen, Howard J. Markman, Galena K. Rhoades, and Donnella L. Prentice. 2010. Decreasing divorce in army couples: Results from a randomized controlled trial Using PREP for Strong Bonds. *Journal of Couples and Relationship Therapy* 9:149–60.

Stevenson, Betsey, and Justin Wolfers. 2007. Marriage and divorce: Changes and their driving forces. National Bureau of Economic Research Working Paper 12944. Cambridge, MA.

Thomas, Adam. 2012. Policy solutions for preventing unplanned pregnancy. Center on Children and Families Brief No. 47. Washington, DC: Brookings Institution.

Thomas, Adam and Isabel V. Sawhill. 2002. *For richer or for poorer: Marriage as an antipoverty strategy.* Washington, DC: Center on Children and Families, Brookings Institution.

University of Chicago Crime Lab. 13 July 2012. BAM—Sports Edition.

U.S. Census Bureau. 2016. Historical tables: FM-1, Families by presence of own children under 18, 1950 to Present. Available from https://www.census.gov/hhes/families/data/families.html.

Ventura, Stephanie J., Brady E. Hamilton, and T. J. Mathews. 2014. National and state patterns of teen births in the United States, 1940–2013. *National Vital Statistics Reports* 63 (4) 1–34.

Waite, Linda, and Maggie Gallagher. 2000. *The case for marriage: Why married people are happier, healthier, and better off financially*. New York, NY: Doubleday.

Wang, Wendy, and Kim Parker. 2014. *Record share of Americans have never married*. Washington, DC: Pew Research Center.

Weiner, Greg. 2016. Moynihan and the neocons. *National Affairs* (winter):155–67.

Western, Bruce, and Christopher Wildeman. 2009. The black family and mass incarceration. *The ANNALS of the American Academy of Political and Social Science* 621:221–42.

Wilcox, W. Bradford, Joseph Price, and Robert I. Lerman. 2015. *Strong families, prosperous states: Do healthy families affect the wealth of states?* Washington, DC: American Enterprise Institute and Institute for Family Studies.

Wilcox, W. Bradford, and Nicholas H. Wolfinger. 2016. *Soul mates: Religion, sex, love, and marriage among African Americans and Latinos*. London: Oxford.

Wildeman, Christopher, Sara Wakefield, and Hedwig Lee, eds. 2016. Tough on crime, tough on families? Criminal justice and family life in America. *The ANNALS of the American Academy of Political and Social Science* 685.

Wildeman, Christopher, and Bruce Western. 2010. Incarceration in fragile families. *Future of Children* 20 (2): 157–77.

Wilson, William Julius. 1987. *The truly disadvantaged: The inner city, the underclass, and public policy*. Chicago, IL: University of Chicago Press.

Wilson, William Julius. 2009. The Moynihan Report and research on the black community. *The ANNALS of the American Academy of Political and Social Science* 621:34–46.

Wilson, William Julius, and Kathryn M. Neckerman. 1986. Poverty and family structure: The widening gap between evidence and public policy issues. In *Fighting poverty: What works and what doesn't*, eds. Sheldon Danziger and Daniel Weinberg, 232–59. Cambridge, MA: Harvard University Press.

Winner, Brooke, Jeffrey F. Peipert, Qiuhong Zhao, Christina Buckel, Tessa Madden, Jenifer E. Allsworth, and Gina M. Secura. 2012. Effectiveness of long-acting reversible contraception. *New England Journal of Medicine* 366:1998–2007.

Wood, Robert G., Sheena McConnell, Quinn Moore, Andrew Clarkwest, and JoAnn Hsueh. 2010. *Strengthening unmarried parents' relationships: The early impacts of building strong families*. Princeton, NJ: Mathematica Policy Research.

Wood, Robert G., Quinn Moore, Andrew Clarkwest, Alexandra Killewald, and Shannon Monahan. 2012. *The long-term effects of building strong families: A relationship skills education program for unmarried parents*. Princeton, NJ: Mathematica Policy Research.

Zolna, Mia R., and Laura D. Lindberg. 2012. *Unintended pregnancy incidence and outcomes among young adult unmarried women in the United States, 2001 and 2008*. New York, NY: Guttmacher Institute.

Elections in America

Elections in America

By
LARRY M. BARTELS

With America in the midst of a historic election year, this issue of *The ANNALS* offers a sampling of current scholarly work on party politics, campaigns, voting behavior, and electoral accountability.

Half a century ago, in a posthumously published book titled *The Responsible Electorate*, the eminent political scientist V. O. Key, Jr. insisted on the "fundamental significance" of how the American public and its political leaders understand electoral politics. "Most findings of the analysts of voting," Key (1966, 5) wrote, "never travel beyond the circle of the technicians; the popularizers, though, give wide currency to the most bizarre—and most dubious—theories of electoral behavior." Bizarre and dubious theories, Key worried (1966, 6), would skew "the types of appeals politicians employ as they seek popular support" and "the kinds of actions that governments take as they look forward to the next election":

> If leaders believe the route to victory is by projection of images and cultivation of styles rather than by advocacy of policies to cope with the problems of the country, they will project images and cultivate styles to the neglect of the substance of politics. . . . If they see voters as most certainly responsive to nonsense, they will give them nonsense. If they see voters as susceptible to delusion, they will delude them. If they see an electorate receptive to the cold, hard realities, they will give it the cold, hard realities.

Larry M. Bartels holds the May Werthan Shayne Chair of Public Policy and Social Science at Vanderbilt University. His books include Democracy for Realists: Why Elections Do Not Produce Responsive Government *(with Christopher H. Achen; Princeton University Press 2016) and a newly revised* Unequal Democracy: The Political Economy of the New Gilded Age *(Russell Sage Foundation and Princeton University Press 2016).*

Correspondence: larry.bartels@vanderbilt.edu

DOI: 10.1177/0002716216662035

Political science is arguably somewhat more prominent in shaping public understanding of American electoral politics now than it was in Key's day. Scholars such as John Sides and Lynn Vavreck have become prominent "popularizers" while also building and maintaining respected positions within "the circle of the technicians." Journalists and analysts such as Ezra Klein and Nate Silver mine The Monkey Cage, Mischiefs of Faction, and other blogs, as well as scholarly journals for insights and evidence. *The Party Decides* (Cohen et al. 2008), *Authoritarianism and Polarization in American Politics* (Hetherington and Weiler 2009), and other major academic works shape political reporting on electoral processes and voting behavior.

Nonetheless, bizarre and dubious theories of American electoral politics are by no means rare, and significant differences remain between the perspectives of scholars and those of most journalists, commentators, campaigners, and citizens. Some of those differences emerge clearly in the following articles. For example, we have little to say about election fraud, microtargeting, soccer moms, prediction markets, who is tweeting whom, Michael Bloomberg, or the conservative brain. On the other hand, our accounts of the electoral significance of issues and ideology, racial and demographic change, the nature of populism, and the impact of political campaigning will probably be surprising—and perhaps even unsettling—both to readers of *The New York Times Magazine* and to viewers of Fox News.

Of course, the contributors to this volume are no mere purveyors of academic consensus. Indeed, some of our arguments and conclusions are controversial even among specialists. We have tried to indicate when that is the case. But that sort of contentiousness, too, offers a valuable lesson for anyone who wants to make sense of elections in the United States. Political science, like any science, is a process of discovery and collective scrutiny, not a fixed body of established facts. That is especially worth remembering in the current election year, when some of the most familiar patterns of contemporary American electoral politics seem to have been shattered.

The contributors to this volume signed up for a very difficult task: to write articles in early 2016 that could be published in September and shed light on an election that would not be held until November. The task became even more difficult as it became increasingly clear that 2016 would be a far-from-typical election year. The first drafts of their articles were submitted on March 15—the same day that Donald Trump forced the last viable "mainstream" candidate out of the Republican primary race by trouncing Marco Rubio in Rubio's home state of Florida. The final versions were submitted on April 15—the day before Trump warned of "a rough July" at the Republican convention in Cleveland if he lost the nomination despite having won more delegates than any other candidate in the primaries.

Some of us (for example, Cohen and his colleagues, Rogers, and I) have finessed this uncertainty by focusing on broad historical patterns in campaigning and voting that are likely to be important regardless of the specific circumstances of the 2016 campaign. Others (for example, Noel; and Oliver and Rahn) have used data from the current election cycle to shed more direct light on the political cleavages of 2016. Still others (Sides, Tesler, and Vavreck; Azari and Hetherington; and Jacobson) explicitly consider the specific circumstances of 2016 in light of recent or distant political experience. In combination, these approaches provide a rich and stimulating response to American Academy of Political and Social Science President Kenneth Prewitt's request for a volume "situating the 2016 election in the sweep of American elections."

The Meaning of Elections

Much popular thinking about elections is guided, however unconsciously, by a complex of comforting beliefs that Christopher Achen and I have characterized as "the folk theory of democracy" (Achen and Bartels 2016). This folk theory has deep roots in American political culture, ranging from Abraham Lincoln's stirring call for "government of the people, by the people, for the people," to the Progressive Era's quest to invent new electoral institutions that would "restore the absolute sovereignty of the people," to a cold night in 2008 when a quarter of a million people gathered in Chicago's Grant Park to hear their new president-elect declare that "change has come to America."

The kernel of faith at the heart of the folk theory is the idea that elections give ordinary citizens the power to control their government. Political scientists are by no means immune to the appeal of this idea; but their professional expertise tends to impress upon them the distance between democratic ideals and realities. As the eminent scholar Robert Dahl put it six decades ago, "We expect elections to reveal the 'will' or the preferences of a majority on a set of issues. This is one thing elections rarely do, except in an almost trivial fashion" (Dahl 1956, 131).

Why not? For one thing, the majority for a winning candidate is not "a majority on a set of issues." Although voters' issue preferences seem to have become somewhat more ideologically consistent in recent decades (Pew Research Center 2014), they are far from agreeing with everything their candidate claims to stand for. Indeed, for many issues, it is far-fetched to think of most voters as having any preferences at all (Converse 1964). And when voters do report issue preferences consistent with their candidate choices, it is usually *not* because they tend to vote for the candidate whose positions they prefer, but because they tend to adopt the issue positions of the candidate they prefer for other reasons (Lenz 2012).

In light of these problems with the policy-centric version of the folk theory, many political scientists have come to think of elections primarily as referenda on the incumbent party's performance in office. Voters "need *not* know the precise economic or foreign policies of the incumbent administration in order to see or feel the *results* of those policies," according to one proponent of this view (Fiorina 1981, 5). "In order to ascertain whether the incumbents have performed poorly or well, citizens need only calculate the changes in their own welfare." That sounds relatively easy, sparing voters from the embarrassment of failing to live up to the unrealistic standards of the folk theory. Thus, evidence that voters do indeed reward incumbents for peace and prosperity and punish them for hard

FIGURE 1
District Opinion and Representatives' Roll Call Votes, 2011–13

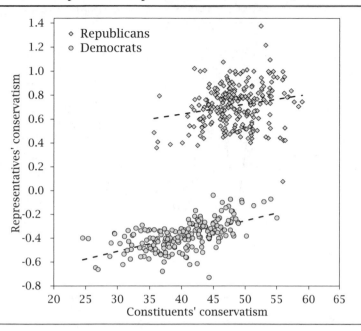

times has often been interpreted as demonstrating that election outcomes "are not 'irrational,' or random" (Kramer 1971, 140) and that "voters are not fools" (Key 1966, 7).

In fact, however, retrospective voting may be harder than it sounds. If voters are myopic in assessing their own well-being, biased in their assessments of good or bad times, and unable to sensibly distinguish good or bad incumbent performance from good or bad luck, then the contribution of retrospective voting to electoral accountability may be much less than advertised (Achen and Bartels 2016, 90–212; Bartels 2016, 74–104). And while incumbents' electoral fortunes may be well explained by election-year income growth, that will be a far cry from a popular "mandate" for any specific policies or program.

Thus, while elections no doubt play some role in constraining the behavior of elected officials, the constraints allow a good deal of leeway for incumbents to pursue their own visions of good public policy. At the congressional level, the result is that Republican and Democratic members of Congress behave very differently, even when they represent congressional districts with identical political views. That fact is evident in Figure 1, which shows the relationship between constituents' opinions and their representatives' roll call votes in the 112th Congress (2011–13). While there is some tendency for more conservative districts to have more conservative representatives, the expected difference in voting behavior between a Democrat representing the most liberal district in the country and a Democrat representing the most conservative district in the country is quite modest by comparison with the expected difference between a

FIGURE 2
Republican Popular Vote Margin in Presidential Elections, 1868–2012

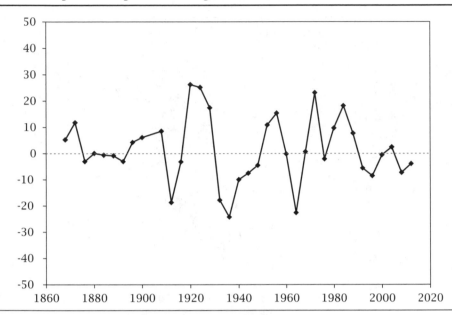

Democrat and a Republican representing identical moderate districts (Achen and Bartels 2016, 46–49).

Presidential candidates likewise seem to take issue stands that reflect their own convictions and those of their core partisans rather than the views of moderate swing voters. The result is a pattern of "leapfrog representation" (Bafumi and Herron 2010) in which small shifts in election outcomes produce wide swings in policy from Left to Right and back again. Voters are by no means irrelevant; but neither are they piloting the ship of state from the voting booth.

2016: A New Era or More of the Same?

For the past 30 years, American electoral politics has been unusually quiescent. That may seem like an odd description of a period that included the rise of the religious Right, the end of six decades of nearly uninterrupted Democratic control of the House of Representatives, a tied presidential election decided by a party-line vote of the Supreme Court, the election of our first African American president, and a gradual but substantial escalation of partisan polarization. Nonetheless, as Figure 2 makes clear, the partisan balance of power nationally has been closer and more stable than at any time in the past century, with no presidential candidate of either party since Ronald Reagan in 1984 winning a popular vote margin of even 10 percentage points. State-by-state analysis indicates that the partisan cleavage underlying this series of close elections has also remained unusually stable, with relatively little erosion or reshuffling of state-level party majorities (Bartels 1998). And individual-level survey data confirm that, despite the extension of partisan conflict to incorporate a variety of highly charged social issues (Layman and Carsey 2002), the long-standing issues of federal power and government spending emerging from the New Deal era have continued to define the most potent division between Republicans and Democrats throughout this period (Bartels 2006).

Perhaps this stable partisan balance will persist in 2016 and for some time to come. However, some analysts have pointed to gradual but substantial demographic change as a source of significant strain on the existing party system. As the proportions of racial and ethnic minorities in the population and in the electorate grow, the competitive balance between an increasingly diverse Democratic Party and an aging, mostly white Republican Party will, they argue, inevitably shift in favor of the former. That might not produce a sharp break with the past but would constitute what Key (1959) once referred to as a "secular realignment" of the party system.

More dramatically, 2016 could turn out to approximate Key's (1955, 4) ideal-type of a "critical election," one in which "the extent of electoral involvement is relatively quite high, and in which the decisive results of the voting reveal a sharp alteration of the pre-existing cleavage within the electorate" that turn out "to persist for several succeeding elections." Presumably, the new entrants to the electorate would be some combination of previously inactive populists mobilized by Donald Trump and Latinos and others countermobilized in opposition to Trump's bombastic rhetoric. Depending on their relative numbers—and on the relative loyalty of current Democrats and Republicans—the result might or might not represent a sharp shift in the even partisan balance of the past 30 years. In any case, it would represent "a sharp alteration of the pre-existing cleavage," with nationalism, trade, and immigration replacing government spending and taxes as the most important issue bases of partisan conflict. But that seems rather unlikely, even in a highly unusual election year.

John Sides, Michael Tesler, and Lynn Vavreck begin our examination of the current political context and where it might lead by laying out "The Electoral Landscape of 2016." They survey the fundamental economic and political factors that have seemed to shape presidential election outcomes over the past several decades, including objective and subjective economic conditions, cycles of incumbency, and assessments of presidential performance. They suggest that these "fundamentals" create strong cross-currents in the current electoral environment. On one hand, the economy is growing and consumers are optimistic, which bodes well for the incumbent party. On the other hand, prospective voters are more pessimistic about the polity and the president than they are about the economy, perhaps due to the growing partisan polarization and racialization of politics in the Obama years. Moreover, Democrats are disadvantaged by the fact that voters tend to feel that it is "time for a change" when the same party has held the White House for eight years. While these factors might seem to add up to a slight Republican advantage, Sides, Tesler, and Vavreck note that "many observers and forecasters gave the Democratic Party an edge," perhaps owing to the Democrats' advantage among the growing share of nonwhite voters.

The first of Gary Jacobson's two contributions to the volume builds on Sides, Tesler, and Vavreck's survey of the current electoral landscape by exploring in detail the long-term political implications of the Obama presidency. Jacobson argues that Obama has largely succeeded in solidifying the support of younger voters, bequeathing a substantial and probably durable partisan advantage to his Democratic successors. Aggregating almost 400,000 responses from 344 separate Gallup surveys conducted since Obama took office, Jacobson tracks partisan loyalties and political attitudes across generations. He finds that Americans born before 1970 have been about equally likely to identify as Democrats or Republicans during the Obama years; but among those who came of age under George W. Bush or Barack Obama, Democrats outnumber Republicans by a solid three-to-two margin. Partly this is a matter of demographic change: whites make up 80–90 percent of Jacobson's oldest cohorts but only 50–60 percent of the youngest cohorts. However, Democrats have also made generational gains among white voters, with the share of Democratic partisans and leaners increasing by almost 10 percentage points as we move from those who came of age during the Reagan era to the youngest cohorts. Moreover, even among Republicans, younger people are less implacably opposed to Obama and his policies than are their elders. For example, while conservatives outnumber moderates by three to one among the oldest cohorts of Republican identifiers, there are about as many moderates as conservatives among those coming of age in 2016, and even some liberals (10 or 12 percent). Of course, they may age into conservatism in the decades to come, but Jacobson judges that "there is no reason at present to think" that the generational tide he portrays "will change any time soon." Thus, he anticipates Democratic gains in the near- and medium-term.

In their article "Back to the Future," Julia Azari and Marc Hetherington consider political change on a much longer time-scale, asking "What the Politics of the Late-Nineteenth Century Can Tell Us about the 2016 Election." They begin by noting a variety of arresting similarities between contemporary politics and those of the late nineteenth century. Although the parties are flipped, the current geographical cleavage between the major parties is nearly identical to that of the 1890s. Partisanship is at a high point now as it was then, both in Congress and in the electorate. Voting patterns are highly nationalized, presidential elections are unusually close, and the partisan balance in Congress is precarious. According to Azari and Hetherington, Gilded Age politics was turned on its head when new issues like economic populism disrupted familiar party coalitions. Thus, they suggest that "if the parties contest the 2016 election on the same familiar ground (race, size of government, muscularity of foreign policy), we will get a familiar result. But, should Donald Trump's scrambling of the GOP during the nomination process produce new fault lines (protectionism and economic populism) in the fall, it could break the mold."

Some Dogs That Mostly Don't Bark

As we have seen, political scientists' accounts of electoral politics focus primarily on "the fundamentals"—the state of the economy, cycles of incumbency and opposition, and long-term shifts in the balance of partisan loyalties due to demographic change or "issue evolution" (Carmines and Stimson 1989). But consumers of campaign journalism are likely to absorb a very different view—one in which day-to-day events such as speeches, debates, and campaign ads produce constant shifts in the polls and, presumably, in the candidates' ultimate electoral prospects. Obviously, this view is well suited to generate ratings and page views. It also meshes nicely with the perspective of political professionals, who focus primarily on day-to-day events by default, because the "fundamentals" are long-term features of the strategic landscape beyond their day-to-day influence. In the apt metaphor of John Sides and Lynn Vavreck (2013, 11–31), candidates and their teams must "play the hand they're dealt," strategically deploying campaign resources in hopes of producing marginal gains in support.

Thomas Wood is in the unusual position of being both a scholar of electoral politics and an experienced campaign practitioner. In "What the Heck Are We Doing in Ottumwa, Anyway?" Wood examines how presidential campaigners allocate one specific kind of campaign resource—candidate visits. Experienced campaigners believe that candidate visits generate favorable national and local press coverage and bolster the spirits of local activists and supporters. However, Wood's detailed analysis of media coverage in the 2012 presidential campaign finds that the effect of candidate visits on local media coverage was "very modest." He also draws upon a wealth of survey data to assess the impact of specific visits by Mitt Romney and his running mate, Paul Ryan, on individual voters. He concludes that the candidates' visits probably produced shifts in vote intentions, especially among political independents. However, those shifts were generally small and seemed to fade even over the course of a few days. Wood suggests that campaigners' reliance on visits despite this "tenuous impact" may reflect "the importance of tradition, inertia, and the lack of alignment between a candidate's interests and the interests of their senior staff." He speculates that campaign resources might better be spent "on those activities that have been shown to more reliably influence voters—such as building out campaign infrastructure at the local level and providing more resources for voter contact."

If campaigning matters less than many people imagine, the same is true of the competing candidates' stands on the major political issues of the day. Whereas many analysts and observers in the grip of the folk theory of democracy assume that a national election is, first and foremost, a referendum on the opposing candidates' platforms, political scientists generally attempt to forecast or explain election outcomes with no reference at all to those platforms, relying instead on measures of economic conditions, incumbency, and the like.[1] Partly that is a matter of expediency: it is difficult to characterize candidates' issue positions systematically, especially in real time. But it is also a matter of parsimony: with "fundamentals" accounting for most of the observed historical variation in election outcomes, it is by no means obvious that the statistical value added from measuring issue positions would be worth the trouble.

Martin Cohen, Mary McGrath, Peter Aronow, and John Zaller set out to assess systematically the electoral cost of ideological extremism in presidential elections since 1948. They measure the ideological positions of the competing presidential candidates in each election using a combination of expert judgments and the perceptions of well-informed voters in contemporaneous surveys. Then they incorporate the relative extremism of the candidates in each election as an additional explanatory variable in statistical models of presidential election outcomes. They find "little evidence of an electorally important relationship between candidate extremism and vote outcomes." The landslide defeats of Barry Goldwater in 1964 and George McGovern in 1972 might suggest that voters strongly punish extremist candidates, thus providing substantial electoral incentives for moderation. But in a broader historical context, those outcomes seem to have had less to do with Goldwater and McGovern's ideological extremism than with the fact that both were challenging incumbents who presided over election-year economic booms. Ronald Reagan in 1980 and Barack Obama in 2008 were at least as extreme as Goldwater and McGovern by Cohen and his colleagues' measure, but they ran in years when recessions offered favorable economic conditions for challengers, and both won easily despite their unfavorable ideological positions. Overall, the difference in expected vote share between the most moderate candidates in the postwar era and the most extreme candidates amounted to less than 3 percentage points—potentially decisive in a close election, but "negligible" compared with the effects of other economic and political factors.

If the electoral penalty for ideological extremism is as modest as Cohen and his colleagues suggest, that may go a long way toward explaining presidential candidates' "Failure to Converge" on the centrist issue positions favored by supposedly pivotal swing voters. Some observers have suggested that candidates fail to converge because they must compromise between the preferences of swing voters and those of their core supporters, who provide resources, enthusiasm, and reliable turnout. Thus, the increasingly "polarized" state of contemporary American politics is often attributed to the extreme views of the parties' (generally meaning the *other* party's) core supporters. My own assessment of the positions of Democratic and Republican core partisans on a variety of specific issues indicates that they have indeed become more polarized, with the average distance between them increasing by about 30 percent between 1980 and 2012. However, they are still not sufficiently extreme to make the positions of presidential candidates plausibly interpretable as compromises between the preferences of swing voters and core partisans. Indeed, the positions of presidential candidates have often been even more extreme than those preferred by their core partisans. The positions of Democratic candidates, especially, seem to reflect durable convictions more than they do the preferences of the Democratic base, much less swing voters. The routine failure of presidential candidates to adopt centrist positions on major issues is a signal embarrassment to the folk theory of democracy, in which citizens use elections to produce policies in accordance with their preferences.

Intraparty Cleavages

My analysis of the parties' respective bases focuses on their generally—and increasingly—extreme policy preferences. Hans Noel offers a different perspective on the views of party activists, drawing on surveys conducted in the run-up to the 2016 nomination process. Those surveys show, not surprisingly, that Republican activists are overwhelmingly conservative or "very conservative," while Democratic activists are overwhelmingly liberal or "very liberal." While distinctions between more or less extreme flavors of each party's dominant ideology sometimes engender intraparty conflict, Noel's analysis highlights a different sort of internal cleavage: between activists who endorse "compromise to get things done" and those who want political leaders to "stick to their principles, no matter what." (The latter stance is somewhat more common among more extreme ideologues, but the correlation is modest.) Within the Democratic Party, supporters of Hillary Clinton and Bernie Sanders were virtually indistinguishable on this score in summer 2015; but by the time of the first caucuses and primaries, Clinton's supporters were more likely to favor "compromise to get things done," while Sanders' supporters were more likely to favor "sticking to their principles." On the Republican side, the cleavage between purists and pragmatists was both starker and of longer standing, with Ted Cruz the clear favorite of those favoring "sticking to their principles," Marco Rubio the clear favorite of those favoring "compromise to get things done," and Donald Trump attracting substantial support from both of these groups. As Noel puts it, "Both parties include an ideological core and a set of party regulars who work to expand that core into a workable governing coalition. The Democrats have, for now, tamed their ideological core. The Republicans have not, and their conflict left things open for a hostile takeover."

The catch-all nature of Trump's appeal is equally evident in Eric Oliver and Wendy Rahn's analysis of the "Rise of the *Trumpenvolk*." Oliver and Rahn provide both a detailed analysis of "populism" in American public opinion and a guide to its role in the 2016 campaign. They identify and measure three distinct dimensions of populism: anti-elitism, mistrust of experts, and American nationalism. Several candidates in 2016 seem to have tapped into one or another of these elements of populism. Bernie Sanders's supporters ranked highest in anti-elitism ("the rich control both political parties"; "the system is stacked against people like me"), but very low in mistrust of experts and American nationalism. Ted Cruz's supporters were highly mistrustful of experts ("when it comes to really important questions, scientific facts don't help very much"), but very low in anti-elitism. Marco Rubio's supporters were strongly nationalistic ("how important is being an American to who you are?"), but also quite tolerant of elites. Only Donald Trump's supporters recorded very high average scores on all three of these separate dimensions of populism. In effect, Trump built a broader populist coalition than any of his rivals. Oliver and Rahn also offer a historical explanation for the prominence of populism in the contemporary political environment. They posit a growing "representation gap" reflected in public agreement with statements like "public officials don't care much about what people like me think" and "the people in Washington are out of touch with the rest of the country." Partisan polarization (as measured by party line voting in Congress) closely tracks and helps to explain these sentiments, providing a fertile setting for the latest upwelling of populist politics in America.

Political Institutions, Electoral Accountability, and Popular Responsiveness

In today's polarized political environment, as we have seen, the positions of candidates and party activists are often far from those of most voters. Since the electoral penalty for extremism is small, extremists are frequently elected and reelected. The result, according to Oliver and Rahn, is populist frustration stemming from a "representation gap." When either party gains firm control of the levers of government, that "representation gap" may be manifested in the adoption of policies "out of touch" with the views of the other party, if not of the country as a whole. A case in point is the Democrats' adoption of "Obamacare" during the brief period in which they enjoyed unified control of the federal government and a filibuster-proof majority in the Senate. More often, however, the fragmentation of power in the American political system, the close electoral balance between the contemporary parties, and the disdain of politicians and activists for "compromise to get things done" result in gridlock and perceived unresponsiveness. In either case, the upshot is a failure of electoral accountability.

One of the most distinctive features of the American electoral system is the length of the ballot, which often includes a plethora of federal, state, and local races and, in some jurisdictions, referenda and initiatives as well. In principle, all of these elections give voters unparalleled control over public officials and public policies. In practice, as Steven Rogers shows, voters are mostly incapable of holding state legislators (at least) accountable for their performance in office. More than 40 percent of state legislative elections are uncontested, and one-third of incumbents are unchallenged in both the primary and the general election. State legislators who share a party affiliation with an unpopular president are more likely to be challenged and more likely to be defeated. Indeed, the number of state legislative seats a party gains or loses in each election is very strongly correlated with the number of congressional seats it gains or loses—despite the fact that policies and performance in each state have little to do with policies and performance at the national level. The president, it seems, is the overwhelming focus of voters' political hopes and fears, and state legislative candidates are mostly just along for the ride.

Under some circumstances, this focus on the president might provide coherence to American politics, helping to coordinate the various branches and levels of government. But in recent years, at least, that has not been the case. Gary Jacobson's concluding essay on "Polarization, Gridlock, and Presidential Campaign Politics in 2016" explores the paradox of electoral coherence and governmental incoherence in Washington. How, he asks, have increasingly strong partisan loyalties and "thoroughly nationalized federal elections" mostly produced divided government and policy stalemate? While state legislative elections hinge on national partisanship and views of the president, so too—and increasingly—voting in House and Senate races reflects national rather than local forces. In 2012, Jacobson notes, only twenty-six House candidates managed to win in districts carried by the opposing party's presidential candidate. (In close elections in the

1960s, '70s, and '80s, such split outcomes were about five times as common.)
Nevertheless, in an era of relatively equal partisan strength, quirks of political
geography and differential turnout have frequently produced divided control of
Congress and the White House. Whereas Democrats have won at least slim
popular pluralities in five of the six most recent presidential elections, their votes
have been geographically concentrated in a minority of congressional districts
(mostly urban, often heavily black and Latino), allowing Republicans to win control of the House with fewer than half the votes.[2] In midterm elections—where
electorates tend to be smaller, whiter, and older—Republicans have been even
more advantaged. Thus, according to Jacobson, "even a solid Democratic victory
in 2016 would not loosen the Republican grip on the House and would simply
extend Obama-era conflicts. A Republican victory would produce a unified
national government but with a policy agenda that, if actively pursued, would
face intransigent Democratic opposition, centered in the Senate, and would
polarize the electorate even further."

Of course, the architects of the American political system might have viewed
"incoherent government" in Jacobson's sense as a feature, not a bug. While they
recognized the need for a more powerful central government than existed under
the Articles of Confederation, their aim was decidedly *not* to translate the will of
national majorities directly into public policy. Their complex machinery of inter-
secting branches and layers of government was intended to curb the "mischiefs of
faction," which James Madison (1787/1901, 45) famously defined as "a number of
citizens, whether amounting to a majority or a minority of the whole, who are
united and actuated by some common impulse of passion, or of interest, adverse to
the rights of other citizens, or to the permanent and aggregate interests of the
community."

The resulting "status quo bias" in American politics is nicely illustrated by
Martin Gilens's (2012, 73–74) analysis of the fate of hundreds of potential
national policy changes proposed in opinion surveys between 1981 and 2002. For
each potential policy change, Gilens recorded the proportion of Americans favoring the change at the time of the survey and whether the proposed change was
actually implemented in the next four years. He found that when the public was
evenly split between favoring and opposing a change, that change was implemented only 28 percent of the time. Even changes favored by 80 percent or more
of survey respondents (240 of the cases Gilens examined) were adopted only
48 percent of the time. Support from a majority of the public is far from being
either a necessary or a sufficient condition for policy change in the American
political system.

Alas, neither Madison nor anyone else has come up with a reliable way to
ascertain when a majority's impulses and interests are "adverse to the rights of
other citizens, or to the permanent and aggregate interests of the community."
Thus, political institutions designed to curb the mischiefs of faction also thwart
the ability of the system to respond to genuine public needs. And in our current
polarized environment, Democrats and Republicans seldom agree on what the
public needs. Many of the same people who bemoan (or, for now, simply wish
away) the institutional hurdles that would face President Clinton (or President

Sanders) thank their lucky stars for the institutional hurdles that would face President Trump (or President Cruz)—and vice versa.

Ironically, then, as Jacobson concludes, "the most likely outcome is that despite all the discontent, anger, and disdain for politics and politicians roiling the electorate in 2016, something close to the status quo will prevail . . . with most of the familiar players and problems returning once again when the new Congress convenes in 2017." In that case, presumably, the discontent, anger, and disdain will persist. Perhaps that is what we should expect, given the chronic mismatch between our unrealistic expectations of popular responsiveness derived from the folk theory of democracy and our complex political institutions reflecting Madison's republican abhorrence of the "mischiefs of faction."

Notes

1. Every four years, the political science journal PS publishes a symposium including a variety of pree-lection forecasts based on statistical models of this sort. See, for example, Campbell (2012).

2. Successful gerrymandering by Republican state legislatures accounts for part of this advantage; but given the geographical concentration of Democrats in many areas, affirmative political engineering would be required to draw politically neutral congressional districts.

References

Achen, Christopher H., and Larry M. Bartels. 2016. *Democracy for realists: Why elections do not produce responsive government*. Princeton, NJ: Princeton University Press.

Bafumi, Joseph, and Michael C. Herron. 2010. Leapfrog representation and extremism: A study of American voters and their members in Congress. *American Political Science Review* 104:519–42.

Bartels, Larry M. 1998. Electoral continuity and change, 1868–1996. *Electoral Studies* 17:301–26.

Bartels, Larry M. 2006. What's the matter with *What's the Matter with Kansas?* *Quarterly Journal of Political Science* 1:201–26.

Bartels, Larry M. 2016. *Unequal democracy: The political economy of the New Gilded Age*. 2nd ed. New York, NY and Princeton, NJ: Russell Sage Foundation and Princeton University Press.

Campbell, James E. 2012. Forecasting the 2012 American national elections. *PS: Political Science and Politics* 45:610–13.

Carmines, Edward G., and James A. Stimson. 1989. *Issue evolution: Race and the transformation of American politics*. Princeton, NJ: Princeton University Press.

Cohen, Marty, David Karol, Hans Noel, and John Zaller. 2008. *The party decides: Presidential nomination before and after reform*. Chicago, IL: University of Chicago Press.

Converse, Philip E. 1964. The nature of belief systems in mass publics. In *Ideology and discontent*, ed. David E. Apter, 206–61. Glencoe, IL: Free Press.

Dahl, Robert A. 1956. *A preface to democratic theory*. Chicago, IL: University of Chicago Press.

Fiorina, Morris P. 1981. *Retrospective voting in American national elections*. New Haven, CT: Yale University Press.

Gilens, Martin. 2012. *Affluence and influence: Economic inequality and political power in America*. New York, NY and Princeton, NJ: Russell Sage Foundation and Princeton University Press.

Hetherington, Marc J., and Jonathan D. Weiler. 2009. *Authoritarianism and polarization in American politics*. New York, NY: Cambridge University Press.

Key, V. O., Jr. 1955. A theory of critical elections. *Journal of Politics* 17:3–18.

Key, V. O., Jr. 1959. Secular realignment and the party system. *Journal of Politics* 21:198–210.

Key, V. O., Jr., with the assistance of Milton C. Cummings, Jr. 1966. *The responsible electorate: Rationality in presidential voting 1936–1960*. New York, NY: Vintage Books.

Kramer, Gerald H. 1971. Short-term fluctuations in U.S. voting behavior, 1896–1964. *American Political Science Review* 65:131–43.

Layman, Geoffrey C., and Thomas M. Carsey. 2002. Party polarization and "conflict extension" in the American electorate. *American Journal of Political Science* 46:786–802.

Lenz, Gabriel S. 2012. *Follow the leader? How voters respond to politicians' policies and performance*. Chicago, IL: University of Chicago Press.

Madison, James. 1787/1901. The numerous advantages of the union. In Alexander Hamilton, John Jay, and James Madison, The Federalist. New York, NY: P. F. Collier & Son.

Pew Research Center. June 2014. *Political polarization in the American public*. Washington, DC: Pew Research Center. Available from http://www.people-press.org/files/2014/06/6-12-2014-Political-Polarization-Release.pdf.

Sides, John, and Lynn Vavreck. 2013. *The gamble: Choice and chance in the 2012 presidential election*. Princeton, NJ: Princeton University Press.

The Electoral Landscape of 2016

By
JOHN SIDES,
MICHAEL TESLER,
and
LYNN VAVRECK

As 2015 got underway, most Americans were poised for another Bush vs. Clinton presidential election, but by the middle of the year it was clear something unexpected was unfolding in the race for the White House. In this article, we illuminate the political landscape heading into the 2016 election, paying special attention to the public's mood, their assessments of government, their attitudes about race and members of the other party, and the health of the nation's economy. Fundamental predictors of election outcomes did not clearly favor either side, but an increasing ethnic diversity in the electorate, alongside a racially polarized electorate, was favorable to Democrats. Ultimately, an ambivalent electorate divided by party and race set the stage for a presidential primary that played directly on these divisions, and for a general election whose outcome initially appeared far from certain.

Keywords: economy; anger; party identification; 2016 election; Barack Obama; trust in government; recession

In the 1953 film *The Wild One*, a woman approaches Marlon Brando's character, Johnny Strabler, the leader of a gang called the "Black Rebels Motorcycle Club" that had just

John Sides is an associate professor of political science at George Washington University. He is coauthor (with Lynn Vavreck) of The Gamble: Choice and Change in the 2012 Presidential Election *(Princeton University Press 2013) and various articles on public opinion, campaigns, and elections. He is cofounder of The Monkey Cage, a* Washington Post *blog about political science and politics.*

Michael Tesler is an assistant professor of political science at University of California, Irvine, and author of Post-Racial or Most-Racial: Race and Politics in the Obama Era *(University of Chicago Press 2016) and coauthor of* Obama's Race: The 2008 Election and the Dream of a Post-Racial America *(University of Chicago Press 2010). He is a contributor to The Monkey Cage, a* Washington Post *blog about political science and politics.*

Correspondence: jsides@gwu.edu

DOI: 10.1177/0002716216658922

rolled into town. She asks, "What are you rebelling against, Johnny?" His famous reply: "Whaddaya got?"

Brando's famous line—indeed, his entire persona, with his sideburns and black leather jacket—evoked something new and even dangerous. At a time when much of America was enjoying the new comforts of life in the suburbs and the convenience of the automobile, the television, and fast food restaurants, Johnny Strabler tapped into some sort of contempt or frustration—but even he could not quite say what it was.

As the presidential campaign got underway in 2015, most Americans were not wearing leather jackets or riding motorcycles. In fact, they were increasingly optimistic about the economy, more than they had been for much of the past decade. But in the minds of many observers, there was an inchoate rebelliousness among Americans that sounded an awful lot like "Whaddaya got?"

Americans were said to be angry, anxious, and fearful. They were said to "be poised for a major reset" (Todd 2015). Some polls appeared to back up this characterization of the electorate. In October 2015, 69 percent of Americans agreed with this statement: "I feel angry because our political system seems to only be working for the insiders with money and power, like those on Wall Street or in Washington, rather than it working to help everyday people get ahead." And 54 percent agreed that, "The economic and political systems in this country are stacked against people like me."[1] Between November 2015 and March 2016, the share of news stories about the presidential election that contained the word "angry" increased by 200 percent.

"Voter anger" would be a common refrain throughout the campaign, and there clearly were signs of anger in the electorate. But there were also signs of other, more positive sentiments. Americans felt far more favorably about the economy than they had during the presidential campaigns in 2008 or 2012. Indeed, they felt as favorably about the economy as they had more than 10 years ago. This optimism reflected the slow but steady economic recovery after the recession and financial crisis of 2007–9.

What was most striking about Americans in 2015 was not their diffuse "anger" but an unusual disjuncture: despite their optimism about the economy, they were distinctly less positive about the overall direction of the country and about their president, Barack Obama. This disjuncture suggests that Americans were not so much "angry" as ambivalent. They saw both good and bad in the country. For example, in that same October poll where a majority said they were "angry" about

Lynn Vavreck, a professor of political science and communication studies at University of California, Los Angeles, and contributing columnist to The Upshot *at the* New York Times, *is a coauthor (with John Sides) of* The Gamble: Choice and Chance in the 2012 Presidential Election *(Princeton University Press 2013), and the author of* The Message Matters *(Princeton University Press 2009) about presidential campaigns from 1952 to 2008. She is an inaugural Andrew F. Carnegie Fellow.*

NOTE: We thank Larry Bartels and the other contributors to this volume for helpful suggestions. We are equally grateful to Vanderbilt University's Center for the Study of Democratic Institutions, which hosted us at a critical juncture in the writing of this article.

the political system, 58 percent agreed that they were "cautiously optimistic about where things are headed."[2]

What was behind this disjuncture? One factor is partisanship. Even as the recovery proceeded apace, Democrats and Republicans held divergent views of the economy and Obama. This helped to depress approval of Obama in particular. In an era where opposite partisans are increasingly unwilling to support the president except under extraordinary circumstances, it may be harder to gain some measure of bipartisan support, even when economic times are good.

A second key factor is race. The Obama administration was not just eight years of a Democratic president; it was also eight years of a black president. Obama's impact on public opinion was profound. During his administration, Americans' racial identity became a more potent force in public opinion. Gaps between the political opinions of whites and blacks were frequently larger than they had been in the past.

Moreover, white Americans' opinions of blacks and other minority groups became more intertwined with their partisan identities and more potent predictors of their opinions about the economy and many other issues—virtually anything even remotely associated with Obama. This growing "racialization" of public opinion began before Obama became president, but it became more pronounced during his time in office.

The public's ambivalence—and these sharp cleavages based on party and race—have resonated throughout the 2016 presidential campaign. For example, even before the Republican primary got underway, there was already significant economic discontent among Republicans. The racialization of public opinion helped to create an increasing fraction of Republicans who expressed unfavorable attitudes toward various minority groups. Both economic discontent and hostility to certain minority groups would help to fuel the surprising success of Donald Trump.

In the Democratic party, where racialization has meant a growing liberalism on racial issues, both of the frontrunners—Hillary Clinton and Bernie Sanders—were freed to advocate for an agenda that spoke more directly than the party had in decades to the interests of the minority groups that were increasingly important to the Democratic coalition.

In the general election, the crucial fundamentals of presidential elections did not clearly favor either side, at least as of early 2016. A growing economy benefited the incumbent Democrats. And with the ethnic diversity of the electorate increasing year by year, a racially polarized electorate was increasingly favorable to Democrats, too.

On the other hand, even though Obama is not on the ballot in 2016, he matters a great deal. Presidential approval is crucial to presidential election outcomes—and Obama's approval rating lagged the growing economy. Democrats also confronted the simple challenge of earning a third consecutive term in the White House.

Ultimately, an ambivalent electorate divided by party and race sets the stage for a presidential primary that plays directly on these divisions, and for a general election whose outcome we would typically expect to be far from certain.

FIGURE 1
Trends in Key Economic Indicators, 2008–15

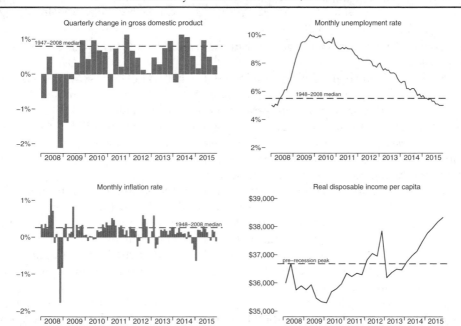

SOURCE: St. Louis Federal Reserve's FRED database.

Was It "Morning in America" Again? The Economic Recovery of 2010–15

Obama took office amid the worst recession since the Great Depression. This recession—the "Great Recession"—was particularly punishing because it was paired with a financial crisis, and some research suggests that this combination leads to an even more sluggish recovery (Reinhart and Rogoff 2009; Danziger 2013). The Great Recession bore this out.

For example, the deep recession that occurred in 1981–82—during Ronald Reagan's first term—actually saw unemployment peak at a higher level (10.8 percent) than it did in the 2007–9 recession (10 percent). But after the 1981–82 recession was over, the economy grew at a much more rapid pace. Unemployment returned to its prerecession value in less than three years. By contrast, this took almost eight years after the Great Recession began.[3]

Despite this sluggish pace, an economic recovery did occur. Figure 1 depicts the recovery by examining trends in four economic indicators: the quarter-to-quarter change in gross domestic product, which captures the overall size of the economy; the monthly unemployment rate; the monthly inflation rate; and real disposable income per capita, which is equal to personal income minus income tax payments and is adjusted for inflation. This figure begins in 2008, during the height of the recession, and continues through the end of 2015.

The recovery did not really begin until 2010. At that point, gross domestic product began to expand. On a quarter-to-quarter basis, the average growth in gross domestic product from 2009 to 2015 was somewhat below its historical median from 1947 to 2008, and there were a few quarters where growth was nearly nonexistent or even negative. But the overall trend was toward economic expansion.

As the economy expanded, unemployment began to fall and—with the exception of the first quarter of 2013—disposable income began to increase. By the end of 2015, the unemployment rate of 5 percent was below its median value over the 60 years from 1948 to 2008. Disposable income was nearly $2,000 above its prerecession peak in the second quarter of 2008. Meanwhile, the inflation rate—measured as month-to-month changes in the consumer price index—was consistently low, compared to its historical median.

This combination of falling unemployment and low inflation was particularly distinctive. These two indicators are often combined into the "misery index," where the combination of high unemployment and high inflation, characteristic of the late 1970s, is the most "miserable" possibility. But by 2015, the misery index was nearly as low as it had been since 1950 (Dews 2016). This implied the opposite of stagflation: an active demand for goods and services along with low unemployment and inflation.

In short, as the election year was getting underway, the U.S. economy had made important progress since the Great Recession. And, perhaps more importantly, Americans realized it.

One of the longest measures of Americans' views of the economy is the Index of Consumer Sentiment, which is tracked by the University of Michigan and dates back to 1960. The index is based on responses to five questions, three of which measure people's views of their current financial circumstances and economic conditions in the country and two of which measure their expectations about the near future.[4]

Figure 2 presents the trend in this index since 1980, when it is possible to separate the electorate by upper-, middle-, and low-income terciles. After Obama took office, there was an initial increase in consumer sentiment that soon plateaued before diving down again during the debt ceiling crisis in summer 2011— the possibility that Congress might cause the United States to default on its debts by not raising the debt ceiling provoked anxiety among financial markets and Americans alike.

But after that crisis passed, consumer sentiment resumed its swing toward greater optimism. By the end of 2015, even with a slight downturn in the second and third quarters of that year, consumer sentiment was as positive as it had been since the mid-2000s. It was also as positive as it had been in the mid-1980s during the recovery from the recession of 1981–82. For example, among all Americans, the value of consumer sentiment at the end of 1983, as Reagan's reelection campaign was gearing up, was 91.6. At the end of 2015, it was almost exactly the same: 91.0.[5]

Other measures of economic sentiment showed a similar trend. For example, in a February 2009 Pew Research Center survey, 71 percent said that economic conditions in the country were "poor," 24 percent said "only fair," 4 percent said

FIGURE 2

The Index of Consumer Sentiment among Income Groups, 1980–2015

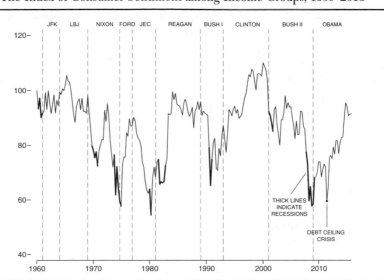

SOURCE: University of Michigan, Survey Research Center; http://www.sca.isr.umich.edu/.

"good," and less than 1 percent said "excellent." By December 2015, only 28 percent said poor, 45 percent said fair, 24 percent said good, and 3 percent said excellent. The December figures were essentially identical to those in August 2004. Similarly, through 2014–15, fewer Americans said that they were "falling behind financially."[6]

Figure 2 also shows that these positive sentiments about the economy were broadly based in the electorate. Throughout 2015, much had been written about the challenges facing the middle and working classes. The middle class was described as "losing ground" and "falling behind financially" (Pew Research Center 2015). The working class was described as "feeling screwed" (Arnade 2015).

It was true that the income gains visible in Figure 1 were not evenly distributed across the electorate. As of 2014, real incomes for a majority of American families were still below their prerecession levels. This was particularly true among the lowest income group.[7] Consistent with this, Figure 2 shows that people with high incomes have had a more positive view of the economy relative to those with low levels of income.

But at the same time, evaluations of the economy among all of the income groups had become more positive since the end of the Great Recession.[8] While middle- and low-income households may have experienced the economic recovery differently than those with higher incomes, it was not evident in these data.

Indeed, what is distinctive about the Obama years—especially compared with the Reagan years—is how small the gap was between income groups. The average gap between upper and lower income groups in their opinions of economic performance from 1981 to 1988 was 21.3 points. From 2009 to 2015, it was 13.4 points. This was also lower than during the administrations of George H. W. Bush (14.7), Bill Clinton (16.7), and George W. Bush (18.4). Evaluations of the economy were more consistent across income levels under Obama than in recent history.

How can perceptions of the economy be so favorable, even among groups that had not yet recovered fully from the Great Recession? One explanation involves the Index of Consumer Sentiment, combined with the most recent trends in family incomes. The index asks respondents to evaluate their financial situation compared to a year ago. As of 2015, the trend in the previous year was positive: even if family incomes had not fully recovered from the recession, they were recovering nonetheless. There was a notable increase in the incomes of most income quintiles between 2013 and 2014, which likely continued into 2015 as well.

These short-term trends were especially important because of how the economy typically matters in elections. Previous research (e.g., Bartels 2008; Achen and Bartels 2016) shows that voters are much more sensitive to election-year trends in the economy than the economy's long-term performance. This "myopia" means that even if many Americans' incomes were below their prerecession levels, the positive trend would be more electorally consequential.

Thus, at the eve of the election year, Americans—including Americans of all income levels—were relatively optimistic about the economy. That they felt as positively as they did at the end of 1983 is particularly noteworthy. When Ronald Reagan ran for reelection in 1984, he contrasted the country's economic growth to what it had been under Jimmy Carter in 1980. It was "morning again in America," said one famous Reagan advertisement. The difference in 2015 is that it somehow did not seem like "morning" at all.

A Distinctly Political Dissatisfaction

Based on consumer sentiment alone, Americans seemed to think that better days were upon them or at least on the horizon. But people were not yet expressing an unguarded optimism. As of 2015, there were significant currents of dissatisfaction with the country, the federal government, and Barack Obama. This disjuncture between views of the economy and political attitudes is unusual. Typically, people's perceptions of the economy loom large in their political attitudes. When they perceive that the economy is doing well, they evaluate elected officials more favorably (Stimson 2004). They trust the government more (Chanley, Rudolph, and Rahn 2000; Keele 2007). They think that the country as a whole is going in the right direction.

But as of 2015, increasingly favorable economic evaluations had not yet affected these other attitudes. There was instead a persistent mistrust in government, dissatisfaction with the overall state of the country, and disapproval of Obama. Figure 3 shows trends in these political attitudes. From 2009 to 2015, even as consumer sentiment was increasing, trust in government, the perception

FIGURE 3

Trends in Presidential Approval, Political Trust, and Evaluations of Country, 2009–15

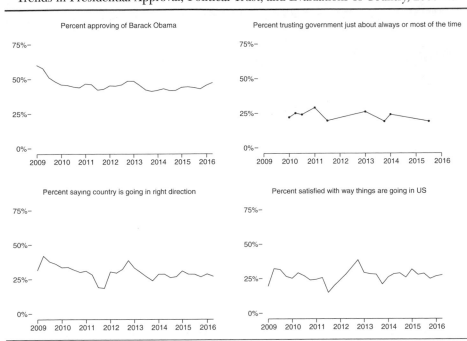

SOURCES: Pollster.com (presidential approval), Pew Research Center surveys 2010–15 (trust), Pollster.com (right direction, satisfaction). All data aggregated to the quarterly level except political trust.

that the country is going in the "right direction," and satisfaction with how things are going in the country were either stagnant or decreasing slightly. Fewer Americans believed that the country was going in the right direction at the end of 2015 than did so at the beginning of 2009—at the height of the Great Recession.

Even though economic evaluations at the end of 2015 were as positive as in the mid-2000s, fewer people said that the country was going in the right direction: 26 percent in the last quarter of 2015 as opposed to 40 percent in the third and fourth quarters of 2004. Trust in government was higher then, too: in a March 2004 Pew poll, 36 percent said they trusted the government just about always or most of the time, compared with 19 percent in fall 2014.[9]

Other surveys showed a similar finding. In the Public Religion Research Institute's American Values Survey, conducted in fall 2015, respondents were asked whether "America's best days are ahead of us or behind us." Americans were evenly divided, with 49 percent saying "ahead of us" and 49 percent saying "behind us." In 2012, however, they were more likely to say "ahead of us" (54 percent) than "behind us" (38 percent). Remarkably, given their increasingly

FIGURE 4
The Relationship between Consumer Sentiment and Presidential Approval

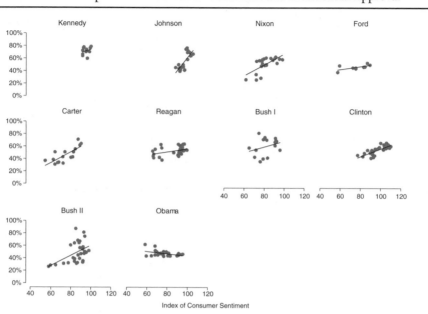

SOURCE: University of Michigan, Survey Research Center; www.sca.isr.umich.edu/.

favorable views of the economy, 72 percent also said that the country was "still in a recession"—even in 2015. And 53 percent said that the "American culture and way of life has mostly changed for the worse" (Jones et al. 2015).

Americans' ambivalence extended to Barack Obama as well. Four years prior, as 2011 came to an end, views of Obama were actually more positive than objective economic conditions and other factors would have predicted (Sides and Vavreck 2013). Four years later, as Obama entered the last year of his presidency, there was reason to believe that he would become even more popular. Although presidential approval typically declines the longer a president is in office, even after accounting for other factors (see Sides and Vavreck 2013, 20), Obama was presiding over a growing economy. The public's increasingly positive evaluations of Obama could have translated into increasing approval ratings.

But as of the end of 2015, this had not happened. In fact, Obama has been the only president since John F. Kennedy whose approval ratings did not tend to increase alongside evaluations of the economy. Whereas in 2011 Obama was able to escape some of the blame for the Great Recession, in his second term, he seems to have also escaped the credit for the recovery. Figure 4 compares presidential approval and consumer sentiment for each president since Kennedy.

For every president except Obama, the relationship is positive: as consumer sentiment becomes more positive, so does presidential approval. In Obama's case, the line is actually negative. Obama was relatively popular right after he was inaugurated—a brief honeymoon bump—but his approval rating fell quickly within his first several months in office. Even as economic evaluations began to improve, his approval barely budged.[10] If presidential approval were simply a function of consumer sentiment and nothing else, Obama should have been more popular than he was—approximately 11 percentage points more popular. But his approval ratings proved far stickier than consumer sentiment alone would predict.[11]

Partisan Divides in the Electorate

One reason for the stickiness in Obama's approval ratings was the partisan divide over his presidency. Partisan divisions in political attitudes are, of course, nothing new. These divisions have sharpened over many years as American political parties have become more ideologically sorted. Democrats are increasingly self-described liberals and Republicans are increasingly self-described conservatives (Levendusky 2009). The parties are also better sorted in terms of certain political issues, such as abortion (Adams 1997, Baldassarri and Gelman 2008).

Moreover, both Democrats and Republicans in the electorate are simply more hostile toward the opposite party. This growing hostility translates into opinions about everyday life: partisans are now more concerned that their son or daughter might marry someone in the opposite party (Iyengar, Sood, and Lelkes 2012). Experiments show that people are remarkably willing to discriminate against members of the opposite party (Iyengar and Westwood 2014) and even find members of the opposite party less physically attractive (Nicholson et al., 2016). This does not mean that the parties have become monoliths or that people have become orthodox liberals or conservatives. But it does mean that party differences and antagonisms are growing.

This trend was very much in evidence as the 2016 campaign began. Democrats and Republicans evaluated the country in different ways. Unsurprisingly, seven years of a Democratic president meant that Democrats felt far more positively than did Republicans. This was manifest in perceptions of the economy. Partisans typically think the economy is doing better when their party controls the White House. Some research also shows that this partisan bias increased substantially between 1985 and 2007, particularly during the Bush administration (Enns, Kellstedt, and McAvoy 2012). It then declined during the Great Recession, when the downturn was so severe that the vast majority of Americans—both Democrats and Republicans—evaluated the economy unfavorably.

But as the economic recovery proceeded, partisan bias reasserted itself and was very much evident in 2015. YouGov/*Economist* polls conducted between June and December 2015 found that Democrats believed their personal finances were doing much better than Republicans did. Among Democrats, 27 percent said that they were better off financially than a year ago, 48 percent said that their finances were about the same, and 20 percent said that they were worse off financially. By contrast, only 11 percent of Republicans said they were better off financially, while 43 percent said they were worse off.

FIGURE 5
Trends in Presidential Approval by Party, 1948–2015

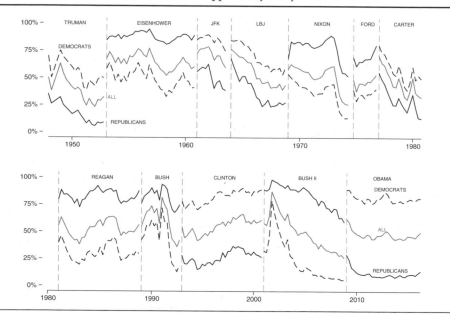

This partisan divide was important enough to override the impact of social class. Although high-income people expressed more financial satisfaction than low-income people—among Democrats, Republicans, and independents alike—partisanship took precedence. In fact, Republicans in the highest income quintile, those making more than $100,000 per year, were actually slightly less satisfied than Democrats in the lowest income, those making less than $20,000 per year. Economic dissatisfaction was in large part a partisan phenomenon.

Democrats and Republicans also differed in their trust in government. Typically, Republicans' trust in government depends a great deal on whether a Republican is in the White House. Democrats show some of this bias, but to a lesser degree (Hetherington and Rudolph 2015). As of February 2014, 33 percent of Democrats, but only 19 percent of Republicans, said that they trusted the government to do what was right just about always or most of the time.

Similarly, Republicans were far more pessimistic about the state of the country. In these YouGov/Economist polls, a whopping 87 percent of Republicans said that the country was on the wrong track. Only 38 percent of Democrats thought so, while the plurality (48 percent) thought the country was headed in the right direction.

Given the partisan polarization on these dimensions, it is hardly surprising that Republicans and Democrats had very different views of Barack Obama. Figure 5 shows the trend in presidential approval for every president from Truman to Obama—both for all Americans and for Democrats and Republicans separately. Obama stands out in two respects. First, his approval ratings were remarkably stable over time. The absence of a large-scale war, a foreign policy crisis, a major political scandal, or an economic recession that began under his watch meant that Obama's approval ratings saw none of the wide swings that characterized the approval ratings of most previous presidents.

Second, partisan differences in assessments of Obama were larger than they had been for any previous president. On average, Obama's approval rating among Democrats was nearly 70 points higher than his approval rating among Republicans. This was even larger than partisan differences during the administrations of George W. Bush (60 points) and Bill Clinton (55 points), both of whom held office when partisan polarization was increasing (Jacobson 2007).

This partisan polarization helps to explain why increasingly positive evaluations of the economy did not appear to improve Obama's approval rating. Part of the reason is that the parties saw the economy differently. But another reason is that, in an age of polarization, Americans may give little credit to a president not of their own party. A good comparison is again to the last quarter of 1983, when consumer sentiment was essentially the same as at the end of 2015. At that point in time, 87 percent of Republicans approved of Reagan and so did 30 percent of Democrats. At the end of 2015, Obama's support in his own party was almost as high (79 percent), but it was much lower among Republicans (10 percent)— exactly where it had been for almost six years.

Racial Divides in the Electorate

These partisan divides in the electorate were only part of the story, however. Eight years of a black president meant that the divides were also about race and ethnicity. Indeed, partisan divides in American politics have increasingly become racial and ethnic divides. That the 2016 election came at the end of Obama's presidency in particular was crucial to the election. Eight years of an African American president magnified this "racialization" of politics.

To be sure, the roots of racialization were in place even before Obama became a national figure. Americans' partisan attachments became more closely aligned with racial attitudes in the post–civil rights era as politicians from the two parties increasingly diverged in both their policies and rhetoric about race. Among white Republicans, racial resentment and opposition to preferences for blacks have increased, while these attitudes have become less common among white Democrats (Carmines and Stimson 1989; Stimson 2004; Valentino and Sears 2005; Tesler 2016).[12]

But the presidential campaigns and administration of Barack Obama accelerated and intensified racialization. Among whites, attitudes such as racial resentment and opposition to affirmative action became tightly linked to partisanship (Tesler 2016). During the 2008 campaign, attitudes about African Americans were more strongly related to white Americans' voting preferences than they had been in any modern election or than they would have been if Hillary Clinton or John Edwards had been the 2008 Democratic nominee (e.g., Jackman and Vavreck 2012; Kinder and Dale-Riddle 2012; Tesler 2016; Tesler and Sears 2010).

FIGURE 6
Growing Partisan Divisions on Racial Attitudes

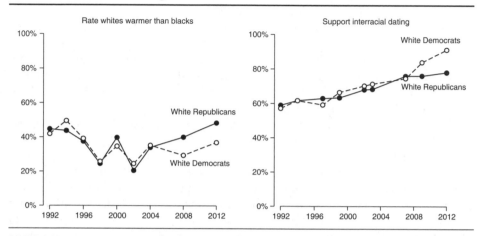

SOURCE: American National Election Studies (thermometer ratings): 1992, 1994, 1996, 1998, 2000, 2002, 2004, 2008 and 2012, and Pew Values Surveys (interracial dating): 1992, 1994, 1997, 1999, 2002, 2003, 2007, 2009, and 2012.

Racialization affected more than evaluations of just Barack Obama. Attitudes toward a whole host of issues or people linked to Obama became more influenced by both racial attitudes and race—a phenomenon termed the "spillover of racialization" (Tesler 2016; see also Henderson and Hillygus 2011; Knowles, Lowery, and Schaumberg 2010). Even racial attitudes that had never divided white Democrats from white Republicans became polarized by partisanship after Obama took office. Figure 6 shows that white Republicans were significantly more likely than white Democrats both to evaluate whites more favorably than blacks and to oppose interracial dating.

Racialization in the Obama era also had implications beyond the attitudes of whites toward blacks. Because Obama was repeatedly characterized as Muslim or foreign-born, a general aversion to all minority groups, and to Muslims in particular, became more strongly correlated with white Americans' voting preferences in both the 2008 and 2012 presidential elections (Kam and Kinder 2012; Tesler and Sears 2010; Tesler 2016). Consequently, Democrats and Republicans became increasingly divided in their attitudes about Muslims. Figure 7 shows, for example, that the percent of Republicans rating Muslims favorably fell during Obama's presidency, while the percent of Democrats rating Muslims favorably rose. [13]

Racialization also had implications for attitudes toward immigration. Figure 7 shows growing partisan polarization on whether there should be tighter restrictions on immigration. The trend is more evident among white Democrats than white Republicans, but other questions show changes in the views of Republicans as well. For example, Republicans' feelings toward undocumented immigrants became less favorable in the Obama years (see also Abrajano and Hajnal 2015).

FIGURE 7
Growing Partisan Divisions on Attitudes toward Muslims and Immigration

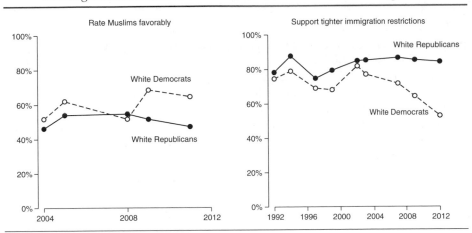

SOURCE: Pew Global Attitudes Project (favorability toward Muslims): 2004, 2005, 2008, 2009, and 2011, and Pew Values Surveys (immigration).

The growing alignment between party identification and attitudes about racial and ethnic issues occurred alongside important trends in the party identification of nonwhites. That the electorate is becoming less white is well known, and this trend seems certain to continue. It has been less certain, however, whether most nonwhites would become consistently aligned with one political party (Hajnal and Lee 2011).

In the years leading up to 2016, the answer became clearer: nonwhites began to move strongly toward the Democratic Party. The percentage of Asian Americans voting for Democratic presidential candidates increased sharply (Ramakrishnan 2012). An increasing number of Latinos also identified with the Democratic Party during Obama's presidency. Latinos were 15 percentage points more Democratic in 2012 than they had been on average from 2002 to 2007.[14] This increase was most heavily concentrated among Hispanics who felt cooler toward whites (Tesler 2016), as Latinos increasingly viewed Republicans as a party of whites.

The Democratic Party further solidified its support among blacks as well. In the two decades leading up to Obama's presidency, black identification with the Democratic Party had actually declined (Hajnal and Lee 2011). This trend reversed itself after 2008: African Americans were upward of 10 percentage points more Democratic than they had been before Obama's election (Hajnal and Lee 2011; Jones 2014).

These racial divides in the electorate mattered a great deal to the landscape of the 2016 election. For one, race helps to explain apparent voter anger as well as the disjuncture between a growing economy and Obama's approval rating. Racial attitudes evoke angry emotions in ways that other political attitudes do not (Banks 2014). The fact that race and racial attitudes were more strongly associated with evaluations of the economy during Obama's presidency (Tesler 2016) may help to explain why many in the country were angry despite a growing economy.

For another, the growing nonwhite portion of the electorate—combined with its growing attachment to the Democratic Party—was reshaping the nature of the party coalitions. In 2008 and 2012, nearly half of Obama supporters were non-white. The previous Democratic president, Bill Clinton, won two terms with a coalition that was only one-quarter nonwhite (Abramowitz 2014).

Even without Barack Obama on the ballot in 2016, trends in previous dec-ades—trends that only accelerated when Obama was president—made issues concerning race, ethnicity, and religion central to the strategies of the 2016 presi-dential candidates and immanent in the election-year discourse.

The Implications for 2016

In the months leading up to the 2016 campaign, there was an undercurrent of pessimism in the Republican Party. In early 2014, some party strategists seemed to think the presidential election was out of reach. In a piece titled "The Republican Party's Uphill Path to 270 Electoral Votes in 2016 Elections," the *Washington Post*'s Dan Balz (2014) wrote: "A recent conversation with a veteran of GOP presidential campaigns raised this question: Which, if any, of the recent battleground states are likely to become more Republican by 2016? The consen-sus: very few." By fall 2015, at least some conventional wisdom still favored the Democrats. *Bloomberg*'s Mark Halperin (2015) declared "The Most Likely Next President Is Hillary Clinton."

Others agreed. Forecasts based on betting markets—which have historically performed well in predicting election outcomes—consistently favored the Democrats. At the end of 2015, these prediction markets put the Democrat's chance of victory at more than 60 percent. A January 2016 survey of seventeen academic experts on elections by the site PollyVote was similarly bullish about the Democratic Party's prospects for victory in November (Graefe 2016). Their sur-vey predicted a four-point Democratic victory, with only one expert out of seven-teen expecting the Republicans to win back the White House.

What is fascinating about these predictions is that they did not necessarily align with the traditional fundamentals of presidential general elections. One of these fundamentals is the national economy. Incumbent presidents, or their party if the president is not running, tend to do better when the economy is improving. The trend in the economy is the most important, and in particular the trend in the election year. Figure 8 provides a demonstration, showing the strong correla-tion between election-year changes in gross domestic product and real disposable income and the incumbent party's share of the major-party vote.

A second fundamental is related: the incumbent president's approval rating. Even if the president is not running, he casts a long shadow over the race. In 2016, higher approval ratings for Obama would buoy his party's chances, other

FIGURE 8

The Relationship between Economic Growth and Presidential Election Outcomes

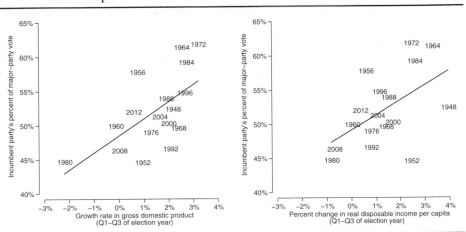

things equal. A third factor presented Democrats with a major disadvantage going into the election year: their party was running for a third consecutive presidential term in office. Across time and space, the longer a party has been in power, the less likely citizens are to vote for its candidates (Achen and Bartels 2016; Nannestad and Paldam 2002; Paldam 1986; Wlezien, forthcoming). Alan Abramowitz (2008) has described this phenomenon in U.S. presidential elections as the "time for a change" factor. The "time for a change" penalty may derive in part from the fact that public opinion typically moves in the opposite direction as the president is pushing public policy. Over two terms, the gap between the president's policies and public opinion will grow even further.

To understand the effect of these factors, we estimated a simple statistical model of the incumbent party's percent of the major-party vote in presidential elections from 1948 to 2012. We include a measure of economic growth (the change in gross domestic product from the first quarter to the third quarter of the election year), the president's approval rating as of June of the election year, and whether the incumbent party had served one term or two or more terms in the White House.

The results are intuitive. For every percent increase in gross domestic product over these quarters, the incumbent party's share of the vote increases by 1.7 points. For every five-point increase in presidential approval, the incumbent party's vote share increases by 1.0 point. The "time for a change" factor imposes a significant penalty: an incumbent party seeking a third (or greater) term receives 3.7 points less of the vote.[15]

If we assume that the election year would resemble the end of 2015—when gross domestic product had grown by about 0.74 percentage points in the last two quarters of the year, and when Obama had an approval rating of about 45 percent—this model would actually favor the Republican candidate. The predicted vote share of the Democratic candidate would be 48 percent. To be sure, the forecast comes with uncertainty: the 95 percent confidence interval spans 41 percent to 58 percent. But a 48 percent vote share still implies that the Republicans' chances of victory would be well above 50 percent—closer to 75 percent, in fact.

The same finding emerges if we substitute a different measure of the economy—change in real disposable income per capita from the first to third quarters of the election year. Assuming that disposable income would grow as fast as it did in the last two quarters of 2015 (just under 1 percent), this model predicts a somewhat closer election, with the Democratic candidate winning 49 percent, but this would still imply that the Republican candidate had about a 62 percent chance of winning.

There is nothing magical about this kind of forecasting model or any such model (for an excellent critique and extension, see Lauderdale and Linzer 2015). We do not believe that such models are perfect predictors, tell us everything about presidential elections, or imply that the campaign is irrelevant. Figure 8, for example, shows that election outcomes vary quite a bit from a prediction based solely on changes in the economy.

But these models do provide a useful baseline. It is significant, then, that so many observers were more bullish on the Democrats than these fundamentals would suggest, based on at least the past seventeen presidential elections. What might create this discrepancy?

One potential factor is the changing demographic composition of the electorate. White Americans were expected to compose only about 70 percent of the electorate in 2016—a 13 percentage-point decline since Bill Clinton won reelection in 1996. Much of that decline was due to the expanding Latino and Asian American shares of the electorate. And with both Latinos and Asian Americans around 30 percentage points more likely than whites to have voted Democratic in 2012, the changing demographic compositions of the electorate may put the Democrats at a greater advantage than they had been in recent elections.

The question, however, is whether increased Democratic support from nonwhite voters may be offset by greater Republican support and higher turnout from whites (see Enos 2015; Bartels 2014). In 2015, however, the prevailing concern was that Republicans would be on the losing end of the country's changing demography. As Republican Senator Lindsay Graham put it in June 2015, "My party is in a hole with Hispanics—the first rule of politics when you're in a hole is stop digging" (Rappeport 2015).

Conclusion

In early 2016, two *Washington Post* writers, David Maraniss and Robert Samuels, set out to gauge the mood of Americans by traveling the country for more than a month. What they found was much more than simple "anger." What they found sounded like ambivalence:

> For every disgruntled person out there who felt undone by the system and threatened by the way the country was changing, caught in the bind of stagnant wages or longing for an America of the past, we found someone who had endured decades of discrimination and hardship and yet still felt optimistic about the future and had no desire to go back. In this season of discontent, there were still as many expressions of hope as of fear. On a larger level, there were as many communities enjoying a sense of revival as there were fighting against deterioration and despair.

This is precisely what we have documented in a quantitative fashion. The economy has improved since the Great Recession, and voters realize it, but their assessments of Barack Obama and the country as a whole were less favorable than the economy alone might have predicted.

Underlying dissatisfaction with Obama, and part of any broader anger in the electorate, were both political partisanship and race. Republicans felt less favorably about the economy than did Democrats, and their persistent disapproval helps to explain why Obama's approval ratings were so stable even as the economy improved.

Moreover, under Obama partisanship, many other attitudes had come to be increasingly correlated with race and racial attitudes. The Democratic Party increasingly comprised racially liberal whites and minorities. The Republican Party increasingly comprised people who were unfavorable toward African Americans, immigrants, and Muslims.

These factors clearly resonated in the 2016 presidential primaries. In the Republican primary, Donald Trump drew support from Republicans who were anxious about their financial situation as well as Republicans who expressed less favorable views of many different minority groups than and anxiety about the status of whites (Sides and Tesler 2016; Tesler and Sides 2016; Pew Research Center 2016). Some other Republican candidates, notably Ted Cruz, also took quite conservative positions on immigration. To Republicans like Lindsay Graham, this was evidence that some Republicans were still digging that hole.

Meanwhile, a Democratic coalition comprising racially liberal whites and minorities meant that the Democratic presidential candidates did not have to soft-pedal racial issues to avoid alienating white swing voters, as was typical even as late as the 1990s (see Kinder and Dale-Riddle 2012). Hillary Clinton and Bernie Sanders ran to Barack Obama's left on matters of racial equality, with Clinton even repudiating some of Bill Clinton's criminal justice and immigration policies for their adverse effects on racial and ethnic minorities.

Looking toward the general election, the American public's ambivalence, coupled with the challenge of winning a third term, should have made the election a toss-up and perhaps even given the Republicans the advantage. But Democrats also seemed poised to benefit from an increasingly diverse electorate, thanks to two mutually supportive trends—the growing divide between Democrats and Republicans on racial issues and the movement toward the Democratic Party among nonwhite voters. Perhaps for this reason, many observers and forecasters gave the Democratic Party an edge early in the election year. Were that Democratic advantage to persist, it would produce a striking irony: an allegedly rebellious and angry electorate seeking "a major reset" ended up returning the incumbent party to the White House for a third term.

Notes

1. This was an NBC News/*Wall Street Journal* poll conducted from October 25–29, 2015. See http://msnbcmedia.msn.com/i/MSNBC/Sections/A_Politics/15463percent20NBCWSJpercent20Late%20October%20Poll%20%284%29.pdf.

2. The entirety of the question read: "I feel cautiously optimistic about where things are headed. It is important to remember how bad the economy was just a few years ago. The economy is improving, more Americans now have health insurance and those with preexisting conditions are covered, more jobs are being created, and things seem to be gradually getting better."

3. The 1981–92 recession is dated to July 1981, when the unemployment rate was 7.2 percent. The unemployment rate declined to 7.2 percent for the first time in June 1984. At the beginning of the Great Recession, in December 2007, the unemployment rate was 5 percent. It declined to that number in October 2015.

4. Those questions are: "We are interested in how people are getting along financially these days. Would you say that you (and your family living there) are better off or worse off financially than you were a year ago?" "Now looking ahead—do you think that a year from now you (and your family living there) will be better off financially, or worse off, or just about the same as now?" "Now turning to business conditions in the country as a whole—do you think that during the next twelve months we'll have good times financially, or bad times, or what?" "Looking ahead, which would you say is more likely—that in the country as a whole we'll have continuous good times during the next five years or so, or that we will have periods of widespread unemployment or depression, or what?" and "About the big things people buy for their homes—such as furniture, a refrigerator, stove, television, and things like that. Generally speaking, do you think now is a good or bad time for people to buy major household items?" More information about the Index of Consumer Sentiment, including links to data is here: http://www.sca.isr.umich.edu/.

5. The index can be broken down into two components: current economic conditions (how the economy is doing now) and consumer expectations (how the economy will do in the future). Both increased at a similar rate and were at a level similar to the mid-2000s or mid-1980s, suggesting that Americans were not, for example, positive about the present day but pessimistic about the future. Compared to the first quarter of 2009, when Obama took office, the index of consumer confidence increased by 61 percent by the end of 2015, while the index of consumer expectations increased by 53 percent.

6. For the Pew Research Center data, see http://www.people-press.org/files/2015/12/12-22-15-Economy-topline-for-release.pdf. Gallup data also show a similar trend: http://www.gallup.com/poll/125735/economic-confidence-index.aspx.

7. See the census data here: http://www2.census.gov/programs-surveys/cps/tables/time-series/historical-income-families/f03ar.xls.

8. The same is true among educational groups, which are defined as those with a high school degree or less, those with some college, and those with a college degree.

9. These data are available from http://www.people-press.org/files/2015/11/11-23-2015-Governance-topline-for-release.pdf.

10. In a least squares regression of approval on consumer sentiment, the coefficient for Obama (2009–15) is –0.20, with a standard error of 0.08. The results for the other presidents are: Kennedy (b = 0.52; se = 0.62), Johnson (b = 2.08; se = 0.43), Nixon (b = 0.86; se = 0.22), Ford (b = 0.24; se = 0.10), Carter (b = 0.86; se = 0.19), Reagan (b = 0.25; se = 0.11), George H. W. Bush (b = 0.45; se = 0.39), Clinton (b = 0.62; se = 0.09), and George W. Bush (b = 0.81; se = 0.26). The same finding emerges if approval is first regressed on the noneconomic factors in the model in Sides and Vavreck (2013), and then the residuals from this regression are plotted in the same fashion. This suggests that the unusual relationship between approval and consumer sentiment during the Obama years cannot be explained by these noneconomic factors.

11. We estimated a model of quarterly presidential approval from the years prior to the Obama presidency (1960–2008) that included consumer sentiment and fixed effects for each president. We then used the results of this model to predict Obama's approval. In the fourth quarter of 2015, the model predicted that 56 percent of Americans would approve of Obama, whereas his actual approval rating was 45 percent. The fuller model of presidential approval in Sides and Vavreck (2013), which includes objective measures of the economy, the length of time the president has been in office, and several other factors, shows that Obama's approval was one to two points lower than the model would predict.

12. Kinder and Sanders's (1996) racial resentment measures whether Americans think deficiencies in black culture are the main reason for racial inequality with questions like, "It's really a matter of some people not trying hard enough; if blacks would only try harder they could be just as well off as whites."

13. The decline in Republicans' assessments of Muslims was even more pronounced in American National Election Study surveys. Republicans' mean thermometer ratings of Muslims (on a 0–100 scale) dropped from 50 in 2004 to 42 in 2008 to 36 in 2012. A 2014 Pew Research Center survey similarly showed that the average thermometer rating of Muslims among Republicans and Republican leaners was just 33. For more, see http://www.pewforum.org/2014/07/16/how-americans-feel-about-religious-groups/.

14. See http://www.pewhispanic.org/2014/10/29/chapter-3-latinos-and-the-political-parties/.

15. Another factor that may also matter is whether the incumbent president is running for reelection, since incumbents appear to have certain advantages and therefore win more often than they lose. In post–WWII elections, incumbency appears less important than the number of terms that the president's party has controlled the White House, but in a larger set of presidential elections it appears more significant: on average, incumbents received an additional 2.5 points of vote share in presidential elections between 1828 and 2004 (Mayhew 2008). Thus, in 2016, the incumbent Democratic Party would expect to be at a disadvantage not only because it was seeking a third term, but also because there was no Democratic incumbent running.

References

Abrajano, Marisa, and Zoltan L. Hajnal. 2015. *White backlash: Immigration, race, and American politics*. Princeton, NJ: Princeton University Press.

Abramowitz, Alan I. 2008. Forecasting the 2008 presidential election with the time-for-change model. *PS: Political Science and Politics* 41 (4): 691–95.

Abramowitz, Alan I. 2014. How race and religion have polarized American voters. The Monkey Cage, *Washington Post*. Available from http://www.washingtonpost.com.

Achen, Christopher, and Larry M. Bartels. 2016. *Democracy for realists: Why elections do not produce responsive government*. Princeton, NJ: Princeton University Press.

Adams, Greg D. 1997. Abortion: Evidence of an issue evolution. *American Journal of Political Science* 41:718–37.

Arnade, Chris. 14 October 2015. Working-class Americans feel screwed. I heard it across the entire country. *The Guardian*. Available from http://www.theguardian.com.

Baldassarri, Delia, and Andrew Gelman. 2008. Partisans without constraint: Political polarization and trends in American public opinion. *American Journal of Sociology* 114 (2): 408-46.

Balz, Dan. 18 January 2014. The Republican Party's uphill path to 270 electoral votes in the 2016 elections. *Washington Post*. Available from https://www.washingtonpost.com.

Banks, Antoine J. 2014. *Anger and racial politics: The emotional foundation of racial attitudes in America*. New York, NY: Cambridge University Press.

Bartels, Larry M. 2008. *Unequal democracy: The political economy of the new gilded age*. New York, NY: Russell Sage Foundation.

Bartels, Larry M. 16 April 2014. Can the Republican Party thrive on white identity? The Monkey Cage, *Washington Post*. Available from https://www.washingtonpost.com.

Carmines, Edward G., and James A. Stimson. 1989. *Issue evolution: Race and the transformation of American politics*. Princeton, NJ: Princeton University Press.

Chanley, Virginia A., Thomas J. Rudolph, and Wendy M. Rahn. 2000. The origins and consequences of public trust in government: A time series analysis. *Public Opinion Quarterly* 64 (3): 239–56.

Danziger, Sheldon, ed. 2013. The effects of the Great Recession. *The ANNALS of the American Academy of Political and Social Science* (650).

Dews, Fred. 11 January 2016. "Misery index" at lowest level. Brookings Institution. Available from http://www.brookings.edu.

Enns, Peter K., Paul M. Kellstedt, and Gregory E. McAvoy. 2012. The consequences of partisanship in economic perceptions. *Public Opinion Quarterly* 76 (2): 287–310.

Enos, Ryan D. 2014. The causal effect of intergroup contact on exclusionary attitudes. *Proceedings of the National Academy of Sciences* 111 (10): 369–70.

Graefe, Andreas. 1 February 2016. Experts still see Democrats in the lead. PollyVote. Available from http://pollyvote.com/en/2016/02/01/experts-still-see-democrats-in-the-lead/.

Hajnal, Zoltan L., and Taeku Lee. 2011. *Why Americans don't join the party: Race, immigration, and the failure (of political parties) to engage the electorate*. Princeton, NJ: Princeton University Press.

Halperin, Mark. 2015. The most likely next president is Hillary Clinton: And Republicans are in denial about it. Bloomberg Politics. Available from http://www.bloomberg.com/.

Henderson, Michael, and D. Sunshine Hillygus. 2011. The dynamics of health care opinion, 2008–2010: Partisanship, self-interest and racial resentment. *Journal of Health Politics, Policy, and Law* 36 (6): 945–60.

Hetherington, Marc J., and Thomas J. Rudolph. 2015. *Why Washington won't work: Polarization, political trust, and the governing crisis*. Chicago, IL: University of Chicago Press.

Iyengar, Shanto, Gaurav Sood, and Yphtach Lelkes. 2012. Affect, not ideology: A social identity perspective on polarization. *Public Opinion Quarterly* 76 (3): 405–31.

Iyengar, Shanto, and Sean J. Westwood. 2014. Fear and loathing across party lines: New evidence on group polarization. *American Journal of Political Science* 59 (3): 690–707.

Jackman, Simon, and Lynn Vavreck. 2012. How does Obama match-up? Counterfactuals & the role of Obama's race in 2008. Unpublished manuscript.

Jacobson, Gary C. 2007. *A divider, not a uniter*. New York, NY: Pearson.

Jones, Jeffrey M. 2014. U.S. whites more solidly Republican in recent years: Party preferences more polarized by race and ethnicity under Obama. Gallup. Available from http://www.gallup.com/poll/168059/whites-solidly-republican-recent-years.aspx.

Jones, Robert P., Daniel Cox, Betsy Cooper, and Rachel Lienesch. 2015. *Anxiety, nostalgia, and mistrust: Findings from the 2015 American Values Survey*. Washington, DC: Public Religion Research Institute. Available from http://publicreligion.org/site/wp-content/uploads/2015/11/PRRI-AVS-2015.pdf.

Kam, Cindy, and Donald R. Kinder. 2012. Ethnocentrism as a short-term influence in the 2008 election. *American Journal of Political Science* 56 (2): 326–40.

Keele, Luke. 2007. Social capital and the dynamics of trust in government. *American Journal of Political Science* 51 (2): 241–54.

Kinder, Donald R., and Allison Dale-Riddle. 2012. *The end of race?* New Haven, CT: Yale University Press.

Kinder, Donald R., and Lynn M. Sanders. 1996. *Divided by color: Racial politics and democratic ideals*. Chicago, IL: University of Chicago Press.

Knowles, Eric D., Brian Lowery, and Rebecca L Schaumberg. 2010. Racial prejudice predicts opposition to Obama and his health care reform plan. *Journal of Experimental Social Psychology* 46:420–23.

Lauderdale, Benjamin E., and Drew Linzer. 2015. Under-performing, over-performing, or just performing? The limitations of fundamentals-based presidential election forecasting. *International Journal of Forecasting* 31 (3): 965–79.

Levendusky, Matthew. 2009. *The partisan sort: How liberals became Democrats and conservatives became Republicans*. Chicago, IL: University of Chicago Press.

Maraniss, David, and Robert Samuels. 17 March 2016. The great unsettling. *Washington Post*. Available from https://www.washingtonpost.com.

Mayhew, David R. 2008. Incumbency advantage in U.S. presidential elections: The historical record. *Political Science Quarterly* 123 (2): 201–28.

Nannestad, Peter, and Martin Paldam. 2002. The cost of ruling: A foundation stone for two theories. In *Economic voting*, eds. Hans Dorussen and Michaell Taylor. London: Routledge.

Nicholson, Stephen P., Chelsea M. Coe, Jason Emory, and Anna V. Strong. 2016. The politics of beauty: The effects of partisan bias on physical attractiveness. Original paper. *Political Behavior*. doi:10.1007/s11109-016-9339-7

Paldam, Martin. 1986. The distribution of election results and two explanations for the cost of ruling. *European Journal of Political Economy* 2:5–24.

Pew Research Center. 9 December 2015. The American middle class is losing ground. Available from http://www.pewsocialtrends.org.

Pew Research Center. 31 March 2016. Campaign exposes fissures over issues, values and how life has changed in the U.S. Available from http://www.people-press.org.

Ramakrishnan, Karthick. 29 November 2012. Asian Americans voted Democrat. We should not be surprised. The Monkey Cage, *Washington Post*. Available from http://themonkeycage.org.

Rappeport, Alan. 8 July 2015. Lindsey Graham says Republicans are "in a hole" with Hispanics. *New York Times*. Available from http://www.nytimes.com.

Reinhart, Carmen M., and Kenneth Rogoff. 2009. *This time is different: Eight centuries of financial folly*. Princeton, NJ: Princeton University Press.

Sides, John, and Michael Tesler. 4 March 2016. How political science helps explain the rise of Trump (Part 3): It's the economy stupid. The Monkey Cage, *Washington Post*. Available from https://www.washingtonpost.com.

Sides, John, and Lynn Vavreck. 2013. *The gamble: Choice and chance in the 2012 election*. Princeton, NJ: Princeton University Press.

Stimson, James A. 2004 *Tides of consent: How public opinion shapes American politics*. New York, NY: Cambridge University Press.

Tesler, Michael, and David O. Sears. 2010. *Obama's race: The 2008 election and the dream of a post-racial America*. Chicago, IL: University of Chicago Press.

Tesler, Michael. 2016. *Post-racial or most-racial? Race and politics in the Obama era*. Chicago, IL: University of Chicago Press.

Tesler, Michael, and John Sides. 3 March 2016. How political science helps explain the rise of Trump: The role of white identity and grievances. The Monkey Cage, *Washington Post*. Available from https://www.washingtonpost.com.

Todd, Chuck. 3 November 2015. America: In search of a political reset in 2016. NBC News Available from http://www.nbcnews.com.

Valentino, Nicholas A., and David O. Sears. 2005. Old times there are not forgotten: Race and partisan realignment in the contemporary South. *American Journal of Political Science* 49:672–88.

Wlezien, Christopher. Forthcoming. Policy (mis)representation and the cost of ruling: U.S. presidential elections in comparative perspective. *Comparative Political Studies*. doi:10.1177/0010414015626446

The Obama Legacy and the Future of Partisan Conflict: Demographic Change and Generational Imprinting

By
GARY C. JACOBSON

Past research has shown that the perceived successes or failures of presidents have a durable influence on the partisan leanings and political attitudes of people who come of political age during their administrations. Here, I examine data from 344 Gallup surveys with a total of 399,755 respondents interviewed during the Obama presidency to (1) document the extent to which generational imprinting is visible among citizens and demographic subgroups in their party identification and ideology, (2) determine how the political identities and ideologies of people who have come of age during Obama's presidency have evolved compared with those of earlier presidential generations, (3) explore the implications of the population's changing demographic makeup and the political attitudes expressed by younger age cohorts for the future partisan balance of the American electorate, and (4) consider how the competition to succeed Obama is likely to affect partisan identities forged during his administration.

Keywords: generational imprinting; president; party identification; ideology; 2016 election

Every modern president has strongly influenced his party's popularity, reputation for competence, perceived ideology, electoral fortunes, and attractiveness as an object of identification (Jacobson 2009, 2012, 2015a, 2016c). The president's influence on individual party identification is arguably the most consequential of these effects because of both its immediate electoral impact and its potential durability. The president's influence on individual and mass partisanship over both the short and long runs is well documented in the literature (MacKuen, Erikson, and Stimson 1989; Green,

Gary C. Jacobson is Distinguished Professor of Political Science Emeritus at the University of California, San Diego. He specializes in the study of U.S. elections, parties, interest groups, public opinion, and Congress. His most recent book is A Divider, Not a Uniter: George W. Bush and the American People *(Longman 2007).*

Correspondence: gjacobson@ucsd.edu

DOI: 10.1177/0002716216658425

Palmquist, and Schickler 1998; Erikson, MacKuen, and Stimson 1998; Jacobson 2012, 2016c; Miller and Shanks 1996). In accord with Mannheim's classic theory of generational imprinting (Mannheim 1928/1972; see also Delli Carpini 1989), durable long-term effects appear as systematic variations in aggregate partisanship, reflecting the era when citizens first came of political age (Ghitza and Gelman 2014; DeSilver 2014; Hopkins 2014; Pew Research Center 2011, 2015; Jacobson 2016c).

Bartels and Jackman (2014) developed a Bayesian model to explain such variations based on the idea that events in particular historical periods "shock" the existing patterns of opinion and that the shocks experienced when people first become politically aware weigh more heavily in shaping political attitudes than those experienced later in life. The dominance of early political experiences is especially pronounced in the development of partisan attitudes, and Bartels and Jackman's theory and findings are fully consistent with the classic Michigan model of party identification (Campbell et al. 1960), in which attachment to a party is a component of social identity, a mode through which people define themselves to themselves and others: "I am a Catholic, a Mets fan, an Italian American, and a Republican." Partisan identities so conceived are adopted early in adulthood, stabilize quickly, and thereafter become highly resistant to change; people do not lightly revise their social identities, and political events and personalities have the most lasting influence when they occur as partisan identities are being formed. Hence "the influences of the political environment are most noticeable among new voters, whose partisan attachments often bear the stamp of the political zeitgeist that prevailed when they reached voting age" (Green, Palmquist, and Schickler 2002, 108).

The concept of generational imprinting implies that the present foreshadows the future: events and personalities that shape the political attitudes prevalent among younger cohorts when they enter political life will continue to register in future years as they pass through the life cycle (although not without some potential modification by later political experiences; see Bartels and Jackman 2014). A political snapshot of age cohorts at any given point in time will thus display both the impact of past "shocks" and bear implications for the future distribution of political identities and attitudes.

In this article, I develop a portrait of the political generations active during the Obama administration by examining data aggregated from 344 Gallup surveys (399,755 respondents) taken between January 2009 and June 2015 that are archived at the Roper Center at Cornell University. Among the most important patterns revealed by this analysis is the emergence of a decisive Democratic advantage among cohorts entering the electorate during the three most recent presidencies, raising the obvious question: Why? The answer turns out to be a combination of demographic and attitudinal changes that, if the past is any guide, will benefit the Democratic Party for decades into the future. Moreover, if the image of the Republican Party projected by its leading candidates for the nomination in 2016 prevails, the effect is certain to be magnified, and mainstream Republicans dismayed by the prospect of Donald Trump winning the nomination have every reason to be worried.

FIGURE 1
Party Identification, by Year Respondent Turned 20 (Leaners Included)

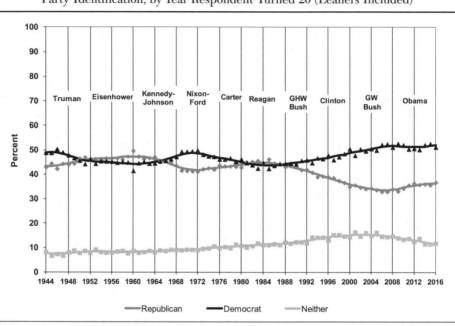

SOURCE: 344 Gallup polls, 2009–2015.

Party Identification across Generations

The systematic generational differences of individual and aggregate party identi-fication that were detected in previous studies reappear in the Gallup data from the Obama era. Figures 1 and 2 display data on partisanship with and without partisan leaners (respondents who initially decline to identify with a party but subsequently say they lean toward one of them).[1] The figures' horizontal axes indicate the year the respondent turned 20, but by shifting attention right or left, the results can be applied to any age or range of ages one might want to treat as pivotal. The annual data points fit the lowest-smoothed trend line very tightly— no surprise because each point averages data from about 5,400 observations, with only the two youngest cohorts (turning 20 in 2015 and 2016) having fewer than 2,000. For this reason, some of the figures presented later in this article display the smoothed trends exclusively.

Different people assume political identities at different ages and over different lengths of time, of course,[2] but the broad generational patterns summarized by these figures, nearly identical in both figures,[3] are clear. People who entered the electorate during the New Deal remain slightly more Democratic. If partisan leaners are included, cohorts entering from the Eisenhower and Kennedy admin-istrations currently favor the Republicans; Democrats retain an edge under

FIGURE 2
Party Identification, by Year Respondent Turned 20 (Leaners Excluded)

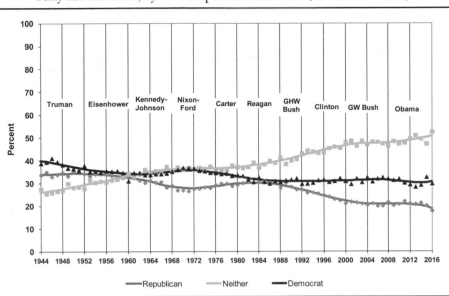

Source: 344 Gallup polls, 2009–2015.

Kennedy if leaners are excluded. Democrats have a clear advantage among cohorts who arrived with Nixon, Ford, and Carter, but the Reagan generation continues to favor the Republican Party. Citizens coming of political age since the Clinton administrations are predominantly Democratic in their partisan leanings by either measure, and by quite large margins in the G.W. Bush and Obama administrations. People in more recent cohorts are much more likely to initially declare themselves independents, but a large majority of them lean toward one of the parties; the proportion of pure independents is actually slightly lower among the Obama cohorts than among their slightly older contemporaries.

These cross-generational patterns reflect the broad popular success or failure of succeeding administrations as measured by survey data on presidential approval and standard historical narratives (Ghitza and Gelman 2014, 11–21).[4] But this is far from the full story, for it cannot account for the wide Democratic advantage among citizens who entered the electorate during the three most recent administrations. To be sure, Clinton's comparative success and G.W. Bush's comparative failure in delivering peace and prosperity and their consequent approval ratings help to explain the Democrats' edge; approval of Clinton's performance averaged 61 percent during his second term, approval of Bush's, 36 percent. But considering past historical patterns, this seems insufficient to account for the size of the Democrats' lead among cohorts coming of age during these administrations. And Obama's approval ratings averaged only 47 percent after his first year in office, yet the Democratic advantage among the young people entering the electorate during his presidency has remained very large.

FIGURE 3
Democratic Share of Party Identifiers, by Race/Ethnicity and Year
Respondent Turned 20 (Leaners Included)

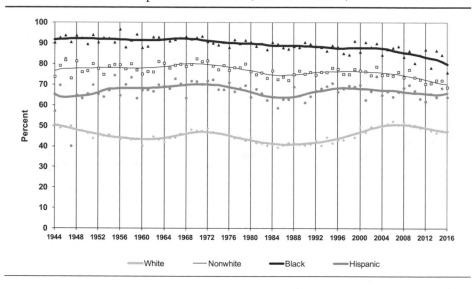

Figure 3, which displays the Democrats' share of major party identifiers (including leaners) by age cohorts of whites, blacks, Hispanics, and all nonwhites, suggests that most of the explanation must lie in demographic change. Only among whites do we observe a larger Democratic share of partisan identifiers in younger cohorts entering during the three most recent administrations. For nonwhites, no such difference is evident; indeed, the trend, if any, is in the other direction. Democrats continue to enjoy a very large advantage among nonwhites, but it has not grown wider for younger cohorts, and generational differences within subgroups are much more modest than for the population as a whole.

What has changed is the demographic profile of successive age cohorts. Figure 4 shows how the demographic composition of the population (as sampled by Gallup) has been evolving, with each succeeding age cohort containing a smaller proportion of whites and a larger proportion of nonwhites, particularly Hispanics. The patterns observed in Figures 1 and 2 are thus primarily compositional effects: the Democrats' widening advantage stems primarily from the growing share of nonwhites in younger cohorts. The youngest white respondents divide themselves nearly evenly between the parties. Younger nonwhites are actually slightly less Democratic than older nonwhites (although interestingly, the Obama generation of blacks is the least Democratic of any), but the growing proportion of nonwhites, even though they are less uniformly Democratic in partisanship, has given the youngest cohorts their decisive Democratic tilt.

Demographics alone pose a challenge to the Republican Party, for the proportion of whites among cohorts entering the electorate will continue to shrink for the foreseeable future. Astute Republican leaders are well aware of this reality and of the consequent need to broaden their party's appeal beyond its older white

FIGURE 4
Racial/Ethnic Composition of the Respondent Population by Year Respondent Turned 20

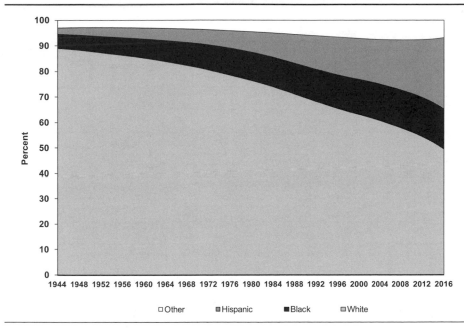

base (Walshe 2013); although, as we saw, most of the candidates for the Republican nomination in 2016 were busy doing the opposite. But additional data examined here suggest that the party's challenge goes beyond coping with demographic change, for the younger cohorts of all partisan persuasions express attitudes and opinions that are substantially less conservative and more pro-Obama than those of their elders.

The Obama Effect

Presidents are of course central to the generational imprinting story, so a review of Obama's public standing is a necessary first step in assessing his potential influence on long-term partisan dispositions. Overall, Obama's presidency has been less than a rousing popular success (the dashed line in Figure 5). After his first year in office, his (smoothed) approval ratings among all respondents exceeded 50 percent only around the time of his reelection. But also notice that Obama's ratings among Democrats have been consistently very high, near or above 80 percent. His ratings among Republicans have been even more consistently very low—flatlining near 10 percent for most of his presidency—and by this measure, Obama has been the most polarizing president on record (with his predecessor G.W. Bush a close second).[5]

FIGURE 5
Approval of Barack Obama's Job Performance, 2009–2015

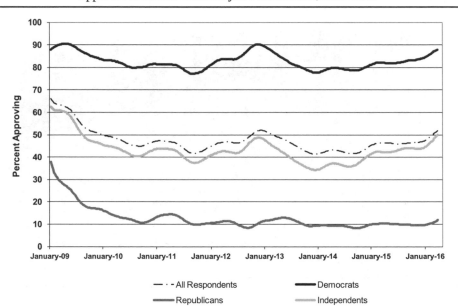

SOURCE: LOWESS smoothed data from 374 Gallup polls.

Obama has also divided the public along generational lines. Younger respondents have given him higher ratings all along, but the gap between them and the oldest age group has tended to widen over time; as he entered his final year in office, it exceeded 20 percentage points (Figure 6).[6] Evaluations of Obama have also split along racial and ethnic lines (Figure 7). Blacks have given him overwhelming support, generally in the 85 to 90 percent range; whites have been much less satisfied by his job performance.

Obama's approval ratings among Hispanics have varied the most.[7] Hispanics initially approved of Obama's performance at very high rates, but approval fell as the administration made little progress on the immigration front. His standing improved steeply after his executive implementation of elements of the DREAM (Development, Relief, and Education for Alien Minors) Act prior to the 2012 election but subsequently dropped by more than 20 points as deportations continued, immigration reform legislation stalled, and Obama delayed further executive action to protect undocumented residents until after the 2014 election in a vain attempt to shield vulnerable Senate Democrats from the backlash it was sure to provoke (Jacobson 2015b, 6). Shortly after the election, he issued another executive order significantly expanding the use of "deferred action" to provide temporary protection from removal for millions of unauthorized immigrants currently in the United States, and his approval rating among Hispanics rose to more than 60 percent once more.

FIGURE 6
Approval of Obama's Job Performance, by Age Group

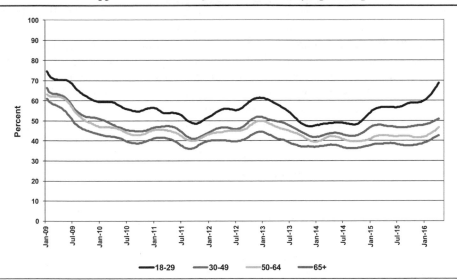

SOURCE: 374 Gallup Polls.

FIGURE 7
Approval of Obama's Job Performance, by Race/Ethnicity

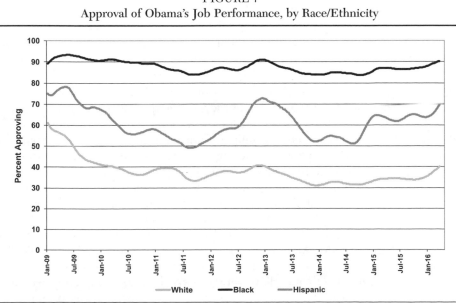

SOURCE: 374 Gallup Polls.

It is no accident that the sharp increase in 2012 coincided with a presidential campaign in which Obama's opponent's solution to the problem of undocumented immigrants was "self-deportation," adding a push to Obama's pull. If current campaign rhetoric is any guide, an even stronger push from the Republican side can be expected from whoever wins the nomination. Hispanics in these surveys seem highly attuned to the handling of the immigration issue, and Republican observers who see "declaring war on America's demography" (Gerson 2015) as a fatal long-term strategy are justified in worrying about virulent anti-immigrant stances adopted by their leading candidates for the nomination, most notably the dominant voice, Donald Trump. California Republican governor Pete Wilson's exploitation of anti-immigrant sentiments to win reelection in 1994 alienated the fastest growing segment of the California electorate and inspired many Latinos to become citizens and voters (Bowler, Nicholson, and Segura 2006). Wilson's contribution to his state party's subsequent decline to near irrelevance stands as an object lesson as well as an illustration of how a salient political event can have enduring consequences for partisanship.[8]

The Future of Polarization

If any single political zeitgeist pervades the Obama era, it is one of extreme partisan polarization (Thurber and Yoshinaka 2015), and we might therefore expect young Democrats and Republicans just entering the electorate to display even more discordant views of the president than their elders do. They do not. Figure 8 shows the average approval ratings offered by partisan age cohorts in Gallup polls taken between January 2014 and June 2015 (a period when Obama's ratings were unusually stable). Younger and older Democrats are equally supportive of the president. But younger Republican cohorts are much more likely to approve of his performance than their elders. The differences are quite striking; only 4 percent of Republicans who came of age during the Eisenhower through Johnson administrations approved of Obama's performance; for the Nixon through G. H. W. Bush generation, it was 9 percent; for the Clinton through G. W. Bush generation, the average was 15 percent, and for those coming of age during Obama's administration, it was 27 percent. A similar if noisier and less pronounced pattern appears among pure independents: younger cohorts are more inclined to view Obama favorably than are their elders. Obama's superior ratings among younger respondents (Figure 6) thus emerge not only because the respondents are more likely to be Democrats, but also because younger Republicans and independents look more favorably on his performance than do their elders.

Younger Americans are clearly less polarized along party lines in their opinions of Obama than are older Americans. They are also less polarized ideologically, because younger cohorts in all partisan categories are much less likely to label themselves conservative than earlier cohorts, partially if not completely accounting for their more favorable views of Obama. Figure 9 displays the proportions of respondents who say they are conservative, moderate, or liberal according to the year they turned 20. The decline across cohorts for "conservative" and upward trends for "moderate" and "liberal" are unmistakable, although the generational trends are interrupted for a period by respondents who came of age during Reagan's presidency. Conservatives outnumber liberals more than two to

FIGURE 8
Approval of Obama's Performance by Party and Year
Respondent Turned 20, 2014–2015

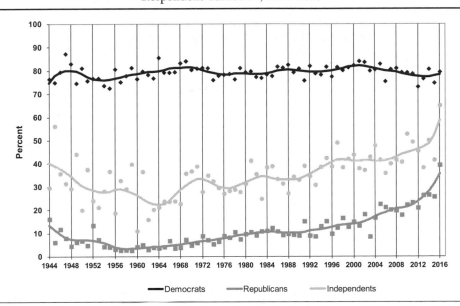

SOURCE: 55,212 respondents in 47 Gallup polls taken between January 2014 and June 2015.

FIGURE 9
Ideology by Year Respondent Turned 20

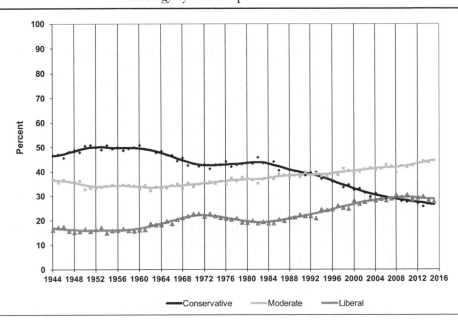

FIGURE 10A
Ideology of Republicans by Year Respondent Turned 20

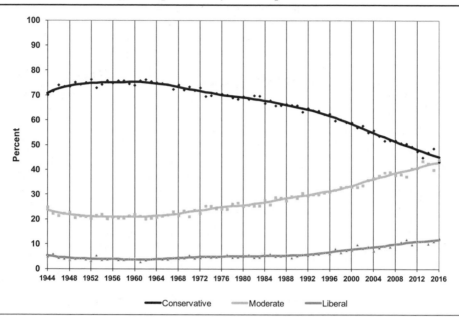

one in the generations that entered their 20s before the 1990s, but this gap becomes progressively smaller in later age cohorts; among people entering the electorate during the Obama presidency, liberals actually outnumber conservatives, although moderates easily outnumber both.

This development cannot be explained by changing demographics, for the same patterns apply to whites and nonwhites alike, although the latter tend to be less conservative and more liberal in every age cohort. Nor can it be explained by the partisan composition of succeeding age cohorts, for the same trends appear among Republicans, Democrats, and pure independents (see Figures 10a, 10b, and 10c). The most striking intergenerational differences appear among the Republicans, with the percentage of conservatives in the most recent cohorts thirty points lower—and the proportion of moderates twenty points higher—than in cohorts who came of political age in the 1960s; the proportion of liberals, while still very low, is also twice as large for the Obama generation as for Republicans entering the electorate before 1980. Among Democrats, successive cohorts are increasingly liberal and decreasingly conservative, with the proportion of moderates remaining nearly constant. Similar cross-generational patterns appear among pure independents, with successively fewer conservatives, more liberals, and about the same proportion of moderates.[9]

These intergenerational differences in self-reported ideology are far too large to be explained by the common (e.g., Truett 1993) if empirically challenged (Kinder 2006, Danigelis, Hardy, and Cutler 2007) notion that people tend to become more conservative as they age.[10] They reflect genuine differences on

FIGURE 10B
Ideology of Democrats by Year Respondent Turned 20

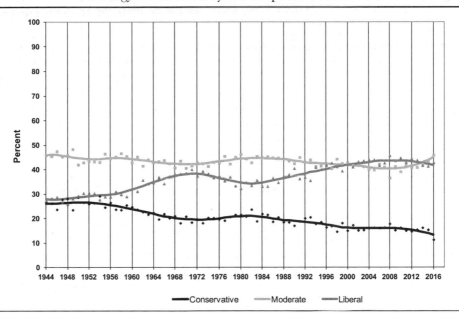

FIGURE 10C
Ideology of Pure Independents by Year Respondent Turned 20

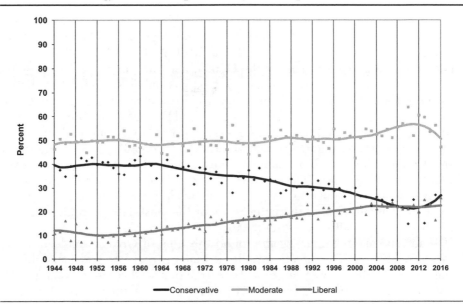

political issues, readily apparent in the distribution of responses to issue questions. Across a range of issues, including immigration, same-sex marriage, health care reform, abortion, and environmental protection, younger Republicans are consistently more liberal than their elders. A generational gradient also appears among pure independents, with more recent cohorts more liberal on every issue; among Democrats older groups actually tend to be a bit more liberal except on same-sex marriage and immigration, although all age cohorts are substantially more liberal than Republicans or independents (for details, see Jacobson 2016a). Younger Republicans are also less likely to consume conservative media and to share the beliefs common among their audiences: compared with older Republicans, those under 30 are significantly less likely to watch Fox News and other conservative outlets, to believe Obama is foreign-born or a Muslim, and to deny that human activity is heating up the planet. They are also less sympathetic to the Tea Party movement (Jacobson 2016a, Figure 13). Although the lesser conservatism of younger Republican cohorts helps to explain why they are less uniformly hostile toward Obama, it is not a complete explanation, for younger conservatives, even conservative Republicans, have more positive views of him than older cohorts. Because younger Republicans tend to hold less conservative views than older Republicans across all issue domains, people who entered the electorate most recently are notably less ideologically polarized along party lines than their elders.

The Durability of Obama's Imprint

When Obama took office in 2009, Democrats held majorities in the Senate and House and among the states' governors and legislative chambers. After Democratic "shellackings" in the 2010 and 2014 elections, Republicans dominated at all of these levels, leaving the Democratic Party in its weakest position nationally since the 1920s (Sabato 2014). Obama's public standing, like that of previous presidents, has also influenced macropartisanship—the aggregate distribution of partisans in the national electorate—and his mediocre ratings after this first year in office helped the Republican Party to recover from the battering it took in this regard during Bush's second term (Jacobson 2012, 2015a). Figure 11 shows the smoothed trends in macropartisanship since 2001 by three measures— the CBS News/*New York Times* surveys (N = 234, leaners excluded) and Gallup surveys with and without leaners (N = 382). By all three measures, Democrats gained substantially during the latter years of the Bush administration but fell back to a narrower advantage after 2009.

Democrats' margins grew again around the time of Obama's reelection but have since fallen off. Democrats are still the majority party (by wider margins, as usual, in the CBS News/*New York Times* data as well as in Pew and ABC News/*Washington Post* data [not shown] than in the Gallup set), but the party remains weaker nationally by this measure than when Obama initially took office.[11] If the whole case rested on the present condition of the Democrats, then

FIGURE 11
Macropartisanship, 2001–2016

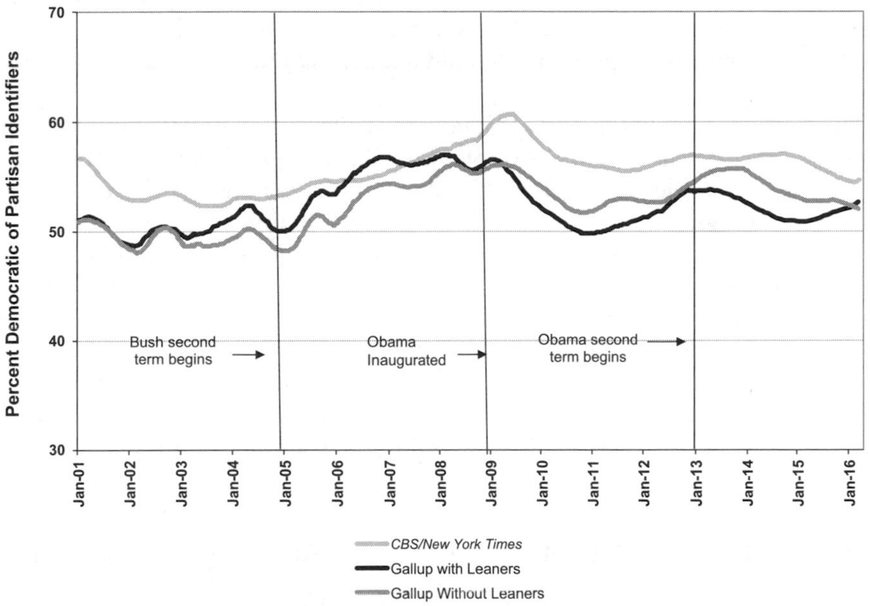

the conclusion would have to be that Obama's presidency has been quite damaging to his party.[12] Obama has also conspicuously failed to achieve his stated goal of bringing Americans together after the divisive Bush era. But considering Obama's impact on people who have come of political age during his administration—and who these people are demographically—his prospective long-term influence on his party's fortunes and on partisan divisions in society looks considerably more favorable.

Democrats, as we have seen, maintained the wide lead in party identification among the youngest cohort of respondents that first emerged during the Clinton and Bush administrations. Demographic trends are the main reason, but at least Obama did nothing to make his party less attractive to younger people of any ethnicity. The slow recovery from the Great Recession has been especially hard on the economic prospects of young people just entering the workforce, as well as on blacks and Hispanics (Thompson 2015; Kochhar and Fry 2014; Brainard 2015), yet they have continued to approve of Obama's performance and favor the Democratic Party at notably higher levels than other groups. The readiest explanation is that the Republican Party has so far failed to present itself as an attractive alternative to Obama's Democrats. Not many people in a generation that is ethnically diverse and comfortable with diversity, worried about a warming planet, supportive of same-sex marriage and LGBT rights, sympathetic to undocumented immigrants, and historically low in religious affiliation are likely to see themselves fitting into the current Republican coalition (Pew 2011). Nor do the party's orthodox economic prescriptions—tax cuts for the wealthy and deregula-tion—seem designed to inspire young people looking for decent paying jobs while burdened with high loads of student debt. Insofar as they have reservations about the Democratic Party, the Obama generation seems inclined toward inde-pendence (at least in response to the initial party ID question) rather than to the Republican Party.

The party loyalties of young respondents are less entrenched and more open to change in response to new experiences (Bartels and Jackman 2014; Green, Palmquist, and Schickler 2002), so the Democratic leanings of the Obama gen-eration are not guaranteed to remain as lopsided as they are at the time of this writing. Yet the newly enfranchised cohorts, including those who consider them-selves Republicans or independents, are notably more moderate or liberal and favorably disposed toward Obama and his policies than their elders, and there is no reason at present to think that this will change any time soon. They are also less ideologically polarized along party lines, and unless a substantial portion of them shifts to the Right on a range of social, economic, and environmental issues—not a likely prospect—they should remain so into the future.

Potential Generational Effects of the 2016 Campaigns

Presidential candidates as well as presidents shape their parties' images and attractiveness as objects of identification. By its choice of nominee (as well as with its formal platform), a party updates its national profile. The candidate becomes the party's preeminent public face, and what people come to think of him or her during the course of the campaign will inevitably color their beliefs and feelings about, and thereby their inclination to identify with, the party that did the nominating (Jacobson 2016c). The competition to replace Obama thus holds the potential to either reinforce or erode partisan identities, particularly among younger citizens presumably less fixed in their political attitudes.

The 2016 Republican nomination contest and its result are almost certain to strengthen rather than undermine the Democratic identities formed during the Clinton, Bush, and Obama presidencies. The two leading contestants, Donald Trump and Ted Cruz, did not alienate younger cohorts in exactly the same way or perhaps to the same degree, but neither of them offered a package of posi-tions, policies, and personal style likely to attract people who currently favor the Democratic Party or who consider themselves independents; their more likely effect was to make moderate younger Republicans reconsider their partisan iden-tities. Both aimed their campaigns at a Republican base consisting of older, white, conservative, religious, married, rural or suburban residents who are angry about national trends that younger voters largely welcome and to a considerable extent embody.

Trump, who assumed a wide and ultimately insurmountable lead in the Republican polls and delegate count during the first quarter of 2016, rose to dominate the field by fanning xenophobic animus against Mexican immigrants and Muslims and antiglobalization sentiments in language that resonated with a substantial minority of Republicans and Right-leaning independents (for more details on the Trump candidacy, see my companion piece in this volume, Jacobson 2016b). His supporters took his crude attacks on detractors and imagined enemies as a sign of authenticity, but more Americans were repelled than were attracted by his bullying, narcissistic rhetoric. Trump consistently received the most lopsidedly negative ratings of any candidate,[13] with young and nonwhite people especially disaffected. For example, the average ratio of favorable to unfavorable opinions of Trump among respondents under 30 in five January 2015–March 2016 YouGov surveys was 21:73; African Americans (16:77) and Hispanics (23:73) were also decisively negative in their assessments.

Even had he not won the nomination, Trump's domination of the Republican stage for so long threatened to redefine who and what the Republican Party stands for in ways that inflicted lasting damage to its image among groups already inclined to favor the Democrats. The effectiveness of his nativist demagoguery pulled his main Republican rivals sharply to the Right on immigration policy affecting both undocumented Latino residents and Muslim refugees. Collectively, the leading Republican candidates explicitly rejected their party's official autopsy of Romney's 2012 loss that had recommended expanding the party's appeal to blacks, Asians, Latinos, women, gays, and young people (Walshe 2013).

Cruz, number two among Republicans in national polls and delegates won, presented a somewhat different threat to the party's image and standing. He was not initially looked upon as unfavorably as Trump was by young and minority voters,[14] but his self-presentation, electoral strategy, and policy positions would be of limited appeal to them. Cruz adopted radically conservative opinions on every issue, placing him further to the Right than any serious Republican candidate in the postwar era (for more detail on Cruz's candidacy, see my companion piece in this volume, Jacobson 2016b). If his extreme proposals regarding immigration (nearly identical to Trump's), abortion (total ban), same-sex marriage (overturn the Supreme Court's decision that made it legal everywhere), climate change (rejecting human causation and any steps to mitigate it), and cabinet departments (dismantling departments including the Department of Education) end up in the Republican platform for 2016, all available survey data tell us they are bound to drive away far more young voters than they attract. Cruz's rhetoric, targeting the most conservative elements of the Republican coalition, was extreme, and nothing in his campaign suggested any inclination or capacity to expand his or his party's appeal beyond its most conservative segments, which include only a tiny fraction of voters who have come of age during recent presidencies.[15]

During the primary season, Trump and Cruz easily outpolled more orthodox Republican candidates such as Jeb Bush or Marco Rubio, who might have been less off-putting to younger voters. Ohio governor John Kasich, a mainstream Republican, managed to win his home state on March 15 but continued to trail Trump and Cruz badly in delegate counts and national polls, making his dropping out in early May inevitable. Kasich was viewed less negatively by young and minority voters than Trump or Cruz, although these voters were also much less likely to know enough about him to have an opinion.[16] His more conventionally conservative positions would have held little appeal to most young voters, but his style and demeanor were less likely to offend, suggesting that his nomination might have been less damaging to his party's standing with the Obama generation than would the nomination of Trump or Cruz. In other words, Kasich would have done his party the least harm.

Trump, Cruz, and most of the rest of the Republican field vowed repeatedly during their campaigns to undo virtually everything that Obama had accomplished. The reason is obvious: the most powerful sentiments animating Republican primary voters are hostility and anger toward Obama that go far deeper than reflexive objections to a mainstream Democrat (Greenberg and Carville 2014; Jacobson 2015c). In catering to this mindset, the Republican Party's two leading candidates adopted extreme positions and ugly rhetoric that will repel the mostly liberal and moderate younger generation that is broadly supportive of the president and his policies. Ironically, the Obama presidency's most valuable long-term gift to the Democratic Party might be indirect and unintended: provoking a virulent partisan backlash that made the Republican Party unmarketable to a rising generation of voters.

On the Democratic side, the choice was between Hillary Clinton, who would at minimum work to protect Obama's major accomplishments on health care, economic regulation, the environment, foreign policy, and immigration; and Vermont senator Bernie Sanders, an avowed democratic socialist who proposed moving much further Left, with a single-payer health care system, highly progressive tax policies, and greatly expanded social programs, including free tuition for students in public universities. Despite some concessions to the Left during the primaries, Clinton was accurately viewed as a moderate Democrat with orthodox positions similar to Obama's and at the median of the Democrats' center-Left coalition (Tesler 2016). Her problems within the party were less about ideology than about personality and character. Among younger Democrats, the 74-year-old Sanders proved to be by far the more popular of the two (indeed, of any candidate of either party), much more so than Clinton even among young women. His support is an indication of how liberal younger Democrats have become (Pew 2015). Millennial voters are clearly far more receptive to Left-wing than to Right-wing populism: compare Trump's net –50 favorable-unfavorable percentages to Sanders' +23 among voters under 30 in the January-March YouGov polls.

Clinton had the smallest capacity to change how people think of the nominee's party of any of the leading prospects in either party. Young Democrats who are not wild about her and would have preferred a more liberal option in Sanders will not thereby be inspired to vote for or identify as Republicans; a generation for whom "socialism" elicits more positive than negative feelings is not poised to enter the Republican ranks.[17] Had Sanders won the nomination, he would certainly alter the image of his party, not in a way likely to diminish its appeal to the Obama generation, but in a way that might make older Democrats reconsider where they fit in (they do not appear to be clamoring for a "revolution" involving a vast increase in the public sector). With the nominations of Clinton and Trump, a Republican far more alienating than attractive to younger voters, the pattern of

Democratic dominance among people first entering the electorate during the past three administrations is likely to persist. If Trump were to win the White House and attempt to fulfill the promises he made during the primary season, the Democratic advantage, driven by both demography and ideology, would likely grow even wider. But no matter how it comes out, the Democratic imprint visible in cohorts who have come of political age during the Clinton, Bush, and Obama administrations is likely to be sustained or even strengthened by the fight over Obama's succession.

Notes

1. For most purposes, treating leaners as partisans is advised, for they share the political attitudes and behavior of self-identified weak partisans much more than those of the "pure" independents or nonpartisans (Keith et al. 1992; Jacobson and Carson 2016, 152).

2. Ghitza and Gelman (2014) estimate the crucial period as between 14 and 24; Delli Carpini (1989, 20) notes other suggested ranges proposed in the generational development literature, including 17 to 25, 18 to 26, 15 to 30, and 20 to 30.

3. The Democratic percentages of major party respondents across these age groups calculated with leaners and without leaners are correlated at .95.

4. A very crude estimate of the relationship derived by regressing the distribution of major party identifiers among people turning 20 in each administration on the president's average approval rating during his final year in office produces coefficients of .132 (SD = .057, p = .046, R^2 = .37) with leaners and .126 (SD = .047, p = .024, R^2 = .45) without leaners (N = 12).

5. Because of the way Gallup reports the data, independents in this chart include leaners as well as pure independents.

6. The opposite was true during the G. W. Bush administration, but the generation gap was much smaller, with ratings offered by the youngest group averaging about four points lower than those offered by older groups during his last two years in office (Jacobson 2011, 247).

7. I refer to Hispanics rather than Latinos to conform to Gallup's usage.

8. In California, Democrats currently hold all statewide elective offices, both U.S. Senate seats, thirty-nine of fifty-four House seats, fifty-two of eighty state assembly seats, and twenty-six of forty state senate seats; Wilson's stand on immigration was, however, only one of a number of factors turning California dark blue.

9. The slight uptick in conservatism in the 2015 and 2016 independent cohorts is based on 181 and 91 respondents, respectively, and thus should not be considered meaningful at this point.

10. In the American National Election Studies, for example, the share of liberals in the 21–30 age group from 1978 to 1986 dropped from 30 percent to 28 percent a decade later (the 31–40 cohort in 1988–1996) and to 25 percent a decade after that (41–50 cohort in 1998–2006). Over the same three decades, the proportion of conservatives increased from 35 percent to 43 percent and then remained at 43 percent. These cohorts did become less liberal and more conservative, but with changes far too modest to account for the cohort differences observed in the Gallup data.

11. Shifts in macropartisanship do not alter the generational patterns identified earlier; they are identical when the data from 2008 and 2009, when the Democratic Party advantage in macropartisanship was at its peak, are compared to later data, except for about a three-point shift toward the Republicans evident across all cohorts (Jacobson 2015a, 24–25).

12. According to Sabato (2014), this is a common effect of two-term presidencies.

13. In twelve surveys asking the favorability question about Trump taken between March 1 and April 4, 2016, the distribution was 32 percent favorable, 65 percent unfavorable: the most negative of any candidate still in the running in April and of any serious presidential candidate in the several decades the question has been asked.

14. The ratio of favorable to unfavorable opinions of Cruz, averaged across the five YouGov polls taken from the end of January through mid-March, was 28:49 among respondents under 30, 24:57 among blacks, and 36:49 among Hispanics.

15. Among respondents under 30 in the 2014 Cooperative Congressional Election Study, only 8 percent were self-identified conservatives with favorable opinions of the Tea Party (Cruz's prime constituency); for comparison, 30 percent of respondents 65 and older were in that category.

16. The ratio of favorable to unfavorable opinions of Kasich, averaged across the five YouGov polls taken from the end of January through mid-March, was 25:32 among respondents under 30, 23:42 among blacks, and 28:34 among Hispanics.

17. In a 2011 Pew survey, the ratio of favorable/unfavorable views of socialism among respondents under 30 was 49:43, compared with 34:58 among the 30 to 49 cohort, 25:68 among the 50 to 64 cohort, and 13:72 among the 65+ cohort (Pew 2011). In the November 2015 CBS News/New York Times poll, 63 percent of the Democrats under 30 expressed positive views of socialism (Russonello 2015).

References

Bartels, Larry M., and Simon Jackman. 2014. A generational model of political learning. *Electoral Studies* 33 (1): 7–18.

Bowler, Shaun, Stephen P. Nicholson, and Gary M. Segura. 2006. Earthquakes and aftershocks: Race, direct democracy, and partisan change. *American Journal of Political Science* 50 (1): 146–59.

Brainard, Lael. 2015. Coming of age in the Great Recession. Paper presented at "Economic Mobility: Research and Ideas on Strengthening Families, Communities, and the Economy" Ninth Biennial Federal Reserve System Community Development Research Conference, April 2, Washington, DC.

Campbell, Angus, Philip E. Converse, Warren E. Miller, and Donald S. Stokes. 1960. *The American voter*. New York, NY: John Wiley & Sons.

Danigelis, Nicholas L., Melissa Hardy, and Stephen J. Cutler. 2007. Population aging, intracohort aging, and sociopolitical attitudes. *American Sociological Review* 72 (5): 812–30.

Delli Carpini, Michael X. 1989. Age and history: Generations and sociopolitical change. In *Political learning in adulthood: A sourcebook of theory and research*, ed. Roberta S. Sigel. Chicago, IL: University of Chicago Press.

DeSilver, Drew. 2014. The politics of American generations: How age affects attitudes and voting behavior. Pew Research Center. Available from http://www.pewresearch.org/fact-tank/2014/07/09/the-politics-of-american-generations-how-age-affects-attitudes-and-voting-behavior/

Erikson, Robert S., Michael MacKuen, and James A. Stimson. 1998. What moves macropartisanship? A response to Green, Palmquist, and Schickler. *American Political Science Review* 92 (4): 901–21.

Gerson, Michael. 13 August 2015. Trump declares war on America's demography. *Washington Post*.

Ghitza, Yair, and Andrew Gelman. 2014. The Great Society, Reagan's revolution, and generations of presidential voting. Working Paper, Columbia University, New York, NY.

Green, Donald, Bradley Palmquist, and Eric Schickler. 1998. Macropartisanship: A replication and critique. *American Political Science Review* 92 (4): 883–99.

Green, Donald, Bradley Palmquist, and Eric Schickler. 2002. *Partisan hearts and minds*. New Haven, CT: Yale University Press.

Greenberg, Stanly B., and James Carville. 2014. *Inside the GOP*. Greenberg Quinlan Rosner Research Report on the Republican Party Project.

Hopkins, Dan. 22 April 2014. Partisan loyalty begins at age 18. *New York Times*.

Jacobson, Gary C. 2009. The effects of the George W. Bush presidency on partisan attitudes. *Presidential Studies Quarterly* 39 (2): 172–209.

Jacobson, Gary C. 2011. *A divider, not a uniter: George W. Bush and the American people*. 2nd ed. New York, NY: Pearson.

Jacobson, Gary C. 2012. The president's effect on partisan attitudes. *Presidential Studies Quarterly* 42 (4): 683–718.

Jacobson, Gary C. 2015a. How presidents shape their party's reputation and prospects: New evidence. *Presidential Studies Quarterly* 45 (1): 1–28.

Jacobson, Gary C. 2015b. Obama and nationalized electoral politics in the 2014 midterm. *Political Science Quarterly* 130 (1): 1–26.

Jacobson, Gary C. 2015c. Barack Obama and the nationalization of electoral politics in 2012. *Electoral Studies* 40:471–81.

Jacobson, Gary C. 2016a. Age, race, party, and ideology: Generational imprinting during the Obama presidency. Paper presented at the Annual Meeting of the Midwest Political Science Association, Chicago, Illinois, 7–10 April 2009.

Jacobson, Gary C. 2016b. Polarization, gridlock, and presidential campaign politics in 2016. *The ANNALS of the American Academy of Political and Social Science* (this volume).

Jacobson, Gary C. 2016c. The coevolution of affect toward presidents and their parties. *Presidential Studies Quarterly* 46 (2): 1–29.

Jacobson, Gary C., and Jamie L. Carson. 2016. *The politics of congressional elections.* 9th ed. New York, NY: Rowman & Littlefield.

Keith, Bruce E., David B. Magleby, Candice J. Nelson, Elizabeth Orr, Mark C. Westlye, and Raymond E. Wolfinger. 1992. *The myth of the independent voter.* Berkeley, CA: University of California Press.

Kinder, Donald R. 2006. Politics and the life cycle. *Science* 312 (June 30): 1905–8.

Kochhar, Rakesh, and Richard Fry. 12 December 2014. *Wealth inequality has widened along racial, ethnic lines since end of Great Recession.* Washington, DC: Pew Research Center. Available from http://www.pewresearch.org.

MacKuen, Michael, Robert S. Erikson, and James A. Stimson. 1989. Macropartisanship. *American Political Science Review* 83 (4): 1125–42.

Mannheim, Karl. 1928/1972. The problem of generations. In *The new pilgrims*, eds. Philip G. Altbach and Robert S. Laufer. New York, NY: David McKay.

Miller, Warren E., and J. Merrill Shanks. 1996. *The new American voter.* Cambridge, MA: Harvard University Press.

Pew Research Center. 3 November 2011. The generation gap and the 2012 election. Available from http://www.people-press.org/2011/11/03/the-generation-gap-and-the-2012-election-3/

Pew Research Center. 30 April 2015. A different look at generations and partisanship. Available from http://www.people-press.org/2015/04/30/a-different-look-at-generations-and-partisanship/

Russonello, Giovanni. 20 November 2015. Poll watch: Democrats, even Clinton supporters, warm to socialism. *New York Times.*

Sabato, Larry. 2014. Why parties should hope they lose the White House. *Politico.* Available from http://www.politico.com.

Tesler, Michael. 27 January 2016. A newly released poll shows the populist power of Donald Trump. Monkey Cage, *Washington Post.* Available from https://www.washingtonpost.com.

Thompson, Derek. 19 May 2015. The economy is still terrible for young people. *The Atlantic.* Available from http://www.theatlantic.com.

Thurber, James A., and Antoine Yoshinaka, eds. 2015. *American gridlock.* New York, NY: Cambridge University Press.

Truett, K. R. 1993. Age differences in conservatism. *Personality and Individual Differences* 14 (3): 405–11.

Walshe, Shushanna. 13 March 2013. RNC completes "autopsy" on 2012 loss, calls for inclusion not policy change. ABC News. Available from http://abcnews.go.com.

Back to the Future? What the Politics of the Late Nineteenth Century Can Tell Us about the 2016 Election

By
JULIA AZARI
and
MARC J. HETHERINGTON

The politics and party system of the late Civil War era are strikingly similar to what we have in the present day. Elections were consistently close; race, culture, immigration, and populism were salient issues; and states almost always voted for the same party in election after election. The states that supported Democrats then, however, mostly support Republicans now, and vice versa. In 1896, though, a new party system began to emerge. In this article, we evaluate bygone elections alongside contemporary ones to assess whether 2016 might be the beginning of something new in American electoral politics. Are national politics likely to follow the familiar pattern of the last four presidential races, or are Americans going to be presented altogether different choices? Our analysis suggests that race and populism are guideposts for potential change in 2016: if the concerns of race continue to define political conflict, the electoral map should change little, but if economic populism eclipses race as it did in 1896, a new political era may be ushered in in America.

Keywords: 2016 election; system of 1896; polarization; populism

Presidential elections have been unusually stable over the past four cycles, with fully forty states voting for the same party in all four contests. The last time there was this kind of

Julia Azari is an associate professor of political science at Marquette University. She is the author of Delivering the People's Message: The Changing Politics of the Presidential Mandate *(Cornell University Press 2014) and co-editor (with Lara Brown and Zim Nwokora) of* The Presidential Leadership Dilemma *(SUNY Press 2013).*

Marc J. Hetherington is a professor of political science at Vanderbilt University. He is coauthor (with Thomas J. Rudolph) of Why Washington Won't Work *(University of Chicago Press 2015), winner of the 2016 Alexander George Book Award from the International Society for Political Psychology.*

NOTE: We thank Larry Bartels for providing much of the historical data that we employ in this article.

Correspondence: marc.j.hetherington@vanderbilt.edu

DOI: 10.1177/0002716216662604

continuity in voting behavior was the late nineteenth century. The volatility of the nomination battle, though, particularly on the Republican side, suggests that 2016 could provide a break from the past. We are not the first to make such an observation, but our reasoning is not based on the unique personal styles of particular candidates. Rather, understanding the stability of election outcomes in recent years means understanding the issues salient to voters and the extent to which voters are given an opportunity to vote for those issues in the election cycle. If the parties contest the 2016 election on the same familiar ground (race, size of government, muscularity of foreign policy), we will likely get a familiar result. But, should Donald Trump's scrambling of the GOP during the nomination process produce new fault lines in the electorate this fall (e.g., protectionism and economic populism), the party mold of recent years could be broken.

To assess whether we will see continuity or change in 2016, we draw on a mostly forgotten series of elections contested more than 100 years ago. Elections of the late nineteenth century were marked by their continuity, and the electoral college maps from the period look much like those today. The parties' strongholds are reversed between the two eras, but the division of states into party coalitions bears more than a passing resemblance (Miller and Schofield 2003). In addition, the level of partisanship apparent in voting behavior in both periods stands out as particularly strong (Bartels 1998). It is probably consequential, too, that congressional roll call voting behavior was highly partisan then as it is now; the polarization of congressional voting behavior by party, based on scores generated by Keith Poole and Howard Rosenthal, reaches its peak in the late Gilded Age[1] and the contemporary period as well, and scholars have established that mass behavior tends to follow elite cues (Key 1966; Zaller 1992).

The late nineteenth century continuity did not last forever, of course. The 1896 contest between Republican William McKinley and Democrat William Jennings Bryan signaled the beginning of a break from the politics of the Civil War. Burnham identifies it as a key turning point in American politics, with its "massive and largely permanent transformation in aggregate electoral behavior" (1970, 71). Issues that had previously been on the backburner of party conflict moved to the fore. Specifically, Gerring (1998) argues that the Democratic Party's full-throated support for populism in the form of Bryan's candidacy is the key to understanding the birth of a new party system. Bryan's candidacy helped to usher in an era in which the Democratic Party emphasized the abuses of economic elites against workers and farmers and embraced government solutions to those problems. This represented a sharp ideological shift from the Democratic Party of previous decades, which had been suspicious of centralized government power. Will 2016 be similar to 1896, with a move away from one set of concerns to another?

We begin by assessing the similarities of the two eras. Some of the issues that are salient now were salient then, including race, morality, immigration, and themes related to populism. Both periods featured similar electoral context, specifically close elections at the national level. Both periods witnessed a nationalization of politics, in which local conditions were rendered secondary in understanding voting behavior. Breathtaking technological innovation also characterized both periods, with one witnessing the dawn of the industrial revolution and the other the dawn of the digital revolution. As a consequence, income and wealth inequality were rampant then, as they are now. Although this list is not exhaustive, it gives us some places to start.

Our analysis suggests that a combination of factors likely undergirds the shape of partisan conflict in both the late nineteenth and early twenty-first centuries. These are (1) racial politics and (2) conflict over the practice of democracy, which we interpret as a consequence of close party margins. Although "culture war" clashes over morality were important in both eras, the religiously conservative side was in the Republican camp both times and hence cannot account for the party flip that occurred after 1896 in the electoral map. Immigration, too, was important in both eras, but, in the late nineteenth century, neither party embraced immigrants, so while that issue distinguishes the two parties from each other now, it did not do so then.

The experience of the late 1890s suggests that the increased salience of economic populism in 2016 could foreshadow a break from the last several elections that could potentially reorder the political map. Economic populism was not a constant force in the late 1800s, but it emerged as important in Democratic circles during Grover Cleveland's presidencies and took hold of the party with Bryan's candidacy in 1896 (and 1900 and 1908). Although populism had great emotional resonance—Bryan was carried off the stage on the shoulders of delegates at the Democratic convention following his famous Cross of Gold Speech—it was not a political winner: the combination of poor rural voters in the Great Plains and poor southern whites (on the wrong side of racial history) was sufficiently unattractive to political coalition partners that the Democratic Party rarely occupied the White House for three decades.

A Shared Pattern of Partisan Competition

Every four years, it feels like the political system is reborn, with at least one new character (and sometimes two) contesting the presidency. The media reinforce this perception by breathlessly covering every twist and turn of the campaign, as though each suggests something new and fresh. Lately, though, this notion does not seem to match reality. The characters change, but the results hardly do.

Something other than shared electoral context must be providing the glue because electoral context varied widely across these four elections. The 2000 and 2008 elections did not include an incumbent. In 2004, the incumbent, George W. Bush, was a Republican. In 2012, Barack Obama, a Democrat, was the incumbent. The economy was quite good in 2000; it was fair in 2004 and 2012; and it was a complete disaster in 2008. Foreign policy was an afterthought in 2000; it was perhaps the central issue in 2004; and it was somewhere in between in 2008 and 2012. Despite these seemingly critical differences in political context of presidential elections from cycle to cycle, voting results were largely identical when viewed at the state level.

The elections contested over the last two decades of the nineteenth century featured the same type of state-by-state continuity in voting that we see today. In addition, those latter day elections were, like now, extraordinarily close in both the popular vote and electoral vote. Indeed, the late 1800s elections were even closer than those today. Because the late nineteenth century is not the most memorable, a brief history lesson might be helpful. In 1880, Republican James Garfield defeated Winfield Hancock by 0.02 percent in the popular vote and 214 to 155 in the electoral college. In 1884, the GOP nominated James Blaine of Maine, who lost to Democrat Grover Cleveland by a mere 0.6 points in the popular vote. The electoral votes of Cleveland's native New York proved the difference.

In 1888, Benjamin Harrison returned the Republicans to the White House. Although he lost the popular vote to Cleveland by 0.8 points, he won the electoral vote fairly comfortably, at least by the standards of the era, by a count of 233 to 168. In the 1892 election, Cleveland returned to the White House in what counts as a landslide for that time, winning by a full 3 percentage points in the popular vote and 132 in the electoral vote count, in his rematch with Harrison. Iowa populist James Weaver won five states that year. Finally, McKinley defeated Bryan in 1896, winning the popular vote by a little more than 4 points and the electoral vote by nearly 100. Some scholars view this election as the dawning of a new electoral order (Key 1955; Burnham 1970).

Perhaps even more remarkable is the similarity of the states that made up each party's voting coalition. Generally speaking, the same states that went together then go together now. We are not the first to note the pattern. Miller and Schofield (2003) observed that thirty-nine of the forty-five states that were part of the Union in 1896 voted for the opposite party in the 2000 election. Twenty-two of the twenty-three states that favored Bryan in 1896 favored George W. Bush in 2000, and seventeen of the twenty-two states that favored McKinley in 1896 favored Al Gore in 2000. This constellation of states has remained largely unchanged for the parties since 2000. In the post–Reconstruction era, we observe a similar continuity in the elections leading up to the one in 1896.

In map 1, we contrast the electoral college map in 1896 with that of 2000, the same contrast that caught Miller and Schofield's (2003) attention for their similarities. The party strongholds are the same, only flipped in terms of affiliation. The South was as solid in 1896 as it was in 2000, only it was a Democratic South then and Republican South now. Most of the northeast and Midwest were Republican areas then and are Democratic areas now. For the references to color, please see the online version.

It is not just that these two snapshots in history are similar. So, too, is the continuity of state-level voting in both the four elections between 1880 and 1896 (excluding 1892 because of Weaver's third party challenge) and those between 2000 and 2012. When we count the number of times that a state cast a plurality of its votes for the Republican presidential candidate in the four elections that compose each of the eras, we find the distributions of party-consistent voting are bimodal for both periods. In the early period, about two-thirds of the thirty-eight states that existed in 1880 either voted Republican all four times or Democrat all four times. Moreover, only one state—Connecticut—voted exactly twice for the

MAP 1
Electoral College Map: 1896, 2000

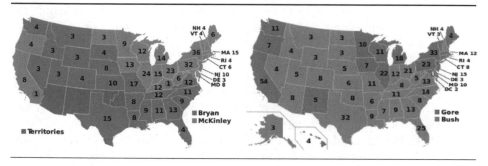

Republicans and twice for the Democrats. In the later period, the percentage of states that were perfectly consistent in their party voting grew to three-quarters of the thirty-eight states that existed in 1880.

Shared Strength of Partisanship

It is not just that states voted in the same direction year in and year out. They also voted in much the same percentages for one party or the other. The consistency of party vote percentages from election to election offers a measure of strength of partisanship in periods that occurred long before the dawn of survey research (Bartels 1998). Bartels's work built both theoretically and methodologically on the work of Donald Stokes (see especially Stokes 1962; Stokes and Iversen 1962; Stokes 1967), who hoped to generalize the survey findings produced by his research team, which produced *The American Voter* (Campbell et al. 1960), to include periods in the presurvey era.

Regardless of the political sources that underlie the similarities in voting behavior, they almost certainly would work through partisanship at the level of the voter. It is strong party loyalties that produce the "normal vote," a continuity in voting behavior that exists in the aggregate from election to election (Converse 1966). We know the effect of partisanship has increased markedly over the last 40 years (Bartels 2000), which would reduce deviations from the normal vote from election to election. By extending the historical analysis originally performed by Bartels (1998), we test whether the same outsized influence of party existed in the late nineteenth century as well.

To approximate a historical measure of partisanship, Bartels regressed the difference between a state's percentage of the Republican vote minus a state's percentage of the Democratic vote in a given year on the same differences recorded in each of the previous three election years in that state. So, for example, the 1896 difference in a given state was modeled as a function of the same differences recorded separately in 1892, 1888, and 1884. This methodology produces a regression coefficient for each of the three lagged elections, which, when

FIGURE 1
The Effect of Partisan Loyalties on the Presidential Vote, 1870–2012

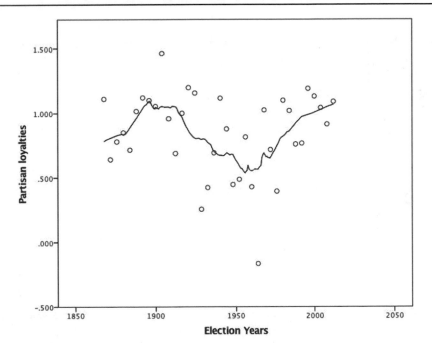

summed, can be interpreted as a measure of partisan loyalty. The regression also produces a standard error, which reveals the effect of subnational forces. Our initial interest is the summation of the coefficients for the three lagged election outcomes, the measure of partisan loyalties.

Following this methodology and extending the data collection as far forward as is now possible, we plot this measure of partisan persistence from the 1870s to 2012. These results appear in Figure 1 as a locally weighted regression trend line from the thirty-seven individual regressions we estimated. What stands out is that the two high water marks for party voting occur in the late nineteenth century and the early twenty-first century. Indeed, there are no other periods in American history that appear like these two. After peaking around 1900, the persistence of party voting from previous elections declines more or less steadily until the 1960s. It starts a march upward from this low ebb in the 1970s, reaching its highest levels in the most recent several elections. In fact, the trend line generated from the last several elections ends at almost precisely the same level in absolute terms where it stood in the late nineteenth century.

In addition, the eras in question both represent substantial moves toward the nationalization of party politics. As Klinghard (2010) argues, the 1880s and 1890s saw a shift from parties that were highly decentralized and localized to an organizational focus of party function. This new system was characterized in part by "presidential dominance" of political party agendas, in addition to changes in the

FIGURE 2
The Effect of Subnational Forces on the Presidential Vote, 1870–2012

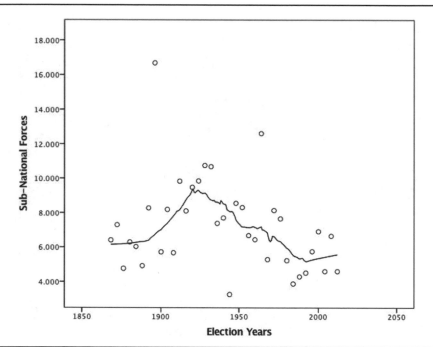

conduct of electoral politics that included direct primaries and increased presidential campaigning. Similarly, scholars have noted a shift from the highly district-focused congressional elections of the mid-twentieth century (see Fenno 1978; Mayhew 2004) to congressional elections fought over national issues (see Jacobson 1996, 2007, 2015).

For our purposes, the nationalization of party politics rests on two premises: the central role of the president and the development of national policy themes to unify an otherwise divided party. Klinghard (2010) emphasizes the role of Grover Cleveland in defining the Democrats' policy agenda: "the departure from tradition—devoting the entire annual message to a single, substantive policy issue—would grab popular attention, inviting public comment and giving the party-in-the-electorate reason to read the message in the privacy of their homes" (p. 167). Similarly, the Democratic politician who sought to succeed Cleveland, William Jennings Bryan, used speeches and populist economic policies to attempt to unite the party's divergent economic constituencies (Klinghard 2010, 168; Bensel 2008; Kazin 2006).

Recall from above that Bartels's analysis identified the standard error of the regression as a measure of the effect subnational forces exerted on presidential votes. Of course, greater nationalization should make subnational forces less important whereas more decentralized party conflict would make subnational forces more important. Figure 2 sketches the change over time in the degree to which the nationalization of politics affected electoral politics. As with the strength of partisanship in voting, the late 1800s and early 2000s stand out for their similarity. The figure shows subnational forces at the beginning of the time series, which begins in the last decades of the nineteenth century, as particularly unimportant. Beginning around the turn of the twentieth century, these forces begin to play a greater and greater role, reaching their peak in the 1920s and 1930s. After that, a slow but steady drop takes place, with the end of the time series producing the lowest ever effects for subnational forces in presidential elections.

Shared Issues

We turn now to a treatment of what the parties at the elite level were offering to voters, working from the assumption that voters generally respond to the stimuli that political elites provide. As we noted above, Miller and Schofield (2003) attribute the similarity in the electoral college map to the importance of cultural and racial issues in both eras. Obviously race and culture are both examples of symbolic—as opposed to programmatic—criteria for voting (Carmines and Stimson 1989; Stimson 2004). Such matters have the power to polarize and thus make the parties that have taken opposite sides on these matters very important to vote choice, which in turn could create polarization.

A culture war?

As remarkable as similarities in voting behavior across the two eras appear, an examination of voting data taken from below the state level reveals important differences. Moreover, these differences may eliminate certain suspects that plausibly explain the electoral college similarities between the two eras. Consider the county-level returns from the 1896 and 2000 presidential elections that are captured in Map 2. In the current day, states mostly have patches of red and patches of blue, corresponding to the population density of the areas within each of the states (Barone 2001). Cities are blue; suburban and rural areas are red. But, with few exceptions, the 1896 county map on the left does not reveal much within-state diversity when compared with 2000.

Consider first the South. The absence of blue patches makes sense in the early era, given that African Americans were largely disenfranchised by 1896, and major populations centers were largely absent. The map plausibly suggests the centrality of race in both eras. Race accounts for the region's rejection of the Republicans in the late 1800s and the Democrats in the 2000s. There is more blue in the 2000 map to be sure, but this is because there are major cities in the South today and because African Americans are no longer disenfranchised to the same extent.

In the non-South, however, the county-level differences evident between the eras are perhaps consequential. Take Pennsylvania as exemplary of the general pattern in the contemporary era. James Carville, for one, has described the Keystone State as Philadelphia and Pittsburgh with Alabama in between. Put another way, its major cities combined with the suburban rings around them tend

MAP 2
County Electoral Map, 1896, 2000

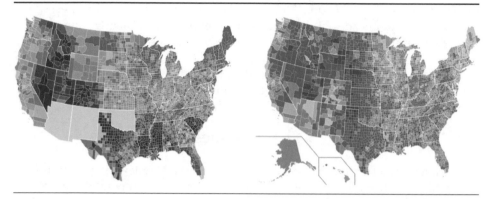

to be Democratic blue. But the rest of the state tends to be dark Republican red. In the 1896 election and consistent with the present day, Philadelphia and Allegheny (home to Pittsburgh) counties were dark red in support of McKinley. However, we see only a few counties in the rural central part of the state that were Democratic blue. Far more were Republican red. For the references to color, please see the online version.

Kleppner (1979) suggests intense ethnoreligious conflict provided post-Reconstruction U.S. politics with its intensity. His work is particularly germane to our inquiry across eras because the notion of ethnoreligious differences shares elements of Hunter's (1991) characterization of a culture war in the late twentieth century based on the orthodoxy or relativism of religious understanding. Hunter's reckoning about present day political conflict features orthodox Christians supporting the Republicans and relativistic Christians (and non-Christians) supporting the Democrats. The problem for a moral "culture war" as an explanation that fits both eras is that the pietistic, evangelical element of the culture war sides with the Republicans in both eras. It was the GOP that supported temperance and Prohibition. Democrats of today do not support modern-day equivalents. Indeed, the reality is the reverse. Moreover, the fact that Republicans of the late 1800s dominated voting in cities, which is where the immigrants—who made up the Papist nonpietistic side of the conflict—disproportionately lived, points out how uncompetitive the "culture war" was in the mid-Atlantic and New England states.

That limitation aside, Kleppner's analysis of the basis for ethnoreligious conflict is, in part, consistent with what divided the voting public then and what divides it now. Specifically, the race issue among northern pietistic Republicans had a strong religious component. The evangelism of that day put strong emphasis on the free will of individual men, making the practice of slavery repugnant to those with an orthodox worldview. If race were the central concern among rural nonsouthern voters, it would provide one possible explanation for the similarity of rural and urban voting in the northeast. Even if this were the case, it is not the same kind of "culture war" that characterizes the present day. We take up the issue of race in more detail below.

Unequal prosperity and populism?

Although the moral culture war does not seem to fit the bill, there might be another similarity in the county electoral maps that is worth noting. The remarkably broad and, with few exceptions, uninterrupted swaths of Republican red above the Mason-Dixon line contrasting with similarly unbroken patches of Democratic blue in the South, Great Plains, and mountain West follow a pattern consistent with the Metropole-Colonies divide described by Burnham (1983). He drew the boundaries of the Metropole as "an area extending from Minneapolis southward along the Mississippi past St. Louis to the Ohio, thence along that river to West Virginia, thence through the southern boundary of West Virginia and eastward across Virginia to Norfolk (the terminus of the coal-carrying Norfolk and Western railroad)" (p. 152). It was home to an overwhelming share of the nation's manufacturing employment, financial services, university endowment, and urban population. The Metropole featured relatively high income; for example, the average per capita income in the mid-Atlantic states was more than twice that of the South Atlantic states (Burnham 1983, 153). The three colonies—western, southern, and plains—were, in contrast, racked by undercapitalization and underdevelopment.

Consistent with the potential importance of populism, two economic issues also figure prominently in the last years of the nineteenth century: tariffs and currency. Klinghard (2005) identifies tariff reform and currency, namely the gold standard, as defining aspects of Grover Cleveland's leadership of the Democratic Party. In his 1888 State of the Union message to Congress, devoted solely to the issue of tariff reduction, Cleveland offered a description of the problem that was tinged with populism: "Corporations, which should be the carefully restrained creatures of the law and the servants of the people, are fast becoming the people's masters." Tariff questions had long divided Republicans, who tended to see protectionist policy as a means to develop American industry, from Democrats who were suspicious of the impact of high tariffs on those outside of the industrial elite. While these were not entirely new policy positions for the two parties (see Gerring 1998), they began to take on heightened significance, particularly toward the end of the Civil War Party era.

Agrarian populism also emerged as a social and political movement in the late nineteenth century. The nomination of Bryan represented a deepening of the distinction between the two parties on economic issues in 1896, specifically. The electoral map at the state level bears this out, with rural western states turning blue and the industrial northeast remaining red.

In sum, party conflict on economic issues was informed late in the era by an overarching theme of economic populism and by questions about how the degree of trade openness affected ordinary workers. Similarly, economic inequality has become a central theme of twenty-first-century politics (Bartels 2008), with these questions animating themes in the 2016 election on both the Left and Right. Economic populism—specifically the abuses of corporations and banks against ordinary citizens—has been a dominant theme in the candidacy of Bernie Sanders. Donald Trump, the unexpected frontrunner for the Republican nomination, has emphasized the need for protection against "bad trade deals." The emergence of economic populism, with attention to corporate power and trade, is one of the most telling indicators of new Gilded Age politics.

Race and immigration

Race and immigration are also shared issues of the two political eras. But it is not clear whether both are central to the party divide of the two periods. For painfully obvious reasons, race is generally considered to have been the driver of political conflict between the North (particularly the Northeast and the upper Midwest) and the South following the Civil War and Reconstruction. Extensive explanations of parties' positions on race were rendered unnecessary because of the depth of sectional political grievances. "Waving the bloody shirt" was all that was required. In the contemporary period, the legacy of the civil rights movement has placed race front and center in understanding political conflict for the past 50 years (Carmines and Stimson 1989). Party platforms make clear that Democrats support rights protection more often than Republicans. On affirmative action, the two parties take opposite positions.

Immigration tells a different story when comparing the two periods. Based on a careful reading of party platforms of the two eras, both parties gravitated toward exclusionary stances between 1876 and 1920, resulting in several rounds of highly restrictive immigration policy. In the contemporary period, significant party distinctions emerge. Republican platforms emphasized criminality and border control more often than did Democratic platforms, although these concerns were often coupled with recognition of the United States as a nation of immigrants. Democratic platforms emphasized reform and bringing undocumented persons out of the shadows.

In short, while race is a consistent source of division between the two national parties in both eras, immigration can be eliminated as a common factor. The two eras look quite different from each other, with agreement on restrictive immigration in the earlier era and substantial policy disagreement in the later one.

What does this suggest for the elections of 2016 and beyond? Although the two parties have built on some shared premises on these two "hot button" issues, intraparty strife may lead to substantial shifts. The Democratic candidates have begun to embrace criminal justice reform as a race issue, and the Black Lives Matter movement has brought systemic and structural racism into the party's discourse on the topic. On the Republican side, the unexpected success of Donald Trump's candidacy has carried the potential to shift at least some factions of the party in a more anti-immigration direction. We also should note that the Gilded Age does not provide much of a road map for what to expect from polarization over the immigration issue; there is a stark contrast between the way the issue maps onto party politics in the two eras we study. This may especially affect the changing electoral map moving forward. In other words, scholars and observers may expect deeper ideological distinctions to emerge on these issues. What remains to be seen is whether these distinctions will be between or within parties.

Political process

Looking at how the two parties discuss issues relating to the political process, we also observe distinctions between the parties both then and now. The emphasis on process, we suspect, reflects the nature of party competition in two ways. First, the substance of the platform language at times reflects genuine differences between the two parties regarding the desirability of direct democracy, the balance between free speech and campaign finance regulation, and the appropriate ways to limit government power.

Second, parties used claims about political process as attacks on opponents. By bringing up questions like patronage and campaign finance, party elites implied that the other party was not playing by the rules or respecting the norms of democracy. For example, between 1876 and 1920, one or both party platforms mentioned civil service reform in nearly every election year. These references were not infrequently accompanied by insinuations that the other party was practicing politics dishonestly. This kind of political rhetoric reflects the tightly competitive political environment in which stakes were high and both parties saw themselves as having a chance to compete for the presidency and for control of Congress.

The 1888 election exemplifies this kind of political conflict, with the popular vote decided in a razor-thin margin and the electoral college reversing the result, allowing Benjamin Harrison to defeat incumbent president Grover Cleveland. In 1892, Cleveland sought to return to office. The 1892 Democratic platform accordingly highlights the abuses of the Republican administration:

> Public office is a public trust. We reaffirm the declaration of the Democratic National Convention of 1876 for the reform of the civil service, and we call for the honest enforcement of all laws regulating the same. The nomination of a President, as in the recent Republican Convention, by delegations composed largely of his appointees, holding office at his pleasure, is a scandalous satire upon free popular institutions and a startling illustration of the methods by which a President may gratify his ambition. We denounce a policy under which the Federal office-holders usurp control of party conventions in the States, and we pledge the Democratic party to reform these and all other abuses which threaten individual liberty and local self-government.[2]

Starting in 1896, Democratic Party platforms also began to feature more advocacy for direct democracy measures, including the direct election of senators and presidential primaries. Several platforms also called for presidential term limits. In these statements and positions, we observe some high stakes conflict over the rules of the game. These stances reflected important policy positions—many of which came to fruition—but also suggested in some instances that the other party had abused its power and thus had made formal changes necessary.

In the later period, fewer questions like direct democracy were on the public agenda than during the Progressive Era. However, on two issues, the parties developed clear and clashing stances. While Democratic platforms stressed voting rights, several Republican platforms (2008 and 2012) stressed preventing voter fraud and preserving the integrity of the electoral process. This issue has had significant policy implications, with thirty-four states adopting some form of voter identification measures. These laws have been controversial because of their potential to disenfranchise low-income and minority voters, and as a result have been a major point of contention between the two parties.

Similarly, Democratic platforms moved toward support for campaign finance reform and condemnation of the status quo in campaign funding. In 2012, the Democratic platform denounced the impact of the *Citizens United vs. United States* decision, while the Republican platform expressed support for the decision as a protection of free speech rights. As with the "voter ID" question, references to campaign finance not only established party positions about major questions of democracy; these platform planks also indicated challenges to the legitimacy of the other party. For the Republicans, this has meant advocacy of voting laws that protect the integrity of the process, thus implying that Democratic victories may not always be legitimate. Similarly, Democratic platforms argue in favor of voter protection, and impugn the status quo in campaign funding. Perhaps it is this type of conflict that best captures the outgrowth of party competition balanced on a knife's edge in both eras.

A final note about political process brings us back to the question of populism. The question of "the people versus the powerful" manifests in this issue area just as it does in economics. Here we observe a slight difference between the eras; the emphasis on expanding the role of the people in democracy was largely the province of the generally more populist Democrats at the turn of the twentieth century. At the turn of the twenty-first, both parties attempted to present their process position in terms of protecting the people from encroaching abuses, whether that be the influence of money in elections or the specter of fraudulent voters. In this sense, both parties compete—using very different ideas—for the populist mantle in twenty-first-century politics.

Back to the Future, and Moving Forward?

As we connect our analysis of the late nineteenth century with the 2016 election, one thing is glaringly obvious: the country is as closely divided now as it was then. It might be that the individual states are becoming decreasingly competitive (Abramowitz 2010), but they aggregate together to produce a competitive national map at the presidential level. Although Republicans enjoy majorities in both houses of Congress—their largest in the House since 1924—their edge in the Senate could be undone in 2016, with several Republican incumbents attempting to protect seats in states that Democrats typically win (Illinois, Wisconsin, Pennsylvania, New Hampshire) and two others in the swing states of Ohio and Florida, which may be swayed by the outcome at the presidential level. The point here is that the divisions are close enough that as of midsummer 2016, it is plausible that either side could control the presidency, the Senate, and, as a consequence, the Supreme Court.

Close divisions in politics, as in sports, ramp up a team mentality. This would be true even if deep policy differences did not exist between the parties. But, exacerbating matters, the two parties are distinct from each other on a wider range of issues than ever before (Layman et al. 2010). Divisions over race issues in addition to questions of women's rights, traditional gender roles (Wolbrecht

2000) and gay rights have made political discourse deeply personal and contentious. Superimposed on the ideological divide that exists around these issues in Congress is the pure partisanship that close margins encourage (Lee 2009). When a party can win the next election, compromise and accommodation are not strategically shrewd moves for the minority party. The majority will get credit for legislative accomplishments. It is smarter to gridlock the system and accuse the majority of being dangerous characters to bolster minority party chances when they next face the voters. When voters receive such a signal from their elites, they will tend to reflect it in their own opinions and behaviors (Key 1966). A partisan elite level produces a partisan mass level (Hetherington 2001). As any sports fan can attest, feelings are strongest during a tight game or a close pennant race. For the last couple of decades, interparty competition has felt like a close playoff series between two evenly matched teams. This is similar to the late nineteenth century, suggesting a map with party divisions like the last four elections.

Also pointing in that direction is the fact that race remains an active concern in American politics. Although overt racism has declined over time, issue areas such as crime and welfare remain highly racialized (Gilens 1999). Moreover, racial attitudes in people's political belief systems increased in the age of Obama. Public support for programs that, in the past, were not driven by racial attitudes, such as health care reform, now are (Tesler 2012). Donald Trump has perhaps deepened racial divisions even further. His bona fides on the issue have been clear for years. Recall that he was a central figure in the "birther" movement, a group that actively questioned the authenticity of President Obama's birth certificate, insisting that he was born in Kenya, which would make him ineligible to be president. Not only has Trump been withering in his criticism of the Black Lives Matter movement on the campaign trail and particularly unforgiving of protestors of color at his rallies, he has gone as far as to question the "spirit" of African American youth (Moodley 2015).

It bears watching, however, whether his more explicit use of race leads to an outcome that differs from when his party appeals to race more implicitly. In the past, Republicans tended to benefit from racial appeals because they were implicit (Mendelberg 2001). For example, when people thought that the infamous Willie Horton ad of 1988 was about crime, it moved a substantial number of people toward George H. W. Bush. When, however, Democrats made the racial undertones of the ad explicit, it lost its power. Trump may be talking about race in a way that makes it no longer an asset to Republicans but rather a liability. Few want to be seen as supporting the same side as fringe groups, and yet Trump has "earned" endorsements from white supremacists. That the use of race has grown so explicit in 2016 runs the risk of repulsing especially college-educated whites who would rather not think of themselves as in a league with white supremacists. If race remains just below the surface and implicit in its use, as it has for decades, it points to a similar electoral college map in 2016 as in the past. More ham-handed use has the potential to repel enough Republicans to create a very different map.

That leaves the role of economic populism in the 2016 election and what this role portends for the electoral map. A reordering of groups is the reason party systems change, and the rise of a new issue that crosscuts the existing party system—like economic populism is doing in 2016 and did in 1896—is what causes the reordering. The populist versus establishment schism we have observed in the Republican Party through the primary season could have enormous implications not only for this election but for the next several. In that sense, the election of 2016 could be a harbinger of a new politics, with somewhat different lines of cleavage between the parties.

It is critical to understand how populism's increased salience might rearrange the groups that usually support the parties. The upside for Republicans is that it has the potential to attract parts of the Democratic coalition, including manual laborers and union members in the all-important Rust Belt states. Propopulist Trump followers believe that such gains could move states like Pennsylvania and Michigan into the Republican column. These optimists point to Bernie Sanders's strong showing in many states with a high percentage of older white voters, many of whom oppose free trade. The downside is that embracing economic populism has the potential to repel some key parts of the current Republican coalition. Big business, for one, likes free trade and the cheap labor it provides. College-educated whites, whose job prospects have not been adversely affected by free trade, seem less well matched to such appeals as well.

This is a major reason establishment Republicans are concerned. Ronald Reagan and George H. W. Bush promoted large tax cuts for the wealthy, a friendly environment for big business, and free trade abroad, suggesting establishment Republican priorities have generally been anathema to populism. The reason the party today includes so many for whom populism is attractive is happenstance. The party's emphasis on concern for "the other" over the past 50 years—whether that "other" is black, immigrant, gay, Muslim, feminist, and so on—attracted a large following of less affluent white voters for whom populism has serious appeal (Hetherington and Weiler 2009). But these voters have little in common with business elites and the country club set that is central to Reagan-Bush Republicanism. Instead, this group of Republicans gave the party establishment fits this year, desiring tough-talking, anti-everything candidates like Donald Trump and Ted Cruz rather than business-friendly Republicans like Scott Walker or Jeb Bush. In short, the rising salience of economic populism splits the Republicans.

Changes to the usual issue agenda do not come out of nowhere. Like the Democratic Party of Grover Cleveland, Republicans have, over the past 15 years, done more than dabble in populist anti-elite anti-Washington rhetoric in their efforts to broaden their electoral coalition, which has laid the groundwork for potential change in 2016. And it has not been just talk. Policy has also been part of the mix. By providing small tax benefits to less affluent voters under the guise of shrinking what they described as an elitist, out-of-touch Washington bureaucracy, Republicans have earned populist support, even as these measures provided truly giant benefits to wealthy individuals (Bartels 2008). The Democratic Party, with its decades-long commitment to using government to redistribute wealth, might seem a more natural vehicle for populism, but it is not a viable alternative for many of these voters because they perceive that the beneficiaries of government programs are minorities, not them (Gilens 1999). Trump, like Bryan in 1896, is not creating something new out of whole cloth but rather is simply making the issue more central than it was before.

Before tacitly endorsing Trumpism, Republicans should recall that the Democrats' full-throated embrace of populism in 1896 did not ultimately serve them well. Not only did Bryan hang himself on a cross of gold that year, he lost in 1900 and 1908 as well, and by increasingly lopsided margins. Beyond the solid South, the Democrats in the early twentieth century won only a few states in the border South and mountain West. It seems possible that a similar fate could befall a Trump-led, populist-fueled Republican Party today.

Such an outcome, however, would require Republican opponents of populism to view the Democrats as a better alternative. In that sense, party system change requires both push and pull. It may be that a Republican embrace of an explicitly racialized form of populism is pushing away business and college-educated whites, but little would change if the Democrats lacked the ability to pull these constituencies into their camp. Business today aligning with the Democrats as a hedge against populism is a much more complicated proposition than business aligning with the Republicans against the populism of the late nineteenth century. Business already favored the Republicans in the earlier era; Bryan's candidacy only pushed it further into the Republicans' embrace.

As odd as it might seem for segments of business to align with the Democrats these days, some evidence suggests it's underway. Hillary Clinton is not Bernie Sanders, the Democratic socialist, or even Barack Obama, the erstwhile community organizer. The latter two would have provided little pull to establishment Republicans. In contrast, Clinton is the senator who formerly represented Wall Street, a charge that Sanders made repeatedly in his efforts to stoke the fires of left-wing populism during the Democratic primaries. In fact, by June 2016, scores of business leaders had announced their endorsement of Clinton, including former chairmen of traditional business giants such as General Motors and AT&T. Even Charles Koch, one of the business-oriented mega-donors to the Republican Party and conservative causes, suggested in an ABC News interview in late April 2016 that Clinton may be a better choice than Trump.

In addition, the digital revolution is in the process of creating a different profile of what business in America is. Companies like Apple, Amazon.com, and HP dot the top 30 of the Forbes 500 along with a large number of financial services and health care firms. Even though Clinton has racked up some surprising endorsements from what Donald Rumsfeld might call "old business," "new business" titans are already firmly in the Democratic camp.

Conclusion

The lesson of the populist-progressive period is that when political conflict between the parties becomes polarized, the same polarizing issues tend to become divisive within parties as well. We find significant parallels between the era around the turn of the twentieth century and the first few decades of the twenty-first century, with fierce, nationalized party competition. As the twentieth century progressed, the party system transformed from one with clear and stark divisions to one with factional divisions within parties and issue cleavages—like race and civil rights—that crossed both parties. If our argument about the emergent economic populism cleavage is correct, then the New Deal period, which reordered politics around new economic questions, may be especially instructive.

The 2016 presidential nomination season provided evidence of something similar, particularly on the Republican side. Such fissures were less apparent in the Democratic coalition, but the closeness of the Clinton-Sanders race suggests they exist. Such internal divisions can often bring about the rise of a new issue that reorganizes political conflict, with populism the most likely suspect. The lessons of history suggest that parties do not remain ideologically distinct and highly competitive indefinitely. The competitive politics of the Gilded Age eventually gave way first to the early twentieth century, in which the Progressive movement eventually engendered divisions in both parties. This movement also resulted in lasting change to the rules of the game—the creation of primary elections and other institutions of direct democracy—alongside policy change. The emergence of new policy issues following the Great Depression allowed an outsized, and thus, diverse, Democratic coalition to come to power.

It is not clear whether the insurgencies of candidates such as Bernie Sanders and Donald Trump constitute significant intraparty movements. Nor has an event on the scale of World War II or the Great Depression reconfigured party commitments. But the fate of previous eras of division suggests that this brand of politics is rarely sustainable in the long term. If not in 2016, it seems change is likely to come soon.

Note

1. "The original Gilded Age in the 19th century is a dramatic case in point. Rapid economic expansion and transformation coexisted with intense partisan conflict and political corruption. Social Darwinism provided a powerful ideological rationale for letting the devil take the hindmost. The mordant novel by Mark Twain and Charles Warner that gave the era its name portrayed a political process in which the greedy and cynical preyed on the greedy and gullible" (Bartels 2008, 24).

2. Party platforms, The American Presidency Project, www.presidency.ucsb.edu

References

Abramowitz, Alan. 2010. *The disappearing center: Engaged citizens, polarization, and American democracy*. New Haven, CT: Yale University Press.

Barone, Michael. 2001. The 49 percent nation. *National Journal* 33 (23): 1710.

Bartels, Larry. 1998. Electoral continuity and change, 1868–1996. *Electoral Studies* 17:301–26.

Bartels, Larry. 2000. Partisanship and voting behavior, 1952–1996. *American Journal of Political Science* 44:35–50.

Bartels, Larry. 2008. *Unequal democracy: The political economy of the new gilded age*. Princeton, NJ: Princeton University Press.

Bensel, Richard. 2008. *Passion and preferences: William Jennings Bryan and the 1896 Democratic National Convention*. New York, NY: Cambridge University Press.

Burnham, Walter Dean. 1970. *Critical elections and the mainsprings of American politics*. New York, NY: Norton.

Burnham, Waltern Dean. 1983. The system of 1896: An analysis. In *The evolution of American electoral systems*, eds. Paul Kleppner, Walter Dean Burnham, Ronald Formisano, Samuel Hays, Richard Jensen, and William G. Shade, 147–202. Westport, CT: Greenwood.

Campbell, Angus, Philip E. Converse, Warren E. Miller, and Donald E. Stokes. 1960. *The American voter*. Chicago, IL: University of Chicago Press.

Carmines, Edward G., and James Stimson. 1989. *Issue evolution: Race and the transformation of American politics*. Princeton, NJ: Princeton University Press.

Converse, Philip E. 1966. The concept of a normal vote. In *Elections and the political order*, eds. Angus Campbell, Philip Converse, Warren Miller, and Donald Stokes, 9–39, New York, NY: Wiley.

Fenno, Richard. 1978. *Home style: House members in their districts*. Boston, MA: Little, Brown, and Co.

Gerring, John. 1998. *Parties and ideologies in America, 1828–1996*. New York, NY: Cambridge University Press.

Gilens, Martin. 1999. *Why Americans hate welfare: Race, media, and the politics of Antipoverty policy*. Chicago, IL: University of Chicago Press.

Hetherington, Marc J. 2001. Resurgent mass partisanship: The role of elite polarization. *American Political Science Review*. 95:619–31.

Hetherington, Marc J., and Jonathan Weiler. 2009. *Authoritarianism and polarization in American politics*. New York, NY: Cambridge University Press.

Hunter, James Davison. 1991. *Culture wars: The struggle to define America*. New York, NY: Basic Books.

Jacobson, Gary. 1996. The 1994 house elections in perspective. *Political Science Quarterly* 111:203–23.

Jacobson, Gary. 2007. Referendum: The 2006 midterm congressional elections. *Political Science Quarterly* 122:1–24.

Jacobson, Gary. 2015. Barack Obama and the nationalization of politics in 2012. *Electoral Studies* 40:471–81.

Kazin, Michael. 2006. *A godly hero: The life of William Jennings Bryan*. New York, NY: Alfred A. Knopf.

Key, V. O., Jr. 1955. A theory of critical elections. *Journal of Politics* 17:3–18.

Key, V. O., Jr. 1966. *The responsible electorate*. Cambridge, MA: The Belknap Press.

Kleppner, Paul. 1979. *The third electoral system, 1853–1892*. Chapel Hill, NC: University of North Carolina Press.

Klinghard, Daniel. 2005. Grover Cleveland, William McKinley, and the emergence of the president as party leader. *Presidential Studies Quarterly* 35:736–60.

Klinghard, Daniel. 2010. *The nationalization of American political parties, 1880–1896*. New York, NY: Cambridge University Press.

Layman, Geoffrey C., Thomas M. Carsey, John C. Green, Richard Herrera, and Rosalynn Cooperman. 2010. Activists and conflict extension in party politics. *American Journal of Political Science* 104:324–46.

Lee, Frances. 2009. *Beyond ideology: Politics, principles, and partisanship in the U.S. Senate*. Chicago, IL: University of Chicago Press.

Mayhew, David. 2004. *Congress: The electoral connection*. 2nd ed. New Haven, CT: Yale University Press.

Mendelberg, Tali. 2001. *The race card: Campaign strategy, implicit messages, and the norm of equality*. Princeton, NJ: Princeton University Press.

Miller, Gary, and Norman Schofield. 2003. Activists and partisan realignment in the United States. *American Political Science Review* 97:245–60.

Moodley, Kiran. 24 June 2015. Donald Trump says African American youths have no spirit. *The Independent*.

Stimson, James A. 2004. *Tides of consent: How public opinion shapes American politics*. New York, NY: Cambridge University Press.

Stokes, Donald. 1962. Party loyalty and the likelihood of deviating elections. *Journal of Politics* 24:689–702.

Stokes, Donald. 1967. Parties and the nationalization of electoral forces. In *The American party systems: Stages of political development*, eds. William N. Chambers and Walter D. Burnham, 182–202. New York, NY: Oxford University Press.

Stokes, Donald, and Gudmund Iversen. 1962. On the existence of forces restoring party competition. *Public Opinion Quarterly* 26:159–71.

Tesler, Michael. 2012. The spillover of racialization into health care: How President Obama polarized public opinion by racial attitudes and race. *American Journal of Political Science* 56:690–704.

Wolbrecht, Christina. 2000. *The politics of women's rights: Parties, positions, and change*. Princeton, NJ: Princeton University Press.

Zaller, John R. 1992. *The nature and origin of mass opinion*. New York, NY: Cambridge University Press.

What The Heck Are We Doing in Ottumwa, Anyway? Presidential Candidate Visits and Their Political Consequence

By
THOMAS WOOD

This article investigates the purpose and effects of presidential campaign visits. I recount common strategic rationales for rallies, town hall meetings, impromptu conversations, and the like, and then show how candidate visits are geographically assigned. I also investigate the impact of campaign visits, finding that while state-level political factors influence the location of visits, the visits themselves have little effect on local media markets. Finally, a bespoke survey is used to measure visits' influence on visited and unvisited respondents in the closing stages of the 2012 presidential election: respondents are shown to have little knowledge about candidate visits, and the visits themselves have only a small and evanescent effect on voter intentions.

Keywords: campaign events; president campaigns; vote choice

When you hear the words "presidential candidate," what image comes to mind? If you are like most people, you probably imagined an older white man, in a business shirt with his sleeves rolled up, beaming either a winning smile or with a furrowed look of empathy, standing on a stage festooned with patriotic bunting. You might also have called to mind supporters wearing white straw hats, or a crowd handpicked to demonstrate the candidate's appeal to all segments of the American public. Whether you are attentive to political minutiae, or you are the type of person for whom an impending presidential election seems to arrive unbidden every four years, the process of running for president, for most Americans, is inextricably linked to the staging and broadcast of campaign visits.

A visit's hokey theatrics are irresistible to both the campaigns and the national press. For

Thomas Wood is an assistant professor of political science at The Ohio State University. He studies public opinion, voting behavior, and political campaigns.

Correspondence: wood.1080@osu.edu

DOI: 10.1177/0002716216661488

the media, visits provide striking images, which their audience uses to determine a candidate's fitness for office. Stories of grand campaign strategy, or wonky scrutiny of policy proposals, are of fleeting interest to a distracted audience. Similarly, the other great demand on a candidate's time (fundraising) is intentionally withheld from media scrutiny, precisely because of its unseemly portents. For these reasons, candidate visits—whether huge rallies in airplane hangars or stadiums and theaters, back-and-forth town halls in a VFW building, or an informal conversation in the vestibule of a Cedar Rapids *Denny's*—are well suited to both the press and the campaigns. The candidate gets to present him- or herself in a controlled environment, in a setting that the audience regards as conventional. The media is provided vivid footage, a speech designed to provide pithy soundbites, and occasional flashes of the candidate thinking on his or her feet.

Despite the foreboding numerical challenge of a single office holder being elected by 330 million citizens, millions of Americans find inventive ways to participate in the presidential race. As Table 1 demonstrates, attendance at candidate visits is a key way that Americans bring the glamour of a presidential campaign into their own lives. In the year preceding the presidential primaries in Iowa and New Hampshire, candidates are frequently seen speaking with very small groups of voters. This standard is impossible to meet in a general election, where a candidate must divide his/her time among a dozen states deemed politically pivotal. Table 1 demonstrates that almost 2 million people attended a presidential candidate's public events in the closing stages of the 2012 election. While the political parties will passively seek out more Americans, and more Americans will engage in less costly expressive acts (such as displaying a candidate's bumper sticker), attending a visit is clearly the principle way that the average battleground-state resident can make a distant candidate seem tangible.

When pushed to justify the use of scarce resources in staging campaign events,[1] campaign consultants claim that visits stimulate voters on three levels. First, the travel to and from the visit location provides the candidate and his/her staff a captive cabin of journalists who might be softened to the candidate. The national press' willingness to cover at least some of the event itself provides a small way to affect the tone of coverage, or so the justification goes. Second, they claim that visits create an opportunity for press coverage on local TV affiliates, which can focus on a candidate's position on a local issue. Finally, consultants claim visits accrue additional, nonmedia advantages at the local level. An event of sufficient size can impress enough voters directly to make some difference in a pivotal state. According to this account, long after the candidate has left, the echoes of their visit remain—in the willingness of locals to write checks or to volunteer.

Contra the consultants, political scientists have provided an equivocal account of visits' electoral impact and implications. Two things temper political scientists' enthusiasm. First, the common political rally or town hall is a mature electoral technology, and neither party likely possesses secret knowledge to make its event uniquely appealing. Therefore, a well-staged visit might provide a temporary bump, but it is likely to be offset quickly. Second, meager visit effects

TABLE 1
Mass Participation in Presidential Campaigns, 2000–2012

Did respondent …	Battleground state residents	Nonbattleground state residents	Difference
… receive voter contact from a major party	50	34	16
… attend a rally or speech	10	4	6
… display candidate bumper sticker or button	19	13	6
… receive voter contact from someone other than a major party	20	15	5
… receive an invitation to register to vote	40	36	4
… donate to a political party	8	7	1
… work or volunteer for a candidate	4	3	1
… donate to a candidate	10	9	1
… donate to a PAC	4	4	0
… attempt to influence the vote of others	37	37	0

NOTE: Cell entries are percentage of state residents who report this participation type. A state was designated a battleground if, in a particular presidential election, it hosted ten or more presidential candidate visits in three months preceding the election.
SOURCE: American National Election Studies cumulative data file (www.electionstudies.org/).

are consistent with the broader campaign literature, which finds presidential campaigns struggling to be heard amid the din of competing political considerations. Unfortunately, both are possibilities—that visits' effects are offset by visits by opponents, or that visits' effects are genuinely small and fleeting—and are difficult to distinguish empirically.

This article first describes consultants' claims about visits and how patterns of visits are determined, briefly contrasting these claims with the social science research on visits. Next, I show how presidential visits were actually allocated to states, TV marketplaces, and counties since the 2000 election to see which theories best explain visit patterns. I then consider news coverage of presidential campaigns, showing the clamorous political environment in which campaign events are staged. Finally, I exploit a bespoke dataset that tracked six presidential visits during the 2012 election to estimate visits' effect on voters' evaluations of candidates. I show that visits are most effective in influencing press coverage at the national level and within battleground states. Visits' effects on voters themselves, however, are much more modest than consultants often claim, and visits appear to have no effects outside the market that hosts a visit. These findings support the notion that overall electoral outcomes are mostly insensitive to campaign strategies.

A Campaign's Rationale for Visits

To affect national press coverage

By the time a presidential campaign gets to midsummer and the two parties have determined (at least to a presumptive standard) their respective candidates, the national media is consumed with coverage of the campaign. At one time, the dominant source of information on candidates and the race was the presidential campaign itself—where candidates went and what they said when they were there. Now, an array of media sources provides public polling, punditry, and predictions to satisfy a voracious and mercurial audience. The United States has become home to an increasingly noisy media environment, with campaigns struggling to assert themselves as an authoritative source on candidates. When learning about a candidate, voters tend to favor the press as the source of news because they have no (apparent) interest in a particular campaign's success or failure, and the media is sophisticated in producing compelling content. Overall, a modern campaign's ability to affect the press coverage of its candidate is at an historical nadir.

What tools remain for a campaign to affect national media dialogue? Campaigns can participate in social media on a candidate's behalf; they can also dedicate hundreds of millions of dollars to TV advertising. Among consultants, candidate visits are a comparably influential tool to affect national press coverage. Most importantly, visits are a valuable service provided for TV journalists, in a tacit exchange for positive coverage. While print journalists can easily cover non-visual policy stories, TV journalists are required to find moving images to complement their story. Candidate events are ideal for this objective: if a TV journalist's particular story of the day is one that casts a candidate in a positive light, the candidate is likely to discuss it explicitly at some event. If the story is negative, their very failure to address it at the event is newsworthy. No matter the story, therefore, campaign visits are a vital source of TV footage, and a campaign's failure to have visits would be a slight to the press.

Second, the very process of moving candidates, their staff, and elements of the national press corps from one campaign event to another is a critical way to build rapport between the candidate and the press. This was the subject of Timothy Crouse's (1973) exposé on the coverage of the 1968 and 1972 presidential elections in *The Boys on the Bus.* According to Crouse, the months spent in close proximity to one another and the creeping convergence of a candidate's political ambitions with the journalist's professional ambitions provide journalists an unconscious willingness to share a candidate's perspective:

> [The journalist] had spent months in making a close, monomaniacal study of the candidate. He had become a very narrow specialist. If there was any justice in the world, the reporter thought, the candidate would come through and justify this fantastic expenditure of time. Otherwise, what a tragic, absurd, depressing waste (p. 56).

To consultants, this serves as perhaps the key personal justification for a candidate's investment in visits. Travel to places allows a candidate and the press to build a rapport, on planes, in hotels, and on buses.[2] Apart from fostering a personal rapport, hosting journalists at events also provides a powerful opportunity to subtly shape their impressions of the horse race. Well-attended rallies overflowing with enthusiastic supporters provide an informal marker of the campaign's public standing.[3]

To affect local press coverage

It's not important that we get coverage for the sake of coverage—that is, to get [Nixon's] name in the papers or to get across any particular thing that he's saying. But it IS important that we get across that he was *here*. Here in New York we're used to having the big wheels come to us; out in corn country, it's a big event. But you don't get that feeling of location in a press conference in a hotel room. That could have been done anywhere. . . . So get him out in the streets, in front of some landmarks, and have him walking, so the cameras are forced to get interesting angles. . . . Show that he's not only interested enough to *come* to Sheboygan, but that he wants to learn a little about Sheboygan, too; establish a rapport, identification.

—William Gavan, "Memorandum," quoted in Joe McGinnis, *The Selling of the President* (1968/2012).

By the late summer, with the party's nomination firmly in hand, consultants are paid to mold the candidate into the best possible fit for each battleground state. This is partially because policy positions adopted to mollify party elites and win a primary campaign might incur political costs in certain battleground states.[4] It is easy for a candidate to say nice things, but actually traveling to a state and spending time with local office holders and public figures is a meaningful (albeit costly) way to show that a state is important to the candidate. The *things* a candidate says while visiting a state are important, too. To a sometimes amusing extent, any tenuous connection between a candidate and the surrounds—a distant relative's attendance at a local college, or a penchant for a local brand of ice cream or type of barbecue—signals common values and sincere regard for the state. For a fleeting moment, local media coverage will consist of the candidate visiting the area and saying pleasant things that are unlikely to be subject to political attack.

At these visits, the local press is usually given privileged access to a candidate. Just as the campaign airplane perceptibly softens the national press corps to the candidate, a presidential campaign will often regard a political correspondent at a local TV affiliate as a "soft touch" whose reluctance to grill a national political figure promises a receptive media setting for the campaign. In these interviews, national political issues may be given some attention, but local issues are the main subject. Local issues pose largely a blank slate for a presidential candidate, and a prime opportunity to explain how this particular issue amply demonstrates his/her promise.

The pattern of visits indicates how strong the notion of using these events to affect local media coverage really is, for Democrats and Republicans, and incumbents and challengers alike. Figure 1 shows the distribution of visits by major party presidential and vice presidential candidate since 2000 for the three months preceding each general election. Clearly, the allocation of visits is quite stable *between* successive elections. States that hosted a large number of visits in a single election, such as Washington in 2000, only to disappear from the presidential battleground,

FIGURE 1
Visit Frequency for Republican and Democratic Party Presidential and Vice
Presidential Candidates During the Three Months Preceding a Presidential Election,
2000–2012

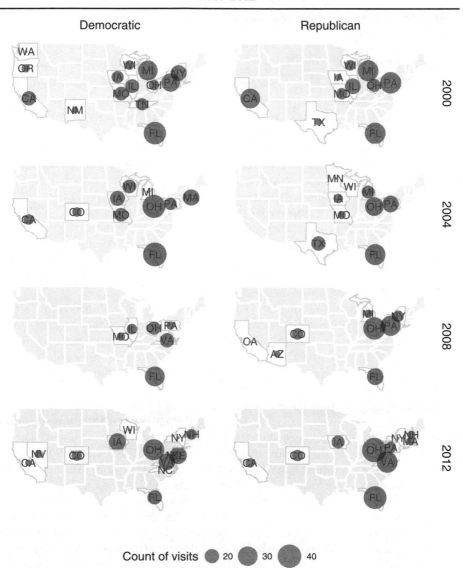

NOTE: A state's count of visits is highlighted only if the state hosted ten or more visits.
SOURCE: *Democracy in Action: The Race to the White House* (2000, 2004, 2008, 2012). See
www.gwu.edu/~action/P2000.html; P2004.html; P2008.html; http://www.p2012.org/.

are comparatively rare. The allocation is also stable *between* parties. Visits in Iowa, Ohio, Florida, Michigan, Wisconsin, or Pennsylvania are comparably attractive to each party. Incumbent presidents seem to have no distinct pattern from challengers. There appears to be a reliable pattern of candidates favoring their home state, even if the state is not politically marginal.[5]

To affect local press resources

The final motivation for a candidate to visit different states is that these visits have the ability to generate political effects net of changed media coverage. It is campaign lore to expect a spike in volunteers at a field office after a candidate visit is announced. Similarly, following a successful visit, campaigns attempt to capture the available information from those who have attended a rally, for example, so that they may be cajoled into providing volunteer labor, giving financial support, or just receiving a reminder to vote. Such advantages are particularly relevant in rural states, where it is more expensive to seek voters out in their homes.

During these visits, presidential candidates also meet in private with local officials. During the primary, these meetings are among the most important commitments a traveling campaign undertakes. By the general election, of course, all elected officials are expected to be supporting their party's nominee. A visit and personal connection, however, can make such offers of support less perfunctory and more meaningful.

In sum, consultants rationalize visits because of their political implications, whether to affect national media coverage, to affect local media coverage within a battleground state, or to improve political support in the immediate vicinity of a visit. Figure 1 suggested that state factors seem to trump national factors in determining where a visit takes place. To provide a more thorough test of the three accounts, Figure 2 shows the relationship between visits and the way states, TV markets, and counties have voted for president in recent elections.

If visits were intended principally to shape a national political dialogue, we should expect no relationship between states' voting history and their visit count. The top row of Figure 2 shows that to host more than twenty events, a state must be politically pivotal (that is, it must mirror the national political division). The middle row tests the extent to which local news coverage affects visits' allocation. This is far from a conclusive case, in that the most visited TV markets are actually those that lean Democratic in presidential voting. This reflects the distribution of voters within a battleground state, since those markets that have the most voters tend to feature large cities, and Democratic presidential candidates tend to fare best in large cities. A more conclusive case is provided in the final row, which shows no relationship between counties' voting patterns and their propensity to host a presidential candidate. Instead, these results suggest that local benefits from a candidate's visit are accrued as a providential happenstance, rather than a formal objective.[6]

The pattern of visits that emerges from Figures 1 and 2 suggests that a blend of rationales one and two account for the places a candidate visits. National factors do not exclusively shape a campaign's allocation of visits. If shaping the narrative in the national media were campaigns' key objective, candidates would

FIGURE 2
Visit Frequency for Democratic (left column) and Republican (right column) Presidential
and Vice Presidential Candidates During the Three Months Preceding a Presidential
Election, 2000–2012, by Geographical Unit and Political Circumstance

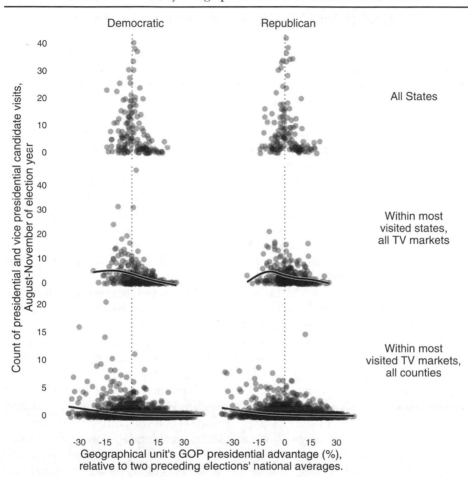

NOTE: The count of visits is mapped to the y axis, while the x axis measures an area's GOP
presidential candidate vote share over the last two elections, relative to the national vote share.
All states are depicted in the top row facet. The second row depicts visits to TV marketplaces
among the most visited states. The third row depicts visits to counties, among the most visited
TV marketplaces.
SOURCE: *Democracy in Action: The Race to the White House* (2000, 2004, 2008, 2012).
Presidential vote taken from CQ: Voters and Elections.

stage visits across the United States. Instead, a tiny number of states host almost
all campaign events. However, it is also clear that state politics is not determina-
tive, since the most marginal TV markets in a battleground state are no more
visited than markets that reliably support one party. While it is vital to hold state

events, the intended impacts on media coverage in a particular state's TV market are only of secondary importance.

Political Scientists' Research on Campaign Visits

Some research supports the claim that elections are tractable to campaign strategy. Daron Shaw's (1999) work supports the claim that campaign visits are influential. Shaw provides a series of estimates that show that visits during the 1992 and 1996 presidential elections had a direct effect on attitudes and also improved tone and quantity of press coverage. Similarly, Shaw and Roberts (2000) find that events influenced prices of political futures contracts in both the 1992 and 1996 presidential elections. J. Paul Herr (2002) finds, in the 1996 election, a large effect of President Clinton's visits on his eventual state-level vote, but only on those visits after October 1; he finds no effect of Senator Dole's visits. Among state executives, Shaw and Gimpel (2012) randomized the visit schedule of the Republican Governor of Texas, Rick Perry, during his January 2006 primary bid for the gubernatorial election. Among the twenty Texas media markets, Shaw and Gimpel chose twelve to host a gubernatorial visit over three consecutive days, and polled 1,000 respondents daily throughout January to model changes in attitudes. Shaw and Gimpel find the primary vote choice strongly responsive to candidate visits: both Republican and Independent respondents in visited markets were between 5 and 6 percentage points more likely to indicate that they would vote for Perry. Visit effects were statistically apparent for almost seven days.

Other research, though, shows trivial effects of campaign visits, supporting the claim that campaigns simply mediate political fundamentals (e.g., economic conditions and demographics) that drive election outcomes. Holbrook (1994) regresses averaged polls on running sums of political events and finds that national conditions were, on average, five times as influential as campaign events over the 1984, 1988, and 1992 elections. Holbrook and McClurg (2005) find that, controlling for other campaign efforts in a state, presidential candidate visits had no effect on turnout in the 1992, 1996, and 2000 elections. Hill, Rodriguez, and Wooden (2010) model polling averages as a function of candidate visits and find effects in only those states that are not subjected to other campaign efforts.

On balance, therefore, campaign events are found to have only a modest effect on voter behavior, such that only in the most marginal elections would the pattern of campaign visits prove decisive. However, most existing studies of campaign visits rely on aggregate measures of voter preferences or gather individual measures of attitudes months after the visits, making it difficult to measure visits' true impact.

Effects on Media Coverage

While visits are plainly intended to affect media coverage, it is far from obvious that they have any systematic effect. Presidential elections are an unparalleled media event. In the closing months of a presidential election, the candidates are assured coverage no matter how they spend their time. During the campaign's closing stage, both candidates undertake a frenetic routine of visits, while the press lavish them with comprehensive media coverage. In effect, we are in the jaws of an uncertain counterfactual—if the candidates staged far fewer campaign events, might they still enjoy the same volume of media attention?

This challenge is clear in Figure 3, which depicts the relationship between candidate visits and the frequency of candidate media mentions (whether in newspapers, in the left column; or in TV news transcripts, in the right column). The second and third rows show these relationships within two frequently visited battleground metropolitan areas (vertical lines indicate candidate visits, with solid lines indicating Democratic visits and dashed lines indicating GOP visits). The top row shows the coverage at the national level. A similar relationship exists for both categories of national coverage: a very modest coverage advantage to the incumbent candidate.[7] A shift in the volume of coverage occurs in the early summer, with volume growing in a linear fashion until it spikes in the days immediately preceding the election. Immediately following the election, coverage of Mitt Romney (the defeated candidate) quickly falls to a trivial amount, while Barack Obama returned to the coverage he enjoyed during the spring.

Coverage inside visited markets demonstrates some peculiarities. For instance, TV news coverage was more inclined to report on President Obama, with this difference remaining approximately constant over the course of the election. The apparent relationship between candidate visits and coverage is much more modest. Compared to the noisy variation in coverage caused by emergent campaign events, and the structural shifts pertaining to the stage of the campaign, the apparent effect of discrete campaign events is hard to discern.

For a precise estimate of visits' media impact, I modeled each candidate's volume of press coverage as a function of a dummy indicator for visits, the month of the year, the day of the week, and lagged measures of the volume and the difference in volume of the preceding news coverage. Each combination of candidate, market, and media type was estimated separately. Figure 4 depicts the estimate of visits' effects on coverage. While we observe some meaningful difference between candidates (Obama's visits enjoyed larger spikes than did Romney's), and some difference according to medium (with biggest spikes in newspapers, rather than TV news), the size of these effects overall was very modest, with no more than three extra stories following a visit. While this analysis does not account for changes in the tone of coverage, these findings do not suggest that visits have a large impact on local media coverage.

Effects on Mass Attitudes

As a final test, I estimate the effect of candidate visits on individual voters. During the 2012 election, 64,312 respondents were surveyed in an instrument that followed the GOP presidential candidates through four visits in four states, with respondents contacted in visited markets and in contiguous markets.[8] The

FIGURE 3

Relationship Between Candidate Visits and News Coverage, 2012 Presidential Election

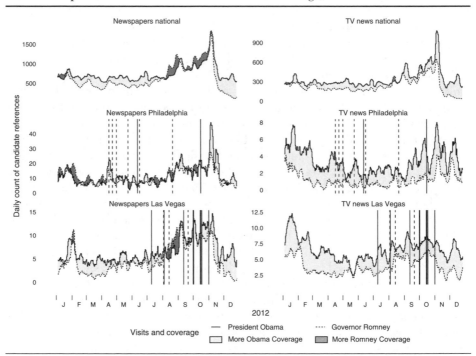

NOTE: References to President Obama are indicated with solid lines and Governor Romney with dashed lines. Ribbons indicate a period when there is an imbalance in the smoothed count of mentions—dark shaded ribbons indicate an imbalance in favor of Governor Romney, light ribbons indicate an imbalance in favor of President Obama. Candidate visits are indicated by vertical lines (again, solid for President Obama, dashed for Governor Romney). For reference, the top row facet shows the national news coverage.

SOURCE: NewsBank Database. Visit data from *Democracy in Action: The Race to the White House* (2000, 2004, 2008, 2012).

sample was drawn from the five states' voter rolls, among registered voters whose previous vote history indicated that they were likely to vote in the 2012 general election. Calls were made via a computerized autodialer. The timing of voter contact was also structured around the visits, so that calls were made on the day before a visit, the day of a visit, and each of the three days following a visit, to estimate how visits' effect changes over time.

First, Figure 5 shows respondents' awareness with candidates' recent visits, controlling for respondents' partisanship, and the type of visit a TV market hosted (whether a market hosted a visit, was contiguous to a visit, or did not host a visit; and whether a market hosted a joint or a single candidate visit.) We observe very strong partisan effects on respondents' perceptions of recent candidate visits. Despite no Democratic candidate visiting these markets in the three weeks

FIGURE 4
Effect of Candidate Visits on News Coverage, 2012 Presidential Election

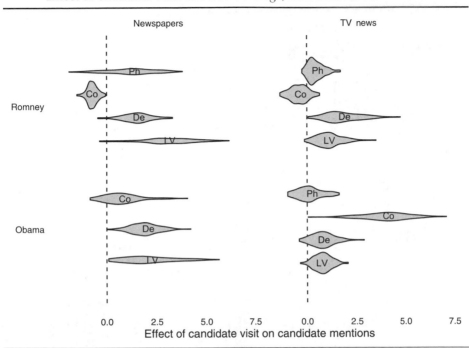

NOTE: Each ribbon shows the estimated effect of an additional candidate visit on the number of candidate mentions in local coverage. "Ph" refers to Philadelphia, "Co" refers to Columbus, Ohio, "De" refers to Denver, and "LV" refers to Las Vegas.
SOURCE: NewsBank Database. Visit data from *Democracy in Action: The Race to the White House* (2000, 2004, 2008, 2012).

preceding the survey, Democrats were between three and ten times as likely to report a recent Democratic candidate visit, compared with independent and Republican respondents. GOP respondents were similarly likely to think their copartisan candidate had been a recent visitor even in an unvisited market. President Obama's higher profile also seems relevant—even in an unvisited market, all partisans were more likely to report familiarity with a recent visit from Governor Romney. This suggests that respondents expect an incumbent's events to be covered more extensively, so that they are comparatively certain when they cannot recall a recent presidential visit.

Visits also seem to achieve negligible spillover effects. Compare, for instance, perceptions in contiguous markets and those in unvisited markets: the distribution of perceptions is indistinguishable. This demonstrates that, within a battleground state, but outside of the specific visited market, coverage of a visit is indistinguishable from generic campaign coverage from across the presidential battleground.

Finally, vote intention seems to be only weakly responsive to campaign visits. Table 2 reports visits' impact as estimated by single multinomial regression

FIGURE 5
Respondent Familiarity with Candidate Visits, by Visit Type and Respondent Partisanship

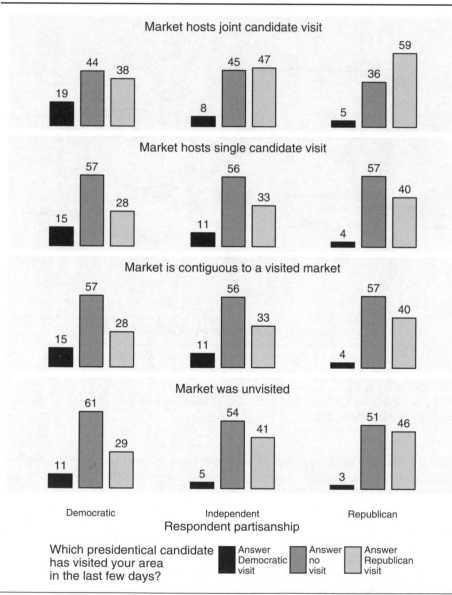

NOTE: Each bar reports the percentage of respondents in that partisanship/visit type combination who report that type of candidate visit. Numbers might sum to more than 100 due to rounding.

model, where vote intention is modeled as three category dependent variables (whether a respondent indicated Obama, Romney, or uncertain vote intention), interacted with a visit dummy, the type of visit, and the number of days since a

TABLE 2

Effect of a Candidate Visit on Respondents' Vote Choice, by Respondent Partisanship and Days Since Candidate Visit

		Democrats		Independents		Republican	
		Obama	Romney	Obama	Romney	Obama	Romney
Days	0	0	0	.01	.01	−.02	.01
Since	1	−.01	.03	−.04	.04	−.02	.02
Visit	2	−.01	.02	−.06	.06	−.03	.04
	3	.01	.02	−.05	.04	−.03	.03
	4	.01	.01	0	.04	.03	.02

NOTE: Cell entries show difference in probability of reporting this vote choice in a visited market compared with an identical respondent in an unvisited market. Probabilities are taken from multinomial logit regression, with separate controls for age, income, race, education, and gender. The predicted probability of reporting an uncertain vote intention is omitted for clarity. Cells with dark type are those where the predicted effects are significantly different from zero.

visit. Controls for respondents' partisanship, age, income, race, and education were also included. In Table 2, I report the mean difference in predicted probabilities of vote intention among respondents in a visited market compared with an identical respondent in an unvisited market. Bold text indicates when a difference is significantly different from zero. As one might expect, independent respondents were most responsive to candidates' visits, increasing their probability of intending to vote for Governor Romney by around 5 percent. Effects are far smaller for partisans: support increasing for the visited candidate by 2–3 percent.

These effects are not only small, they are also ephemeral. No effect is apparent on the day of the visit, and no effect remains apparent after the third day following the visit. Only independents are affected by visits for more than two days. In this way, those who argue that campaigns have minimal influence on electoral outcomes, even in an ideal circumstance, are vindicated.

Conclusion

Of all the tools in a campaigns' strategic arsenal, the campaign visit is distinguished by its unchanging nature. At least since the advent of television news, visits have been used as a powerful lever to affect a candidate's press coverage. The observed pattern of visits within the battleground states—where the most politically pivotal markets were *not* more frequently visited—suggests consultants intend visits to affect the national media narrative rather than local coverage. Visits were found to have a small effect on the candidate's press coverage in visited markets, and survey respondents' awareness that their city had hosted a visit was ephemeral and strongly geographically contained, which limited a campaign visit's influence on vote intention.

Taken together, these findings invite a thought experiment: if visits have only a moderate impact on voters but consume vast amounts of the candidates' and their staff's time, attention, and resources, why not neglect visits and instead redouble candidates' attention to fundraising? New resources could then be spent on those activities that have been shown to more reliably influence voters—advertising, building out campaign infrastructure at the local level, and providing more resources for voter contact—and especially inspire turnout.

In this experiment, travel to the pockets of the country with wealthy donors would double as the candidate's visits schedule; public events could be staged in the largest states (which have many recurrent donors but are rarely battlegrounds) to provide the required rallies to the national press. On the other hand, this strategy might appear so anomalous and so discordant with visits' traditional role as a necessary part of the American electoral tableau, that the financial advantages might be offset, especially if it appeared that the candidate was privileging donors at the cost of being accessible to voters.

It is also possible that visits have some political consequence that has alluded this analysis. For instance, visits might provide a subtle accumulation of popular goodwill for a candidate that has a delayed effect on vote choice. Visits might serve to inoculate a candidate to the attacks of his/her rivals, such that a candidate's support would have declined further, absent the visits. Visits might also serve to solidify the coordination between a presidential campaign and their copartisans running congressional campaigns in battleground states.

Conversely, the results reported above might be a true reflection of visits' tenuous impact. In this case, we might account for visits' privileged command of campaign resources by considering the importance of tradition, inertia, and the degree of alignment between a candidate's interests and the interests of their staff. According to this account, visits remain so frequent because of campaigns' aversion to change and innovation. To adjudicate between these possibilities, further research inside campaigns is required, especially focusing on the strategic calculations of senior staff, making the campaigns themselves the subject of research rather than the host.

Notes

1. Even requesting a justification for visits' efficacy for a presidential candidate is disquieting to some consultants. It is in some ways akin to any other professional being asked to justify their vocation's emblematic activity—surgeons make incisions, carpenters make joints, and campaign staff coordinate candidate events.

2. Occasionally, this is true even of those candidates who are old Washington hands. Nixon was famously aggrieved by the stories that emerged from Senator Kennedy's campaign in 1960, where campaign journalists were frequently hosted. When Nixon ran again in 1968, he was far more attentive to the needs of the campaign correspondents, attempting to foster a rapport and provide recurrent stories.

3. These impressionistic markers of a campaign's vitality are of particular importance to a candidate flagging by technical standards, that is, those candidates at a polling disadvantage. By a scientific standard,

a presidential campaign's ability to turn out supporters at the closing stage of a presidential election is of little or no value as a marker of popular support. However, crowd size—something a candidate can affect— may help to counter popular impressions of impending electoral doom.

4. Governor Romney's 2012 position on wind power subsidies was a particularly vivid example of this tension. In the preceding year, Romney had argued that President Obama's subsidies to green power would prove counterproductive (a claim consistent with conservative economic ideology). This position was politically awkward in the battleground state of Iowa, where subsidies for the wind turbines were championed by the state's GOP. Romney's events in Iowa were designed specifically with this tension in mind, with Romney omitting his criticism of green energy subsidies from his speeches.

5. This relationship is quite strong. Consider, for instance, Gore's focus on Tennessee in 2000, Bush's visits to Texas in 2000 and 2004, Kerry's attention to Massachusetts in 2004, Obama's attention to Illinois in 2008, McCain's visits to Arizona in 2008, and Romney's visits to Massachusetts in 2012. Outside of these attempts to foster a national political image by staging events redolent of a candidate's constituent base, these states are seldom host to presidential candidates.

6. Two stipulations are important for these results. First, these estimates do not control for population size, but correcting for these differences does not meaningfully change the relationship between pivotality and visit frequency. Second, the effect pivotality should influence counties differently. Because presidential elections are won by accruing votes at the state level, visiting pivotal counties is not necessary. However, comparing other characteristics of counties, for instance, their population of eligible voters, or their record of disproportionately supporting one party, does not meaningfully influence this relationship. Overall, then, the evidence for campaigns affecting local coverage is weak.

7. Almost certainly, the coverage advantage provided to President Obama reflects the coarseness of this measure, which simply reports the number of separate articles mentioning a candidate's name. During 2012, President Obama was subject to coverage as a candidate and as an executive, whereas Governor Romney was only mentioned in coverage of the presidential horse race.

8. In each state, the visited (listed first) and contiguous markets (listed second) were: Iowa (Davenport, Cedar Rapids), Ohio (Columbus, Dayton), Michigan (Detroit, Flint), and North Carolina (Raleigh, Greenville). During August and September, an unvisited market (Denver, Colorado) was surveyed to provide greater variance among unvisited markets.

References

Crouse, Timothy. 1973. *The boys on the bus*. New York, NY: Random House.

Herr, J. Paul 2002. The impact of campaign appearances in the 1996 election. *The Journal of Politics* 64 (3): 904–13.

Hill, Jeffrey S., Elaine Rodriquez, E., and Amada E. Wooden. 2010. Stump speeches and road trips: The impact of state campaign appearances in presidential elections. *PS: Political Science & Politics*, 43 (2): 243–54.

Holbrook, Thomas. 1994. Campaigns, national conditions, and U.S. presidential elections. *American Journal of Political Science* 38 (4): 973–98.

Holbrook, Thomas, and Scott McClurg. 2005. The mobilization of core supporters: Campaigns, turnout, and electoral composition in United States presidential elections. *American Journal of Political Science* 49 (4): 689–703.

McGinniss, Joe. 2012. *The selling of the president*. New York, NY: Penguin Books.

Shaw, Daron. R. 1999. A study of presidential campaign event effects from 1952 to 1992. *The Journal of Politics* 61 (2): 387–422.

Shaw, Daron, and Jim Gimpel. 2012. What if we randomize the governor's schedule? Evidence on campaign appearance effects from a Texas field experiment. *Political Communication* 29 (2): 137–59.

Shaw, Daron, and Brian Roberts. 2000. Campaign events, the media and the prospects of victory: The 1992 and 1996 U.S. presidential elections. *British Journal of Political Science* 30 (2): 259–89.

Ideologically Extreme Candidates in U.S. Presidential Elections, 1948–2012

By
MARTY COHEN,
MARY C. McGRATH,
PETER ARONOW,
and
JOHN ZALLER

Scholars routinely cite the landslide defeats of Barry Goldwater and George McGovern as evidence that American electorates punish extremism in presidential politics. Yet systematic evidence for this view is thin. In this article we use postwar election outcomes to assess the electoral effects of extremism. In testing ten models over the seventeen elections, we find scant evidence of extremism penalties that were either substantively large or close to statistical significance.

Keywords: extremism; ideology; presidential elections; political economy

Political narrative and scholarly theory claim that voters exact a penalty on ideologically extreme candidates. In the wake of the 2016 Iowa primary, the *Washington Post* editorial board suggested that Ted Cruz and Bernie Sanders were too extreme for general election voters. Pundits routinely invoke Barry Goldwater and George McGovern as cautionary figures: candidates destined for landslide defeat due to their ideological extremism. This conventional wisdom finds theoretical support in the median voter theorem, a classic model of candidate positioning that demonstrates that if

Marty Cohen is an associate professor of political science at James Madison University. His main research focus is the electoral influence of the religious Right in the Republican Party. He is coauthor of The Party Decides: Presidential Nominations before and after Reform *(University of Chicago Press 2008).*

Mary C. McGrath is an assistant professor of political science at Northwestern University and a faculty fellow at the Institute for Policy Research.

Peter Aronow is an assistant professor of political science and biostatistics at Yale University and a resident fellow at the Institution for Social and Policy Studies.

John Zaller is a professor of political science at the University of California, Los Angeles. He specializes in public opinion, the mass media, and political parties.

Correspondence: zaller@ucla.edu

DOI: 10.1177/0002716216660571

ANNALS, *AAPSS*, 667, September 2016

voters favor a candidate with views closest to their own, a candidate can always capture more votes by moving toward the center, away from the extremes.[1]

Yet evidence that extremism has mattered in presidential elections is thin. Indeed, while a great deal of attention is paid to candidate ideology during the course of a campaign, there is scant evidence that ideological position helps to predict electoral outcomes. Models based on data from the postwar elections have been able to explain much of the variation in presidential vote outcomes with just a few fundamental variables, but ideological extremism is not among them.[2] In this article, we build on two leading models of the presidential vote to learn how a candidate's relative ideological location fares as a predictor of electoral performance, given political and economic fundamentals. Our results do not support the idea that the relative ideological location of candidates is an important factor in predicting presidential elections.

The remainder of this article is organized as follows: First, we describe the two models we take as our starting point: Christopher Achen and Larry Bartels's (2016) "musical chairs" model and Douglas Hibbs's (2012) "bread and peace" model. We then introduce our measures of candidate ideological location and explain the construction of five variations of an incumbent party relative candidate extremism variable based on these measures. Next, we present our analysis, examining the relationship between relative candidate extremism and presidential vote outcomes when the fundamental "musical chairs" and "bread and peace" variables are taken into account. We then provide some context to help gauge the importance of this relationship. We conclude with a discussion. Full replication files—from raw data to results—are available elsewhere.[3]

Baseline Models

We make use of two well-established models of presidential vote outcomes to create a baseline context within which to evaluate the role of candidate ideology: Achen and Bartels's (2016) "musical chairs" model and Hibbs's (2012) "bread and peace" model. Both models account for a great deal of the variation in presidential vote outcomes over the years with just two variables, one political and one economic. The political variable in musical chairs is incumbent party tenure; the political variable in bread and peace is war casualties. For the economic variable, both models employ change in real disposable income (RDI), which Hibbs describes as "the broadest single aggregate measure of changes in the electorate's economic well-being" (2012, 635).[4] As described below, the two models differ dramatically on how far back into a presidential term the voter's economic memory reaches.

The "musical chairs" model

Achen and Bartels (2016) ground their model in two main ideas. First, they maintain that voters focus on their own wallets in deciding how to vote, but have

NOTE: We thank Larry Bartels for advice at several stages of this project and Molly Offer-Westort for helpful comments on the paper.

a very short memory—voters consider only the most recent economic past. To incorporate economic performance in their model, Achen and Bartels test the predictive power of different configurations of quarterly RDI data. They find that presidential vote outcomes most closely correspond with economic growth in the six months immediately preceding the quarter in which the election is held. The best fit of the model is obtained when using RDI data only from the 14th and 15th quarters of a presidential term—adding RDI data from any other quarter weakens the model performance.

Second, Achen and Bartels (2016) note the strong tendency of the American electorate to tire of an incumbent party over time. As a party accrues years in the White House in a continuous stretch, that party's vote share in presidential elections falls (Bartels and Zaller 2001; Mayhew 2008; see also Abramowitz 1988; Bartels 1998; Stokes and Iversen 1962). Achen and Bartels thus include the incumbent party's years in control of the presidency as the second variable in their model. Exactly what the variable signifies is not clear, but it may represent many things: the exhaustion of the governing party's agenda, the eagerness of the opposition to do whatever it takes to win, or a predilection of voters for change.

The dependent variable in musical chairs is incumbent party vote margin, in percentage points, in the U.S. presidential elections from 1952 to 2012. Third-party votes are implicitly included in this measure, which is calculated as (incumbent party percent of the vote) – (challenging party percent of the vote).

The "bread and peace" model

Hibbs (2012) proposed his bread and peace model in 1983 and has used it regularly to forecast and explain presidential elections. While Hibbs, like Achen and Bartels (2016), also employs change in RDI to measure economic performance, bread and peace allows RDI growth from every quarter of a presidential term to factor into the model, albeit discounted over time so that earlier quarters carry less weight. Hibbs applies a decay parameter—λ, estimated within the model as a number between 0 and 1—to progressively discount economic growth in earlier quarters of the presidential term. This discounting takes the following form: Because the election is held one-third of the way through the 16th quarter of a presidential term, RDI growth in this quarter is down-weighted by $\frac{1}{3} * \lambda^0$. The 15th quarter of the presidential term is down-weighted by λ^1, the 14th quarter by λ^2, and so on for the preceding quarters. The closer the estimate of λ is to 1, the smaller the time decay, so that if $\lambda = 1$, economic growth in earlier quarters would matter just as much as economic growth immediately before the election; the closer the estimate of λ is to 0, the greater the time decay.[5, 6] Bread and peace consistently estimates λ to be about .9, making the voter's economic memory very long, as opposed to the short-term memory seen in musical chairs.

The bread and peace model includes a penalty for going to war as the other fundamental determinant of presidential vote outcomes. This variable is measured in the number of U.S. military fatalities per millions of U.S. population during the presidential term. This penalty is applied only for unprovoked, hostile deployment of U.S. military forces. In the 2004 election, for example, the penalty is assessed for the invasion of Iraq, but not Afghanistan, the latter considered to be provoked by the attacks of September 11, 2001. The penalty applies to the party of the president initiating the commitment of forces, and after a one-term grace period, to the party of presidents inheriting such a conflict.

The dependent variable in bread and peace is the incumbent party's share of the two-party vote in the presidential elections from 1952 to 2012. The measure is calculated as: 100*(incumbent votes / (incumbent + challenger votes)).

Candidate Ideology

The purpose of this article is to evaluate the importance of candidate extremism in predicting presidential vote outcomes when other factors, which are well established as fundamental to presidential vote outcomes, are taken into account. The two models described in the previous section provide a baseline for this analysis.

In this section, we describe our measurement of relative candidate extremism. Candidate extremism is at the heart of our analysis, but difficult to measure. To guard against vagaries introduced by any single construction, we build and test five different measures of relative candidate extremism. In the first subsection, we describe three methods of measuring candidate ideological *location*—that is, where each candidate would fall on a spectrum from liberal to conservative. Then, in the second subsection, we calculate *relative candidate extremism* from these location measures. The relative extremism score characterizes how ideologically extreme the incumbent party candidate is relative to the challenging candidate, so that each pair of opposing candidates receives a single score. We use two different methods of calculating relative extremism; applied to the different location measures, this results in five variations of the incumbent party relative candidate extremism measure.

Ideological location measures

Our broadest measure of candidate ideological location combines information from two recognized scales: Steven Rosenstone's (1983) political location scores, and the American National Election Studies (ANES) candidate ideology placement. With these two scales, we can measure the positions of both major party candidates in each election from 1948 to 2012.

Rosenstone (1983) was the first to study effects of the political positions of presidential candidates across a series of elections. To measure these positions, Rosenstone asked a group of American politics scholars and graduate students to place the nominees of each party on 100-point scales denoting policy position. For elections from 1948 to 1980, Rosenstone obtained candidate ratings on two axes, one denoting New Deal liberalism and the other racial liberalism. We use the average of the two ratings in our analysis as a measure of the general ideological location of candidates.

As Rosenstone's measure ends at 1980, we splice in a scale from the ANES to bring our measure up to 2012. Since 1972, the ANES has asked respondents to place candidates on a 7-point scale, from one (extremely liberal) to seven (extremely conservative). The Rosenstone and ANES ratings overlap for three elections. Following Zaller (2003), we use this overlap to rescale the Rosenstone measure, mapping the earlier Rosenstone scores to the 7-point ANES scale. For our measure, we recenter this scale so that it ranges from –3 as the most liberal score to +3 as the most conservative score.

Our first two measures of candidate ideological location use these spliced ANES/Rosenstone scores. We use the rescaled Rosenstone scores for the presidential elections from 1948 to 1968, and mean candidate placements by ANES respondents for the elections from 1972 onward.

Our first and most basic measure of location uses the mean candidate placements from among all self-described presidential election voters in the ANES samples. Our second measure of candidate location refines the ANES ratings in two ways. First, we use only the ratings of respondents who scored in the upper quartile of a three-item measure of political information. The three items, common to all ANES surveys in this study, were knowledge of which party is more conservative, knowledge of which party has a majority of members in the House of Representatives, and interviewer rating of respondents' general level of political information. Then from these well-informed placements we estimate candidate ratings that are purged of partisan bias.

Bias arises from the fact that ANES respondents who self-identified as partisans rated candidates from their own party as less ideologically extreme. That is, respondents who identified as Republican placed Republican candidates closer to the center of the ideology scale than they placed Democratic candidates, and respondents who identified as Democrat exhibited the opposite pattern of candidate placement. Using the response data from all self-described voters in the upper 25 percent of the political information score, we employ a simple model[7] to estimate candidate ideological locations that represent the placements by self-identified independent voters. Our second measure of candidate ideological location thus approximates ratings by well-informed nonpartisan voters. This measure generates about 50 percent more year-to-year variation in perceived candidate location than our first measure, which uses the mean ratings by all self-described voters.

Figure 1 plots candidate locations from the refined measure. The y-axis shows ideological locations in units of the 7-point ANES scale (centered on 0). The x-axis shows election years. As noted above, candidate scores in the elections from 1948 through 1968 are based on the Rosenstone scores recalibrated to the ANES scale. In the measure shown here, candidate scores from 1972 on are based on refined ANES candidate placements: estimates of well-informed, nonpartisan voter ratings. Democratic candidates are represented by solid points; Republican candidates are represented by clear points.

The most notable feature of Figure 1 is the gap between the two parties. Voters, at least the informed and centrist voters driving these ratings, see a large difference between party candidates and comparatively small differences among party candidates. Most of the ratings are consistent with conventional understanding, but some

FIGURE 1
Candidate Positions on ANES/Rosenstone Ideology Scale, 1948–2012

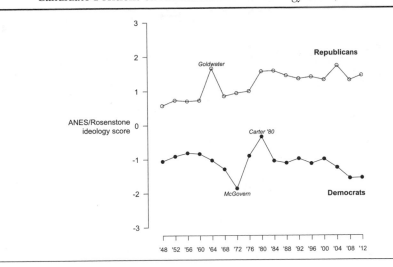

merit notice. George W. Bush's rating changed between his first and second elections. Calling himself a compassionate conservative, he was rated in 2000 as a typical conservative Republican; indeed, he was rated slightly more moderate than the median of all Republican nominees in the entire period. After four years of ideological struggle in Washington, Bush was perceived as the most conservative of all GOP nominees in our dataset. Among Democrats, Carter is notable for being rated as more conservative in his second election, probably due to the challenge for renomination he faced from the Left wing of his party. Finally, Obama's rating in 2008 is the second most extreme Democratic position in the data—perhaps surprising given that Obama ran on promises of avoiding partisanship.

Our first two measures of candidate location, based on the ANES/Rosenstone ratings, deal in perceived rather than actual ideological location. For our third measure of ideological location we turned to NOMINATE scores,[8] which are rooted in actual positions legislators and presidents have taken. NOMINATE scores are available only for candidates who have supported or opposed legislation in the form of roll call votes (as a legislator) or *Congressional Quarterly's* presidential support votes (as president). For eight of our seventeen elections, both candidates have NOMINATE scores as either a legislator or as president.[9] In these eight cases, we can use NOMINATE scores as a measure of candidate ideological location from which to calculate a relative candidate extremism score.

Figure 2 compares the ANES/Rosenstone scores with the NOMINATE scores. The correlation between the two series is +.97, but much of this high value is due to party difference. If the absolute values of the two measures are correlated, the value is +.75. Whether a correlation of .75 is reassuringly high or disappointingly low is hard to say, but it seems high enough to validate both measures as worth taking seriously.

FIGURE 2
Ideology on NOMINATE and ANES/Rosenstone Scales

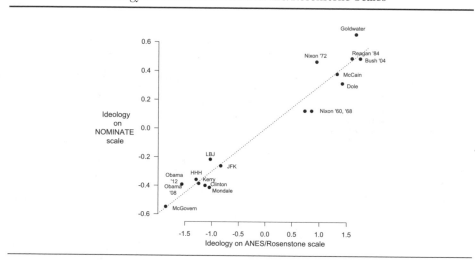

Relative candidate extremism variable

In this section we explain how we use the three measures of candidate ideological location to calculate relative candidate extremism scores. We use two different methods of calculating relative extremism.

The first method relies on the midpoint of the ideology scale as the reference point for determining relative extremism. The Rosenstone, ANES, and NOMINATE scales all have natural midpoints, halfway between most liberal and most conservative.[10] Rosenstone obtained his ratings on a 0 to 100 scale, which makes 50 an implicit moderation point. The NOMINATE scale has an implicit moderation point at 0, with liberal positions scored as negative and conservative positions scored as positive. The ANES uses a 7-point scale with an *explicit* moderation point at the middle position, described to respondents as "moderate or middle-of-the-road."

On both the ANES/Rosenstone and the NOMINATE measures of ideological location, liberal positions are scored as negative and conservative positions are scored as positive. The dependent variable in the musical chairs and bread and peace models, however, is based on the *incumbent*-party vote (rather than the Democratic party vote, for example). This means that we must construct the incumbent-party candidate's relative extremism for each election. To do this, we first transform our scale so that positive numbers represent incumbent-party candidates' ideology (rather than conservative candidates' ideology), and negative numbers represent challenging-party candidates' ideology (rather than liberal candidates' ideology).[11] Then we take the midpoint between each set of opposing candidates to arrive at a single relative candidate extremism score for each election. With this transformed scale, positive values of our relative candidate extremism variable indicate that the incumbent-party candidate is more extreme than the challenger; negative values indicate that the challenger is more extreme than the incumbent.

An alternative approach is to use the mean of voter ideology, rather than simply the midpoint of the ideological location scale, as the reference point for determining relative extremism. From 1972 onward, a suitable measure of voter ideology is available in the ANES 7-point measure of ideological self-placement. The stem for this question is the same as the one used in candidate placement. Based on the self-placement and two candidate placement scales—all recentered to a range of –3 to +3—we measure relative incumbent extremism as follows:

$$\text{Incumbent extremism} = \left[\frac{(\text{Incumbent position} - \text{Voter mean}) +}{(\text{Challenger position} - \text{Voter mean})} \right] / 2$$

$$= \left[\text{Incumbent position} + \text{Challenger position} \right] / 2$$

$$- \text{Voter mean}$$

In the special case in which mean voter ideology is 0, this second method of calculating relative candidate extremism reduces to the first.

Because opinion surveys since the late 1940s have found that more Americans identify as conservative than as liberal, the question arises, Why consider the first approach to measuring candidate extremism at all? Should not extremism always be measured as departure from the mean position of voters rather than an implicit and perhaps artificial zero point?

Despite the common-sense appeal of using mean voter ideology as a reference point for candidate extremism, an argument can be made that using zero as the reference point might be preferable. Even though more Americans call themselves conservative than liberal, a large number do not view themselves as either. The modal self-placements of voters are as middle-of-the-road or centrist, an identification selected by about 25 percent of voters in the 1992 ANES survey. An additional 20 percent said they did not know or had not thought about their ideology. And these figures still understate the weakness of many Americans' sense of ideology. When 1992 voters were asked their position on the ANES liberal-conservative scale in two different surveys, only about one-third stated a position on the same side of center in both interviews.[12] These data suggest that a majority of American voters are close to the middle of the ideological spectrum—if they have firm ideological views at all.

In light of the difficulties of measuring public opinion, and without a clear rationale for preferring either a zero-centered or a voter-mean-centered reference point, we test both methods for calculating relative candidate extremism. From the ANES data, we can calculate zero-centered and voter-centered relative candidate extremism measures for elections from 1972 to 2012. We can also calculate a zero-centered measure of relative NOMINATE extremism, but lacking a measure of voter location on the NOMINATE scale, we cannot build a voter-centered NOMINATE measure. We thus arrive at five measures of relative incumbent extremism, each of which can be tested in the musical chairs and bread and peace models. By testing the measures in these models, we control for the political and economic fundamentals that also influence outcomes, thereby increasing the likely precision of our tests. In testing five measures in each of the two models, we have a total of ten tests of voter sensitivity to extreme candidates in presidential elections.

Analysis

In this section, we present our results on the relationship between our measures of incumbent party relative candidate extremism, as developed in the previous section, and the incumbent party's vote share. We begin with bivariate correlations among the key measures. We then present a visual juxtaposition of two relationships: the correspondence between RDI and vote share shown alongside the correspondence between relative extremism and vote share. Next, we gauge how relative extremism performs as a predictor of vote outcomes when well-established political and economic fundamentals are taken into account. In this same subsection, we present our replications of the musical chairs and bread and peace models, develop two composite models that combine variables from both baseline models, and introduce our extremism variables into these composites. Finally, we present some calculations intended to aid with interpreting the magnitude of our estimates.

Correlations between incumbent extremism and vote share

We begin our analysis by examining bivariate relationships between our relative extremism variables and incumbent party vote share. These data, in the form of correlations, are presented in Table 1.

The first column of Table 1 shows that all five measures of incumbent party relative candidate extremism have the expected negative relationship with incumbent party vote share, but the four measures based on voter perceptions generate small relationships. The correlation between the NOMINATE measure and vote share is stronger—a respectable −.48—but this correlation is based only on the eight cases in which both candidates have NOMINATE scores. When the two zero-centered measures are limited to just these eight cases, both measures show a correlation with vote share of −.44. Thus, the stronger showing of the NOMINATE measure seems based more on the cases for which it is available than a genuinely stronger performance.

It is possible that relationships between relative extremism and vote share will strengthen when political fundamentals are taken into account. Below we consider extremism in the context of these fundamentals. Because the refined, zero-centered measure turns out to have the most statistically reliable relationship with vote share, we feature this measure in the next two subsections. In the final subsection we examine effect sizes for all five measures.

TABLE 1

Bivariate Correlations between Vote Share and Measures of Relative Candidate Extremism

	Incumbent-party vote share	Zero-centered (1)	Voter-centered (2)	Zero-centered (3)	Voter-centered (4)
All-voter perception measures					
(1) Zero-centered (n = 17)	−0.11				
	(17)				
(2) Voter-centered (n = 11)	−0.08	0.18			
	(11)	(11)			
Refined voter perception measures					
(3) Zero-centered (n = 17)	−0.12	0.98	0.10		
	(17)	(17)	(11)		
(4) Voter-centered (n = 11)	−0.07	0.39	0.95	0.35	
	(11)	(11)	(11)	(11)	
(5) NOMINATE locations (n = 8)	−0.48	0.67	0.62	0.68	0.85
	(8)	(8)	(5)	(8)	(5)

NOTE: Cell entries are correlations; numbers of cases are shown in parentheses.

Comparing RDI and extremism as predictors

Panel A of Figure 3 shows the relationship between incumbent-party vote share and RDI, using the musical chairs RDI variable.[13] A strong positive relationship is apparent: higher growth in quarters 14 and 15 generally corresponds to higher incumbent-party vote share. Panel B of Figure 3 shows the relationship between incumbent party vote share and our zero-centered, refined ANES/Rosenstone measure (relative incumbent extremism as measured by the estimated perceptions of informed and mainly centrist voters). If voters penalize candidate extremism and prize moderation, we should see high incumbent vote shares to the left, where negative numbers on the x-axis indicate that the challenger was more extreme than the incumbent; and low incumbent vote shares to the right, where positive numbers indicate that the challenger was more moderate than the incumbent. We do see a slight negative relationship between incumbent party relative candidate extremism and incumbent party vote share, but this relationship is weak and indistinct.

Accounting for political and economic fundamentals

Table 1 and Figure 3 suggest that relative extremism may not be a strong predictor of vote share. For a sharper look, we estimate the relationship between extremism and vote outcomes when political and economic fundamentals are taken into account, as represented by the musical chairs and bread and peace models.

FIGURE 3
Relationship of Vote Share to RDI and to Incumbent Party Candidate Extremism

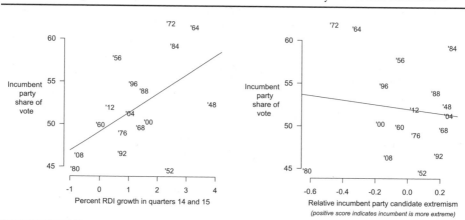

Panel A of Table 2 uses the musical chairs model as a starting point. The dependent variable is incumbent party vote margin, and RDI is measured using the musical chairs version of the variable: change in RDI per capita immediately prior to the election (quarters 14 and 15). Incumbent party fatigue, measured by the number of years the incumbent party has spent in the White House, is also included in each of the specifications in Panel A. Column A1 replicates the original musical chairs model, with updated data from 1948 to 2012. Column A2 creates a composite model by introducing the war fatalities variable from bread and peace into the original musical chairs model. In column A3, we add our main incumbent party relative candidate extremism variable (the zero-centered, refined ANES/Rosenstone measure) to the composite model built in column A2.

Panel B of Table 2 starts with the bread and peace model and builds on it in the same manner that Panel A built upon musical chairs. The dependent variable in Panel B is incumbent party share of the two-party vote, and RDI is measured using Hibbs's definition of the variable, with quarters 1–16 discounted by a decay parameter as described above. The war fatalities variable is included in each of the Panel B specifications. Column B1 replicates the original bread and peace model using updated data from 1952 to 2012. Column B2 incorporates the incumbent fatigue variable from musical chairs to create a composite based on the bread and peace model. Column B3 then adds our main extremism variable to the composite model from column B2.

The composite models in columns A2 and B2—musical chairs plus Hibbs's war casualty variable and bread and peace plus Achen and Bartels's incumbent fatigue variable, respectively—include all three variables that serve as fundamentals in these reputable models of presidential vote outcomes. These composites serve as our baseline models, within the context of which we will assess the importance of relative candidate extremism. We estimate the relationship between incumbent party relative candidate extremism and vote outcomes in

TABLE 2
Relative Extremism Variable in Baseline Models

	Musical Chairs			Bread & Peace		
	A1	A2	A3	B1	B2	B3
Δ RDI in Q14-15	6.40***	6.38***	6.38***			
	-1.4	-0.96	-1			
Δ weighted RDI in Q 1-16				3.29***	2.82***	2.89***
				-0.52	-0.44	-0.44
Incumbent fatigue (yrs. In WH.)	-1.79***	-1.65***	-1.65***		-.46**	-.41**
	-0.26	-0.32	-0.35		-0.18	-0.18
War fatalities		-0.02	-0.02	-.05***	-0.02	-0.02
		-0.03	-0.03	-0.01	-0.01	-0.01
Relative extremism			-0.46			-2.23
			-5.19			-2.04
Decay parameter				0.88	0.83	0.83
				-0.06	-0.07	-0.07
Constant	9.2	8.7	8.6	46.8	50.2	49.6
N of cases	17	17	17	16	16	16
adjusted r-squared	0.81	0.8	0.79	0.83	0.88	0.88
RMSQ	4.62	4.7	4.89	2.3	1.9	1.89

NOTE: Dependent variable for musical chairs is incumbent vote margin. Dependent variable for bread and peace is incumbent vote share. RDI = real disposable income; WH = White House; RMSQ = Root mean squared error.
***$p < .01$. **$p < .05$. °$p < .10$.

137

FIGURE 4
Additional Explanatory Force of Relative Candidate Extremism

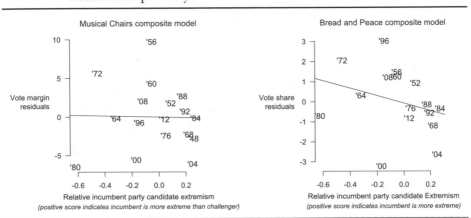

columns A3 and B3. Column A3 shows that, in the context of a musical chairs–based composite, moving the relative extremism score by one ANES scale point corresponds with an estimated .46 percentage point decrease in incumbent party vote margin. Column B3 shows that within the context of a bread and peace–based composite, an increase in relative extremism by one ANES scale point corresponds to an estimated 2.23 percentage point decrease in incumbent party vote share. [14]

The residuals from the composite models in columns A2 and B2 represent the variation in vote outcomes that remains unexplained by the three fundamental variables: change in RDI, incumbent fatigue, and war fatalities. Figure 4 plots the residuals from these two composite models against our main relative extremism variable. This provides a picture of how much of the unexplained variance in vote outcomes might be explained by candidate extremism.

Panel A in Figure 4 shows the residuals from model A2, the musical chairs–based composite. The y-axis shows percentage points of incumbent party vote margin; the x-axis shows relative incumbent extremism, with positive numbers indicating that the incumbent was more extreme than the challenger, negative numbers indicating a challenger more extreme than the incumbent. The relationship between extremism and the vote-margin residuals in panel A is essentially null—within the musical chairs–based model, incumbent extremism does not provide a good explanation of the variation remaining after accounting for the fundamentals. Panel B shows residuals from the bread and peace–based composite, with percentage points of incumbent party vote share on the y-axis. As in panel A, the x-axis scale is incumbent relative candidate extremism. The ability of candidate extremism to explain the remaining variation in vote share from the bread and peace–based model is stronger than in the musical chairs–based model, but the relationship depicted in panel B remains well short of statistical significance: the two-tailed p-value for the coefficient is .26.

TABLE 3
Maximum Effect Sizes for All Models

	Musical chairs			Bread and peace		
	Maximum effect	Two-tailed p-value	df	Maximum effect	Two-tailed p-value	df
All-voter perception measures						
(1) Zero-centered	−0.43	0.90	12	1.24	0.39	10
(2) Voter-centered	1.33	0.60	6	0.30	0.85	5
Refined voter perception measures						
(3) Zero-centered	0.29	0.93	12	1.38	0.30	10
(4) Voter-centered	2.28	0.42	6	0.82	0.64	5
(5) NOMINATE locations	−2.53	0.69	3	1.14	0.77	2

Maximum predicted effect of relative candidate extremism

Table 3 reports the maximum effect of candidate extremism that would be predicted by each of our ten models. All estimates are based on regressions identical in form to those in columns A3 and B3 in Table 2 and fully documented in our replication files. Maximum effect is calculated as the coefficient for the variable × the largest value of that variable. To take one example, the coefficient for the zero-centered refined incumbent extremism variable is −2.23 in the bread and peace composite, as shown in Table 2. The largest value of the zero-centered refined variable occurs in 1980, when Reagan's ideological location was a relatively extreme 1.58 and Carter's location was −.34, the most moderate of any of the thirty-four candidate positions in the dataset. This works out to a relative incumbent extremism score of −.62 for that variable in that election, with the negative direction of the score showing that the challenger, Reagan, was more extreme than the incumbent, Carter. Based on these values, maximum effect is calculated as +1.38. The incumbent Carter should have been expected to gain a small amount of vote share—1.38 percentage points—from being less extreme than his challenger. As Table 3 also reports, the p-value for the coefficient underlying this estimate is .30 and based on ten degrees of freedom.

The ten maximum effect estimates in Table 3 are impressive for their modesty. For all five variables, the largest value represents an election in which the incumbent was less extreme than his challenger, so the relative extremism score employed in these calculations is always negative.[15] Then, under the standard assumption that extremism incurs a penalty, the extremism coefficients should all be negative, producing only positive maximum effect estimates in Table 3. But this minimal expectation that the extremism coefficient should be negative is met in only eight of ten cases. The NOMINATE measure and the zero-centered all-voter measure both produce differently signed estimates in the two baseline models. Notice, moreover, that no maximum effect estimate is substantively large and that the p-values for the coefficients underlying the estimates are extremely weak. It is hard to find evidence in these results that candidate extremism has any consistently important correspondence with vote share in U.S. presidential elections since World War II.

Conclusion

Based on our estimates of the relationship between candidate extremism and vote outcomes, ideological location seems unlikely to be of much predictive importance in elections where one candidate begins with an important advantage. The extreme candidates Goldwater and McGovern, widely cited exemplars of the dangers of extremism, met with landslide defeats. But these candidates faced a double whammy: they were running against incumbents whose parties had been in the White House only one term, presiding over strong economies. Meanwhile, Ronald Reagan in 1980 and Barack Obama in 2008 were rated almost as extreme as Goldwater and McGovern, but were challenging incumbent party candidates with poor economic records. In these more favorable conditions, Reagan and Obama both won comfortable victories.

If extremism does little apparent damage, neither does moderation always pay off. Dewey in 1948, Nixon in 1960, and Carter in 1980 were rated as moderates, and yet each lost—and in two of three cases, lost to candidates who were not at all moderate.

We therefore find little evidence of an electorally important relationship between candidate extremism and vote outcomes—but this is not evidence that no important relationship exists. Still less do our results imply that voters pay no attention to candidates' policy positions in casting their presidential ballots.

The difference between policy voting and ideological voting is made clear by Rosenstone's (1983) analysis. Recall that he measured candidate positions on two policy dimensions, New Deal economic liberalism and racial liberalism. Whereas we collapsed these two dimensions into a single ideological dimension, Rosenstone used them as separate policy dimensions and examined their effects at the level of state electorates over the period 1948 to 1980. He obtained effects that ranged from minimal to moderate to huge, depending on particular states and candidate configurations.[16] The largest effects were for racial liberalism on voting in southern states, flipping some from Democrat to Republican as Republican candidates became more racially conservative. Effects of New Deal liberalism registered more strongly in the North, with states voting more and less Democratic and Republican on the basis of candidates' varying embrace of social welfare protections. The effects of candidates' policy positions were cross-cutting, winning votes in some states and losing them in others. To take an important case, Goldwater's racial conservatism helped him in the South but cost him in the North. While our results show little evidence that voters respond to candidates' ideological positions, Rosenstone's findings indicate that voters may respond to more narrowly defined policy dimensions.

The scholarly work most strongly identified with the importance of ideological positioning is Anthony Downs's *Economic Theory of Democracy* (1957). Although many scholars have been impressed by Downs's elegant reasoning, one who remained dubious of its significance for mass politics was Philip Converse. Converse argued forcefully in his "Nature of Belief Systems in Mass Publics" (1964) that most voters knew and cared little about ideology and that when they changed parties between elections, it was more likely to be because of "the nature of the times"—a term referring mainly to economic conditions—than anything about ideology. This judgment stands up much better to evidence from postwar presidential elections than does Downs's more famous median voter theorem. To many political scientists—including some of the authors of this article—who have taught students, told journalists, and personally believed that extreme candidates have difficulty winning elections, this is a hard lesson, but it is one that needs to be taken seriously.

Notes

1. As such, the median voter theorem predicts that if candidates are simply looking to win, they will converge at the center, since positions that are more extreme would garner fewer votes. Many efforts have been made to reconcile this model with the abundant empirical evidence against this prediction.

2. Evidence of a causal effect of candidate ideology on election outcomes is difficult to find in part because the same factors that are highly predictive of the vote may also influence who is selected as a nominee. For example, if one party knows it is fairly likely to lose the election, it may choose an extreme candidate to satisfy its base.

3. See isps.yale.edu/research.

4. An unexpectedly consequential feature of Hibbs's analysis is his use of a different RDI data series from that used by other scholars. Where most use the "chained dollar" (i.e., inflation-adjusted) RDI series from the Bureau of Economic Analysis (BEA), Hibbs uses current dollar income data from BEA and discounts it by the Consumer Price Index published by the Bureau of Labor Statistics. This arcane difference has a substantial impact on the performance of the bread and peace model. When the BEA's chained dollar RDI data are used instead of the BEA/Consumer Price Index data, the model's r-square falls from .85 to .74.

5. This is because $1^{15} = 1^{14} = \ldots = 1^0 = 1$, so all quarters receive an equal weight of 1; and $0^{15} = 0^{14} = \ldots = 0^1 = 0$, but $0^0 = 1$, so all quarters preceding the election quarter receive a weight of 0.

6. For comparison, musical chairs could be thought of as having a decay parameter of $\lambda = 1$ for the 14th and 15th quarter, and $\lambda = 0$ for all other quarters.

7. Details about this model are presented in the online appendix to this article. See http://ann.sagepub.com/supplemental.

8. Published by Howard Rosenthal and Keith Poole at Voteview.com.

9. We use Nixon's NOMINATE score as a legislator in 1960 and 1968 and his NOMINATE as president in 1972.

10. Technically, NOMINATE scores can range beyond $-1/+1$ in some instances.

11. This simply involves taking the absolute value of every candidate's ideological location score and then multiplying challenging-party candidates' scores by -1.

12. These figures are based on the 1990–1992 ANES panel survey.

13. In all of our analyses, we use updated versions of the musical chairs and the bread and peace RDI variables, calculated from BEA and Bureau of Labor Statistics data obtained in spring 2016.

14. Recall that we rely on Rosenstone's candidate locations, based on expert raters, for the period 1948 to 1968 and ANES voter-derived candidate locations for later years. Thus, we make no use of Rosenstone's measures for the period 1972 to 1980, except for purposes of calibration. We preferred the voter-derived measures because of concern that Rosenstone's experts, who knew who had won elections and were also familiar with Downs's (1957) median voter theorem, might subconsciously rate losers more extreme than

they actually were. Given this, any extremism effect obtained from Rosenstone's measure would be prey to endogeneity bias. But if we suspend this concern and test an all-Rosenstone ideology measure in our two vote models for the period 1948 to 1980, we obtain weak extremism effects, as in other analyses we have reported.

15. For the eight measures based on ANES/Rosenstone, this was the 1980 election. For the NOMINATE measure, which did not include the 1980 case, the maximum effect estimate is based on candidates' locations in the 1964 election, in which Johnson was rated less extreme than Goldwater.

16. See especially Rosenstone (1983) figures 4-2 and 4-3, pp. 79 and 81.

References

Abramowitz, Alan I. 1988. An improved model for predicting presidential election outcomes. *PS: Political Science and Politics* 21 (4): 843–47.

Achen, Christopher H., and Larry M. Bartels. 2016. Musical chairs: Pocketbook voting and the limits of democratic accountability. In *Democracy for realists*, eds. Christopher Achen and Larry M. Bartels. Princeton, NJ: Princeton University Press.

Bartels, Larry M. 1998. Electoral continuity and change, 1868–1996. *Electoral Studies* 17 (3): 301–26.

Bartels, Larry M., and John R. Zaller. 2001. Presidential vote models: A recount. *PS: Political Science & Politics* March:9–20.

Converse, Philip E. 1964. The nature of belief systems in mass publics. In *Ideology and its discontents*, ed. David E. Apter. New York, NY: The Free Press of Glencoe.

Downs, Anthony. 1957. *An economic theory of democracy*. New York, NY: Harper & Row.

Hibbs, Douglas A. 2012. Obama's reelection prospects under "bread and peace" voting in the 2012 U.S. presidential election. *PS: Political Science & Politics* 45 (4): 635–39.

Mayhew, David R. 2008. Incumbency advantage in U.S. presidential elections: The historical record. *Political Science Quarterly* 123 (2): 201–28.

Rosenstone, Steven J. 1983. *Forecasting presidential elections*. New Haven, CT: Yale University Press.

Stokes, Donald E., and Gudmund R. Iversen. 1962. On the existence of forces restoring party competition. *Public Opinion Quarterly* 26 (2): 159–71.

Zaller, John. 2003. Floating voters in U.S. presidential elections, 1948–2000. In *The issue of belief: Essays in the intersection of non-attitudes and attitude change*, eds. Paul Sniderman, and Willem E. Saris. Princeton, NJ: Princeton University Press.

Failure to Converge: Presidential Candidates, Core Partisans, and the Missing Middle in American Electoral Politics

By
LARRY M. BARTELS

The logic of electoral competition suggests that candidates should have to adopt moderate issue positions to win majority support. But U.S. presidential candidates consistently take relatively extreme positions on a variety of important issues. Some observers have attributed these "polarized" positions to the extreme views of the parties' core supporters. I characterize the issue preferences of core Republicans, core Democrats, and swing voters over the past three decades and assess how well the positions of presidential candidates reflect those preferences. I find that Republican candidates have generally been responsive to the positions of their base. However, Democratic candidates have often been even more extreme than the Democratic base, suggesting that electoral polarization is due in significant part to candidates' own convictions rather than the need to mollify core partisans. Neither party's presidential candidates have been more than minimally responsive to the views of swing voters.

Keywords: candidates; core partisans; Democrats; political polarization; presidential elections; Republicans; swing voters

One of the most elegant and influential theories in political science purports to demonstrate that in a competitive two-party system the competing parties must converge to the center of the distribution of voters' preferences, since victory requires support from the moderate voters who hold the crucial balance of power between liberals and conservatives (Downs 1957, 114–41; Enelow and Hinich 1984). However, contemporary American

Larry M. Bartels holds the May Werthan Shayne Chair of Public Policy and Social Science at Vanderbilt University. His books include Democracy for Realists: Why Elections Do Not Produce Responsive Government (with Christopher H. Achen; Princeton University Press 2016) and a newly revised Unequal Democracy: The Political Economy of the New Gilded Age (Russell Sage Foundation and Princeton University Press 2016).

Correspondence: larry.bartels@vanderbilt.edu

DOI: 10.1177/0002716216661145

political parties seem not to have gotten the message. On a variety of major issues, their positions diverge substantially from the center of public opinion, with Democrats well to the Left and Republicans well to the Right, even when they represent the same mostly moderate electorates (Fiorina with Abrams 2009; Achen and Bartels 2016, 45–49).

The left panel of Figure 1 provides an illustration of this phenomenon. The dotted line in the center represents the average ideological position of swing voters in each presidential election from 1980 through 2012 on a scale running from 0 for "extremely liberal" to 100 for "extremely conservative."[1] The double lines above and below represent the positions of the Republican and Democratic presidential candidates, respectively, in each election year as perceived by knowledgeable, politically neutral observers. (These estimates, based on data from the authoritative American National Election Studies surveys, are described in more detail below.) Year after year, and increasingly over time, Democratic candidates are seen as far to the Left of swing voters while Republican candidates are far to the Right; there is no evidence at all of convergence to the center of public opinion.

What accounts for this striking mismatch between the theory of electoral competition and the reality? According to a recent front-page article in the *New York Times* (Martin and Healy 2016), "With partisan preferences increasingly cemented in the American public and a declining share of swing voters, elections are increasingly won through mobilizing party members rather than trying to persuade independent-minded or skeptical voters. That is why most politicians are reluctant to do anything that defies or demoralizes their respective voter bases."

In her 2008 presidential campaign, Hillary Clinton generated headlines when she bemoaned the influence of her own party's core partisans. Clinton—who was falling behind in the delegate count despite strong showings in big-state primaries—blamed her poor showing in party caucuses on an "activist base" characterized by ideological extremism and intensity: "We have been less successful in caucuses because it brings out the activist base of the Democratic Party. MoveOn didn't even want us to go into Afghanistan. I mean, that's what we're dealing with. And you know they turn out in great numbers" (Kleefeld 2008). She argued that she would be her party's strongest candidate in the general election—despite the apparent antipathy of the "activist base"—because of her greater appeal to centrist swing voters.

More commonly, politicians and pundits attribute the ills of the contemporary American political system to the influence of the *other* party's core partisans. According to liberal *New York Times* columnist Paul Krugman (2015), for example,

NOTE: I am grateful to my fellow contributors, and especially to Gary Jacobson, for very helpful comments on a preliminary draft of this article. I am also grateful for criticism and advice on a precursor piece (Bartels 2010) from participants in the 2010 annual meeting of the American Political Science Association in Washington, DC, and the 2011 annual meeting of the European Political Science Association in Dublin, as well as from William Crotty, Marjorie Hershey, Steve Rogers, Lynn Vavreck, John Zaller, and especially Chris Achen.

FIGURE 1
Ideological Positions of Swing Voters, Presidential Candidates,
and Party Bases, 1980–2012

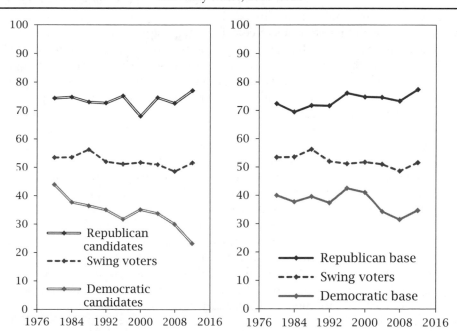

Modern Republican politicians can't be serious—not if they want to win primaries and have any future within the party. Crank economics, crank science, crank foreign policy are all necessary parts of a candidate's resume. . . .What distinguishes Mr. Trump is not so much his positions as it is his lack of interest in maintaining appearances. And it turns out that the party's base, which demands extremist positions, also prefers those positions delivered straight. Why is anyone surprised?

Krugman's complaints about the extremism of the Republican base, in particular, echo a common wisdom among some political scientists. For example, Jacob Hacker and Paul Pierson (2005, 5, 9, 10) argued that Republicans "have moved further and further from the political center. Nothing remotely close to this massive shift has happened on the other side of the spectrum, much less among the great bulk of ordinary voters. . . . What is the great force that pulls Republican politicians to the right? In a word, the 'base.' . . . The base has always had power, but never the kind of power it has today."

The right panel of Figure 1 provides a first, rough check on the plausibility of claims of this sort. The solid lines at the top and bottom of the graph chart the average ideological positions of each party's base—the most enthusiastic and active Republican and Democratic partisans in each election year. (A more detailed explanation of my procedures for identifying core partisans and swing voters is provided in the next section.) The Republican base is, indeed, vastly more conservative than the swing voters in the center of the electorate, while the Democratic base is much more liberal. If presidential candidates attempted to balance the competing demands of centrist swing voters and more extreme core partisans, we would expect them to take positions somewhere in between those of swing voters and their own base. However, in the case of Republicans, a comparison of the two panels of Figure 1 suggests that the ideological positions of presidential candidates have often been just as conservative as those of the Republican base. Even more remarkably, the figure suggests that Democratic presidential candidates have often been even more liberal than the Democratic base—and almost as "extreme," relative to swing voters, as Republican candidates have been.

Obviously, positions this extreme cannot plausibly be interpreted as (even lopsided) compromises between the views of core partisans and swing voters. In that sense, standard explanations emphasizing the strategic importance of mobilizing the base fall short of accounting for the remarkable failure of presidential candidates to cater to the preferences of the broader electorate. While the views of the base are presumably important, they are not sufficient to account for candidates' ideological extremism. We also need some explanation for why the centrist views of swing voters fail to pull candidates at least some way toward the center of the ideological spectrum. The most compelling such explanation is that, contrary to much elegant theorizing, ordinary voters do not choose candidates on the basis of their ideological positions (Achen and Bartels 2016, 21–51). While that is a disquieting and controversial conclusion, it has the virtue of fitting the facts—including the fact that, as Marty Cohen and his colleagues (this volume) note, the electoral penalty for ideological extremism in presidential elections seems to be remarkably modest.

The remainder of this article provides a broader and more systematic assessment of the relationship between the positions of presidential candidates and those of swing voters and core partisans in contemporary American politics. I relate the positions of presidential candidates on a variety of political issues over the past three decades to the preferences of swing voters and their own core partisans. My findings provide ample grounds for alarm for anyone who believes that presidential candidates should be responsive to the views of swing voters. However, they also suggest that this unresponsiveness is not merely a reflection of the political influence of core partisans. While the parties' respective bases are clearly influential, the stable convictions of party elites themselves seem to be at least as consequential in producing the failure of convergence evident in the left panel of Figure 1.

Identifying Swing Voters and Core Partisans

Assessing the influence of swing voters and core partisans obviously requires systematic measurement of their respective political views. Fortunately, data from the American National Election Studies (ANES) surveys make it possible to track the views of representative samples of swing voters and Democratic and Republican core partisans on a variety of important political issues over the nine most recent U.S. presidential elections (1980–2012).[2] But who, exactly, is a "swing voter" or a "core partisan"?

My identification of swing voters in each election year is guided by a simple mathematical theory of how vote-maximizing candidates would target their appeals in a competitive election (Bartels 1998, 2010). In theory, the attractiveness of any specific citizen as a target for persuasion hinges on the product of two factors: the probability that she will turn out to vote and the extent to which her vote is likely to be up for grabs in a close election if she does turn out. Obviously, from a candidate's perspective, there is no point in appealing to someone who will not vote, and only half as much value (other things being equal) in appealing to someone with a 40 percent chance of voting as someone with an 80 percent chance of voting. Equally as obvious, there is no point in appealing to a likely voter who will almost certainly vote against you (or, for that matter, for you) anyway. Swing voters—the most attractive targets for persuasion on the basis of issues or other appeals—are the people who are *both* likely to vote *and* persuadable.

I estimated each ANES survey respondent's likelihood of voting and her "persuadability" on the basis of statistical analyses of self-reported turnout and vote choice. First, I estimated each respondent's probability of turning out on the basis of political and demographic characteristics: strength of party identification and partisan affect, age, education, income, race, sex, marital status, union membership, homeownership, and region.[3] Second, for respondents who reported voting for a major-party presidential candidate, I related vote choices in each election to the same explanatory factors.[4] I used the results of these analyses to estimate each prospective voter's availability for partisan conversion in a close election, whether or not she actually voted. This value is relatively large for prospective voters whose partisan attitudes are near the center of the distribution in a given election year and relatively small for prospective voters whose partisan attitudes are more extreme (regardless of whether they are pro-Republican or pro-Democratic).[5]

Multiplying these two values—estimated probability of turnout and estimated availability for partisan conversion—produces a measure of each prospective voter's attractiveness as a target for partisan persuasion in a close election. The multiplication appropriately discounts the value to candidates of appealing to people who are very unlikely to support them (or very likely to support them) anyway. It likewise discounts the value of appealing to undecided "voters" who are unlikely to vote even if they are convinced to favor one candidate over the other.

By this measure, each ANES survey respondent receives some weight as a swing voter, since there is some (perhaps small) probability that she will turn out to vote and some (perhaps very small) probability that she can be persuaded to change sides. However, weighting each respondent's views by the *product* of her likelihood of turnout and her "persuadability" heavily skews my tabulations of the views of swing voters in favor of the minority of likely voters whose votes are legitimately up for grabs in any given election.

Existing theory provides much less specific guidance regarding the identification of core partisans. As Carmines and Woods (2002, 363–64) put it,

> There is no easy way to identify who should be considered . . . a party activist in the United States. Falling between major officeholders at one end of the continuum and the largely inactive mass electorate at the other end, political activists are a heterogeneous group and include delegates to the national nominating conventions, those citizens heavily involved in campaign activities, major financial contributors to political parties and individual candidates, and even the thousands of minor officeholders and party officials.

The literature on party activists reflects this heterogeneity, with various scholars focusing on national party convention delegates (e.g., Layman 2001, 94–130; Carmines and Woods 2002), state party convention delegates (e.g., Stone and Abramowitz 1983), people who participated in at least three types of campaign activities (Carmines and Woods 2002) or in any political activity beyond voting (Aldrich 1995, 163–93), or even all party identifiers (Holbrook and McClurg 2005). As a result, we have no real scholarly consensus regarding the political views of party activists in contemporary America, much less a persuasive analysis of how they matter.

Elaborations of the basic spatial model of electoral competition have posited a variety of specific reasons why candidates might appeal to their respective party bases. Peter Aranson and Peter Ordeshook (1972) posited that candidates require support from party activists to be nominated. John Aldrich (1983) noted that a party's base may, through a dynamic process of self-selection, come to represent what the party stands for in the minds of party leaders and candidates. Finally, and perhaps most obviously, parties typically rely heavily on core supporters for money, time, and other resources necessary to wage effective campaigns.

If the potential influence of core partisans derives primarily from their willingness to participate and contribute resources on the party's behalf, as all of these accounts suggest, then we need a definition of the parties' bases that captures both high levels of partisan enthusiasm and high levels of political activity. Thus, I identify core partisans in the ANES data by the extent to which they are committed supporters of their party's presidential candidates and politically active in a variety of ways (not only voting, but also persuading others to support their party's candidates, attending rallies, donating money, and working in campaigns). More specifically, I weight the views of Democratic and Republican core supporters in proportion to the product of their partisan enthusiasm and their political activity. The resulting weighted samples of core partisans are quite distinctive in both these respects while still being large enough numerically to play a potentially crucial role in the functioning of the parties.

I measure political activity using a battery of six questions in the ANES surveys, which ask respondents whether they voted (66 percent), tried to convince others how to vote (32 percent), attended a political meeting or campaign rally (6 percent), donated money to a candidate (6 percent) or party (5 percent), or worked for a campaign (3 percent). My index of activism is a simple additive scale counting how many (if any) of these things each respondent reported doing. Almost 30 percent of the respondents reported no activity and another

38 percent reported just one; at the other extreme, 0.5 percent reported all six. The average number of political activities in the weighted sample of Republican core supporters is 2.43; the corresponding average level for Democratic core supporters is 2.28. Thus, a typical core supporter in my analysis did not just turn out to vote, but engaged in at least one or two additional activities such as attempting to persuade others, attending a rally, or contributing money to a candidate or party.

I measure partisan enthusiasm using the index of partisan voting propensity derived from my statistical analyses of reported vote choices. However, the index does not simply reflect each respondent's probability of voting for a party's presidential candidate; rather, it heavily over-weights the most enthusiastic party supporters. For example, someone who is 99 percent likely to vote for the party's candidate gets 80 percent more weight than someone who is "only" 90 percent likely to vote for the party's candidate by this calculation. Further, weighting each core partisan's views by her level of political activity produces an even more enthusiastic cadre of party supporters. For example, most of my weighted sample of Republican core supporters was virtually certain (more than 99.5 percent likely) to support the Republican presidential candidate in a close election; most of my weighted sample of Democratic core supporters was at least 99 percent likely to support the Democratic presidential candidate in a close election.

The Political Attitudes of Swing Voters and Core Partisans

The characterizations of the ideological positions of presidential candidates, swing voters, and the parties' respective bases presented in Figure 1 provide a valuable picture of ideological stability and change over a period of more than three decades. However, ideological self-identification is a rough and often idiosyncratic summary of a wide variety of specific political attitudes. Even many committed partisans mix and match conservative views in some domains and liberal views in others, while many others decline to place themselves or the presidential candidates on the ideological scale.

A clearer assessment of how parties might attempt to appeal to core partisans, and with what consequences, requires more detailed information about the positions of those core partisans on a variety of salient political issues. Thus, in addition to overall liberal-conservative ideology, I focus here on four issues included consistently in ANES surveys—government spending,[6] government jobs,[7] aid to blacks,[8] and defense spending.[9] Obviously, this set of issues is far from exhaustive. Unfortunately, changes in the battery of ANES issue questions from one election year to the next—and especially the limited availability of parallel questions about the presidential candidates' positions—limit the scope of my analysis in this regard.[10]

The potential importance of this limitation is underlined by the fact that, even within this limited set of issues, there is considerable variability in how the positions of swing voters and core partisans have evolved over time. This variability is evident in Figure 2, which shows the estimated average positions of the Republican base, swing voters, and the Democratic base on each of these issues in each election over the past three decades.[11]

FIGURE 2
Issue Positions of Swing Voters and Party Bases, 1980–2012

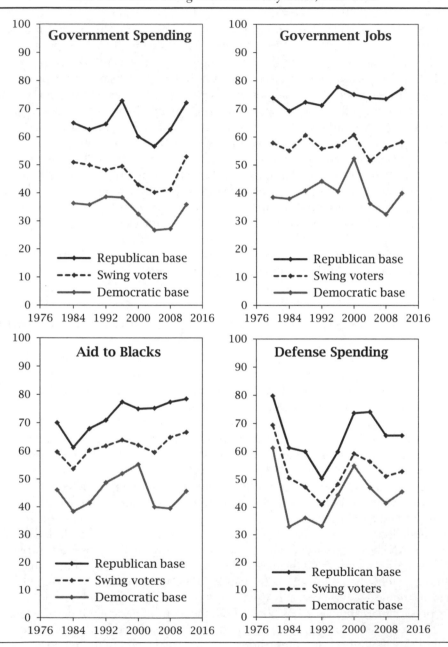

On the issue of government spending, all three groups became gradually more liberal over most of this period before shifting sharply to the Right in 2012. On the issue of government jobs, the views of swing voters and the Republican base have been relatively stable over time, whereas the Democratic base became gradually more moderate through the 1980s and 1990s but sharply more liberal in the 2000s. On the issue of aid to blacks, all three groups became gradually but substantially more conservative through the late 1980s and 1990s; but while swing voters and Republican core partisans continued to become increasingly conservative in the 2000s, the Democratic base shifted sharply to the Left in 2004 and thereafter. And all three groups moved roughly in parallel on the issue of defense spending, registering peaks of support for spending increases in 1980 and 2000 but much less enthusiasm in the brief window of relative tranquility following the fall of the Berlin Wall.

These data allow for a systematic test of the familiar notion that the parties' respective bases have become more "polarized" over the past three decades. Table 1 summarizes overall shifts in the absolute positions of each party's core partisans on each issue over time. The results indicate that the Democratic base became substantially more liberal with respect to overall ideology and government spending, while the Republican base became substantially more conservative with respect to government aid to blacks and, to a lesser extent, ideology and government jobs. Averaging over all five issues, Democratic core partisans moved about three points to the Left on the 100-point scale, while Republican core partisans moved about five points to the Right. These shifts have increased the absolute distance between the parties' respective bases by about 30 percent over three decades. Thus, my analysis provides significant empirical support for the claim that the parties' respective bases have become more polarized in recent years.

Is this increasing polarization primarily attributable to Republicans or to Democrats? The parallel results for swing voters in Table 1 indicate that their views also shifted significantly over time on some issues. Thus, it seems most sensible to assess the extremism of each party's core supporters not in absolute terms, but relative to the positions of swing voters who have themselves shifted over time. For example, while the Republican base shifted thirteen points to the Right on the issue of government aid to blacks, that shift seems less extreme when we note that swing voters moved eight points to the Right. Conversely, the Democratic base's eight-point shift to the Left on the issue of government spending seems less extreme when we note that swing voters moved almost six points to the Left on the same issue.

Figure 3 shows the relative extremism of each party's base for each issue in each presidential election year from 1980 through 2012. The bars in the figure represent the absolute discrepancy of each party's core partisans (Democrats to the left, Republicans to the right) from the average position of swing voters on the same issue in the same year. These discrepancies clearly vary considerably by issue, by party, and over time. With respect to overall ideology, for example, the Republican and Democratic bases were roughly symmetric in their relative extremity in the 1980s, but in the 1990s the Republicans became much more extreme (relative to swing voters) while the Democrats became—temporarily—much less extreme.

TABLE 1
Cumulative Shifts in Issue Positions of Swing Voters, Core Partisans, and Presidential
Candidates, 1980–2012

	Democratic candidates	Democratic base	Swing voters	Republican base	Republican candidates
Cumulative shifts in absolute positions					
Conservative ideology	−14.9	−6.2	−4.5	+5.3	+0.4
	(2.8)	(3.2)	(1.6)	(1.8)	(2.8)
Government spending cuts	−5.8	−8.3	−5.7	+1.4	−1.1
	(3.2)	(5.3)	(6.0)	(7.4)	(9.7)
(Oppose) government jobs	+0.4	−1.6	−1.1	+4.4	+7.7
	(3.0)	(6.1)	(3.1)	(2.5)	(4.5)
(Oppose) aid to blacks	+4.4	+0.7	+8.1	+13.4	+9.3
	(2.7)	(6.5)	(2.9)	(3.6)	(4.5)
Defense spending	+1.6	+0.8	−3.7	+1.1	−3.2
	(4.9)	(10.6)	(8.9)	(10.9)	(9.3)
(Average)	(−2.9)	(−2.9)	(−1.4)	(+5.1)	(+2.6)
Cumulative shifts in relative positions					
Conservative ideology	−10.4	−1.8	—	+9.8	+4.8
	(3.7)	(3.3)		(2.3)	(3.1)
Government spending cuts	−0.1	−2.6	—	+7.1	+4.6
	(7.4)	(3.2)		(3.8)	(6.9)
(Oppose) government jobs	+1.5	−0.4	—	+5.5	+8.8
	(4.3)	(5.0)		(3.2)	(6.1)
(Oppose) aid to blacks	−3.9	−7.3	—	+5.3	+1.0
	(4.5)	(5.5)		(2.2)	(2.9)
Defense spending	+5.3	+4.5	—	+4.8	+0.5
	(5.5	(4.1)		(2.1)	(9.1)
(Average)	(−1.5)	(−1.5)	—	(+6.5)	(+3.9)

NOTE: Linear trends in average placements (with standard errors in parentheses) on 0–100 scales.

Views about government spending followed roughly the same pattern, except that the increased conservatism of the Republican base (relative to swing voters) since the 1990s has been less pronounced and consistent.

The relative moderation of Democratic core partisans in the 1990s—the heyday of the Democratic Leadership Council and "triangulation"—and the shift back to (relatively) more liberal positions after 2000 are even clearer with respect to government jobs and aid to blacks. In both cases, the Democratic base in recent years has actually been more extreme, relative to swing voters, than the Republican base. In the case of government aid to blacks, that discrepancy reflects a sharp left turn on the part of the Democratic base beginning in 2004—before Barack Obama became a salient national figure—after more than a decade of gradual moderation.

FIGURE 3
Issue Extremism of Party Bases, 1980–2012

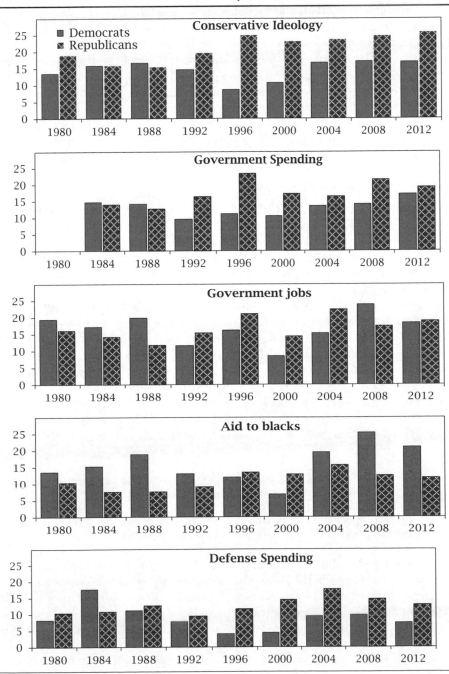

The issue of aid to blacks is the only one of the five considered here on which the Democratic base has generally—and increasingly—been more extreme, relative to swing voters, than the Republican base. (On average, the difference amounted to about five points on the 100-point scale.) On the other hand, the Republican base has been more extreme on the issues of government spending and defense (by about four points) and overall ideology (by almost seven points)—and these differences, too, have generally increased over the three decades covered by my analysis. (The two parties' core partisans have been about equally extreme on the issue of government jobs.) Thus, while a definitive comparison of "extremism" would require us to consider a much broader range of issues, the available data generally support the claim that the Republican base has been more extreme than the Democratic base, especially in recent years.

Do Presidential Candidates Cater to Their Core Partisans?

As we have seen, political scientists and pundits alike have often supposed that the striking departures of presidential candidates from the moderate positions that would presumably appeal to swing voters reflect the influence of their respective partisan bases.

Of course, political parties have always relied on cadres of active, enthusiastic supporters for the energy and resources they need to attract votes. In Boss Plunkitt's day, the Tammany Hall machine provided patronage jobs and "honest graft" in exchange for political labor (Riordon 1905/1963). Nowadays, political parties have much less to offer in the way of patronage than they did a century ago. So what do today's Plunkitts get in return for their effort and resources? According to one popular textbook, "in recent years, most of those who volunteer for party work seem to be motivated by a desire to use the party to achieve policy goals" (Hershey 2009, 87). Thus, as Aldrich (1995, 183, 191) argued, the distinctive policy preferences of

> party activists . . . constrain the actual leaders of the party, its ambitious office seekers, as they try to become the party-in-government by appealing to the electorate. . . . The need for the support of party activists to gain nomination and the value of those activists' working for the nominee in the general election will work against the incentive to moderate and pull [candidates] toward the positions of the party [activists].

Despite the plausibility of this argument, I know of no systematic analysis of the relationship between the issue positions of presidential candidates and those of their core partisans. In this section, I examine that relationship. Given the paucity of available data—estimates of (perceived) candidate positions and those of core supporters for eight or nine election years for each party and issue—my analyses are necessarily rudimentary. Nonetheless, they provide considerable evidence of surprising unresponsiveness to the views of swing voters—and some intriguing evidence as well that the parties' respective bases are not entirely to blame for that unresponsiveness.

I begin by characterizing the positions of presidential candidates on the same four issues considered in the preceding section—government spending, government jobs, aid to blacks, and defense spending. The same ANES survey respondents who reported their own positions on each of these issue scales were also invited to place each of the presidential candidates on the same issues. Figure 4 shows the average placements of each candidate on each issue by politically knowledgeable survey respondents, statistically adjusted to take account of the respondents' own partisan sentiments.[12]

Comparing the positions of presidential candidates in Figure 4 with those of their parties' respective bases in Figure 2 suggests that candidates are often at least as "extreme" as their core partisans. Indeed, the summaries of issue positions presented in Table 2 indicate that, on average, Democratic presidential candidates have been more extreme than the Democratic base on every issue. On the issue of aid to blacks, Democratic candidates have been ten points more liberal than the Democratic base, on average, and more than 25 points more liberal than swing voters. Republican candidates, on the other hand, have been somewhat more moderate than the Republican base on the issue of aid to blacks, somewhat more conservative on defense spending, and in close agreement with the Republican base on government spending and government jobs.

The positions of both parties' presidential candidates have become more extreme over the past three decades. The first and last columns of Table 1 summarize cumulative shifts in the positions of each party's candidates over the whole period represented in Figure 4. These tabulations indicate that Democratic candidates have shifted sharply to the Left with respect to overall ideology, and less sharply to the Left on the issue of government spending. Republican candidates have shifted significantly to the Right on the issues of government jobs and aid to blacks, but not at all on overall ideology, government spending, or defense spending. The net result of these shifts has been to increase the absolute distance between the parties' presidential candidates by 15 to 20 percent over three decades—roughly half the 31 percent increase in the polarization of the parties' core supporters over the same period. This increase in partisan polarization reflects increasing extremism among both Democratic and Republican candidates, though Republicans have moved further and more consistently to the Right, relative to the positions of swing voters, than Democrats have to the Left.

My primary interest here is in whether and how these shifts in the positions of presidential candidates reflect a strategic trade-off between appealing to swing voters and core partisans. The simplest way to think of that trade-off is to suppose that candidates' positions represent compromises between the centrist views of swing voters and the more extreme views of the parties' core supporters, with the relative weight of each depending upon their relative importance in a given electoral context (Bartels 2010). The key question then is how much weight candidates attach to the views of core partisans in this compromise. For each party, the statistical results presented in Table 3 offer two different answers to that question.

The top panel of Table 3 reports the results of statistical analyses relating the issue positions of each party's presidential candidate in each election year to the positions of swing voters and core partisans. The weights attached to the positions

FIGURE 4
Issue Positions of Presidential Candidates, 1980–2012

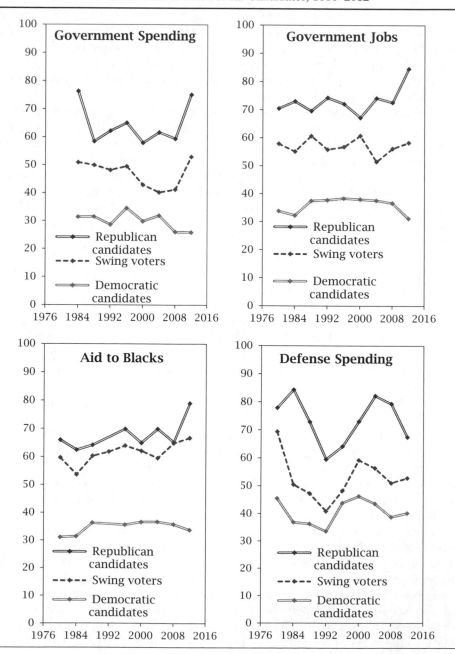

TABLE 2
Average Issue Positions of Presidential Candidates, Core Partisans,
and Swing Voters, 1980–2012

	Democratic candidates	Democratic base	Swing voters	Republican base	Republican candidates
Conservative ideology	34.1	37.6	52.1	73.5	73.6
Government spending cuts	30.0	33.9	47.0	64.6	64.5
(Oppose) government jobs	35.9	40.3	57.0	73.8	73.1
(Oppose) aid to blacks	35.0	45.3	61.4	72.6	67.7
Defense spending	40.5	44.0	52.9	65.6	73.4
(Average)	(35.1)	(40.2)	(54.1)	(70.0)	(70.5)

NOTE: Average placements on 0–100 scales.

of swing voters and core partisans on each issue are constrained to sum to 1.0 for each party, and thus are interpretable as measures of proportional influence. The statistical results for Republicans (in the left columns of the table) indicate that the views of the Republican base had more than 100 times as much influence as those of swing voters on the issue positions of Republican presidential candidates. The results for Democrats (in the right columns of the table) are somewhat less precisely estimated but, remarkably, even more skewed. They suggest that, if anything, the views of swing voters probably had a slight negative impact on the positions of Democratic presidential candidates over the past three decades. If presidential candidates' positions reflect "compromises" between the positions of core partisans and swing voters, they are clearly all about that base. These analyses account for candidates' positions with an average error of 6 to 7 points on the 100-point issue scales.[13]

The bottom panel of Table 3 reports the results of somewhat more elaborate statistical analyses of the issue positions of each party's presidential candidates. Here I relax the assumption that candidates' positions simply reflect compromises between the positions of swing voters and core partisans. Instead, I allow for three-sided compromises among the views of swing voters and core partisans and durable "party convictions" distinct from the preferences of both these groups. While this formulation leaves unaddressed the question of where "party convictions" come from (or precisely who holds them), it provides for more flexible representations of candidates' positions by allowing for the possibility that they are not particularly responsive to either swing voters or core partisans.[14]

For Republicans, the results of these analyses suggest that durable party convictions and the shifting views of core partisans each received about four times as much weight as the views of swing voters. For three of the five issues, the effects of durable convictions and core partisans were largely reinforcing, since the party convictions estimated in the statistical analysis and reported in Table 3 are only slightly (from three to five points) more conservative than the three-decade average positions of the Republican base. The exceptions are government aid to blacks (where the party conviction seems to have been somewhat more moderate

TABLE 3

Presidential Candidates' Responsiveness to Swing Voters and Core Partisans, 1980–2012

	Republican candidates		Democratic candidates	
Swing/base compromise model (N = 35)				
Responsiveness to swing voters	.007 (.026)	(Average error = 6.62)	−.135 (.089)	(Average error = 6.03)
Responsiveness to core partisans	.993 (.026)		1.135 (.089)	
Swing/base/party compromise model (N = 35)				
Responsiveness to swing voters	.107 (.140)	(Average error = 4.85)	.229 (.104)	(Average error = 2.96)
Responsiveness to core partisans	.485 (.137)		.199 (.080)	
Responsiveness to party convictions	.408 (.088)		.573 (.058)	
Conservative ideology	78.9 (8.3)	2.66	23.1 (4.7)	4.07
Government spending	69.9 (8.5)	5.86	22.5 (3.8)	3.16
Government jobs	76.6 (7.7)	4.92	26.1 (4.5)	2.94
Aid to blacks	63.3 (5.3)	3.92	22.1 (5.2)	2.66
Defense spending	91.2 (10.5)	6.88	35.5 (2.6)	1.97

NOTE: Nonlinear seemingly unrelated regression parameter estimates (with standard errors in parentheses).

than the views of the Republican base) and defense spending (where the party conviction seems to have been much more extreme than the Republican base).

For Democrats, the estimated party conviction is substantially more liberal than the Democratic base on every issue. The smallest difference (eight or nine points) appears on the issue of defense spending, while the largest difference (twenty-three points) appears on the issue of aid to blacks. Moreover, those extreme liberal convictions seem from the results reported in Table 3 to have received almost three times as much weight as the views of the Democratic base in shaping Democratic candidates' issue positions. That has tended to make Democratic candidates considerably more extreme than they would have been even if they catered entirely to the views of their core supporters. The apparent weight attached to the views of swing voters has moderated those extreme positions somewhat; nonetheless, the extreme liberalism and apparent weight of Democratic Party convictions in Table 3 account for the fact that Democratic candidates are consistently more extreme than the Democratic base in Table 2.

The combined effect of these forces is evident in Figure 5, which charts discrepancies between the perceived positions of each presidential candidate and the average position of swing voters on each issue in each election year. With respect to overall ideology, the partisan polarization of presidential candidates' positions has been relatively symmetric in most elections, though Jimmy Carter in 1980 and George H. W. Bush in 1988 were (relatively) quite moderate. The pattern for government spending is fairly similar, with Democratic candidates significantly further from swing voters in 1988, 1992, and 2012, but significantly closer in 1984 and (especially) 2004. On the issue of government jobs, Democratic candidates were more extreme than their Republican opponents in the 1980s and again in 2000.

The issues examined in the bottom two panels of Figure 5 provide striking examples of significant durable asymmetries in the extremism of Democratic and Republican presidential candidates. In the case of defense spending, Ronald Reagan came significantly closer than Jimmy Carter to matching the public's enthusiasm for defense spending increases in 1980; but thereafter, public support for further spending increases subsided quickly, leaving Republican candidates in six of the next eight presidential elections much further from swing voters than their Democratic opponents were. The issue of government aid to blacks provides an even more dramatic example of asymmetric extremism. In every one of the eight recent elections for which we have data, the perceived positions of Republican presidential candidates on this issue corresponded fairly closely with the views of swing voters, while the perceived positions of Democratic candidates were vastly more liberal. The discrepancies in 2008 and 2012 were especially large; however, it is evident from Figure 5 that Democratic candidates were far out of step with swing voters on this issue for at least a quarter-century before Barack Obama came on the scene. Whether this consistently liberal position reflects a high-minded attachment to the principle of racial equality or the clout of a key part of the Democratic coalition (African Americans have constituted about one-third of the party's base over this period, by my estimate) or some combination of these and other factors, it is a striking instance of unresponsiveness to the views of swing voters.

The Missing Middle

In some respects, my analysis reinforces a familiar view of contemporary American electoral politics. I find that the preferences of the Democratic and Republican parties' core supporters on a variety of important issues have polarized significantly since 1980, with most of the increase in polarization attributable to the increasing extremism of the Republican base. I also find that the positions of Democratic and Republican presidential candidates have polarized, albeit at a slower rate, due to the responsiveness of candidates' positions to the views of their respective partisan bases. These findings are broadly consistent with both scholarly and popular understandings of contemporary electoral dynamics.

However, upon closer inspection, my findings also reveal some significant anomalies. One important twist is that the asymmetric "extremism" of each party's bases does not seem to translate directly into asymmetric extremism of their

FIGURE 5
Issue Extremism of Presidential Candidates, 1980–2012

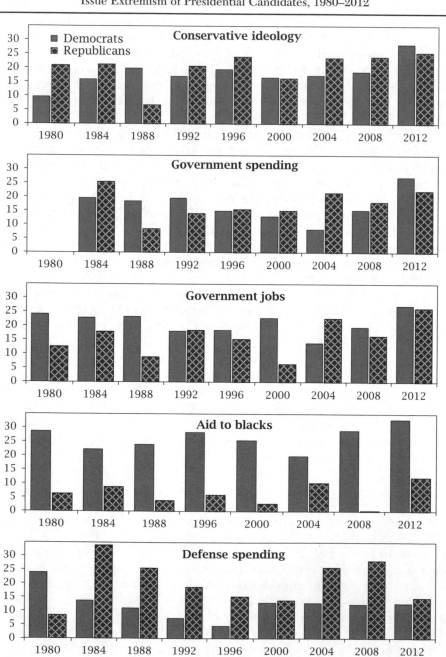

presidential candidates. While the positions of Republican presidential candidates seem to be quite responsive to the views of the Republican base, the positions of Democratic candidates seem to reflect stable partisan convictions much more than they reflect responsiveness to the views of core partisans. The effect has been to make Democratic presidential candidates as extreme as Republican candidates on most issues and much more extreme on some. If extremism is a problem in presidential politics, it seems to be at least as much of a problem for Democrats as for Republicans.

General claims of Republican extremism are often offered with little in the way of systematic evidence. When systematic evidence is adduced, it is mostly limited to the summaries of congressional roll call votes constructed by Keith Poole and Howard Rosenthal (2007), which show Republican legislators moving sharply to the Right since 1980 (e.g., Mann and Ornstein 2012, 57). However, the statistical assumptions required to scale roll call votes consistently over time are quite demanding—and entirely insensitive to shifts in the congressional agenda and the political context. Efforts to incorporate additional information about the substance of what Congress is actually doing at any given time may produce very different conclusions (Clinton, Katznelson, and Lapinski 2016). In any case, it seems well worth bearing in mind that changes in the "extremism" of the two parties' congressional delegations, even if they are real, are not necessarily indicative of parallel shifts in the parties' stances more generally, or more specifically in the positions of their presidential candidates.

Perhaps the apparent extremism of presidential candidates in my analysis is an artifact of some sort of bias in the issue positions attributed to candidates by ANES survey respondents. Perceptions of the positions of presidential candidates are no doubt subject to considerable error due to vagaries of measurement and public inattention. However, it is by no means obvious why even considerable error should significantly skew estimates of candidates' positions based on averaging several hundred or more individual responses, especially when the most obvious potential sources of bias—respondents' own issue preferences—are statistically controlled in the process of measurement. And while some observers have accused journalists of practicing "false equivalence"—imposing an artificial symmetry on the extremism of the Right and Left (e.g., Mann and Ornstein 2012, 186, 194; Froomkin 2013)—it is hard to see why that would produce public perceptions of Democratic candidates' positions that are in some cases significantly more extreme (relative to the positions of swing voters) than those of their Republican opponents.

In any event, my analysis casts doubt on the notion that the influence of the party's respective core partisans is the sole—or even the most important—cause of presidential candidates' distinctly noncentrist issue positions. The views of core partisans are clearly important; but the idea that candidates' positions reflect strategic compromises between the preferences of core partisans and swing voters—a straightforward elaboration of political scientists' standard model of electoral competition—fares poorly here. Even with generous allowance for the possibility that the money and organizational resources provided by the parties' respective bases have become increasingly important in the current electoral environment, the overwhelming weight of core partisans relative to swing voters implied by my statistical results is simply much too large to reflect the relative importance of core partisans in determining election outcomes.[15]

Allowing for the influence of durable party convictions in addition to the preferences of core partisans and swing voters further complicates the picture. Relaxing the assumption that only swing voters and core partisans matter turns out to provide a much better explication of candidates' issue positions. In the case of Democrats, the average error in accounting for candidates' positions is reduced by half, from six points to three, when the statistical analysis is elaborated to incorporate durable party convictions. Moreover, those convictions seem to be more important even than the preferences of the Democratic base in determining candidates' positions. In the case of Republicans, both the estimated weight of party convictions and the improvement in fit produced by allowing for them are somewhat less impressive; nonetheless, it is clear that Republican candidates, too, adopt positions that are something more than compromises between the preferences of swing voters and the Republican base.

Of course, the term "party convictions" is merely a convenient shorthand for whatever forces have impelled presidential candidates to maintain consistent positions over the past three decades, even as the views of core partisans and swing voters have shifted from year to year. If my assessment of their importance is correct, then a concerted attempt to better understand those forces should be high on the agenda of scholars of American electoral politics. If the relevant party convictions are not those of the candidates themselves, perhaps they reflect the influence of much smaller, more extreme subsets of "intense policy demanders" (Cohen et al. 2008, 19–45) or "big donors, ideological activist groups, [and] grassroots conservative [or liberal] organizations" (Hacker and Pierson 2005, 9) distinct from the larger cadres of core partisans identified here. Or perhaps different definitions of who counts as a "party activist" or "core partisan" would produce better evidence of consistency between their policy demands and the positions of presidential candidates.

A clearer conception of whose views matter in determining the positions of presidential candidates, and why, would seem to be a pressing priority for scholars of American party politics. In the meantime, however, we are left with a great deal of evidence suggesting that the views of swing voters do not matter much. For political scientists—whose most elegant and influential theorizing about party politics emphasizes the moderating effects of electoral competition—that is (or should be) a significant intellectual embarrassment. For citizens—who have to live with the consequences—it is (or should be) a significant political challenge.

Notes

1. "Here is a 7-point scale on which the political views that people might hold are arranged from extremely liberal to extremely conservative. Where would you place yourself on this scale, or haven't you thought much about this?" Responses on the 7-point scale are recoded to range from 0 for "extremely liberal" to 100 for "extremely conservative."

2. The data are publicly available from the ANES website, www.electionstudies.org. My analysis is based on the ANES Time Series Cumulative Data File. In addition to employing the standard weight variable included in the ANES data file (VCF0009x), I weighted the respondents in each election year by the inverse of the sample size (more precisely, by the number of people who voted divided by the number of ANES postelection respondents who reported voting). This additional weight has no effect on year-by-year analyses but produces a representative sample of the cumulative electorate for analyses in which the data from all nine election years are combined.

3. I estimated each ANES survey respondent's probability of voting on the basis of a separate probit regression analysis in each election year relating self-reported turnout to respondents' strength of party identification, the absolute difference in their ratings of the Democratic and Republican parties on a "feeling thermometer," age, family income percentile, and indicator variables for college graduates, people with some college, people with high school diplomas, blacks, Hispanics, females, married people, union members, homeowners, and southerners. The results of these analyses are presented in supplementary Table A, available online at http://ann.sagepub.com/supplemental.

4. The results of these analyses are reported in Table B in the online supplement. Since the theoretical analyses on which these calculations are based (Bartels 1998, 2010) ignored minor parties and independent candidates, minor party voters are ignored in this step of my empirical analysis. However, they are included—as are nonvoters—in my subsequent analysis as potential targets of Democratic and Republican electoral appeals based on the attitudes they expressed toward the two major parties.

5. I used the probit regression coefficients to assess the strength of each prospective voter's underlying propensity to favor the Democratic or Republican candidate, then adjusted the propensities to have a median value of zero in each election year, then calculated the normal probability density corresponding to the adjusted propensity for each prospective voter. Centering the distribution of partisan propensities separately for each election year ensures that the prospective voters with the highest values are those who would be pivotal if the election turned out to be close. The adjusted measure of partisan propensity ranges from –5.93 to +5.56. Scores below –1.28 (registered by 24.7 percent of ANES survey respondents) imply Republican voting probabilities below 10 percent; scores above +1.28 (registered by 27.2 percent of respondents) imply Republican voting probabilities above 90 percent.

6. "Some people think the government should provide fewer services, even in areas such as health and education, in order to reduce spending. Other people feel that it is important for the government to provide many more services even if it means an increase in spending. Where would you place yourself on this scale, or haven't you thought much about this?" Responses on a 7-point scale are recoded to range from 0 for "government should provide many more services; increase spending a lot" to 100 for "government should provide many fewer services; reduce spending a lot."

7. "Some people feel that the government in Washington should see to it that every person has a job and a good standard of living. Others think the government should just let each person get ahead on his own. Where would you place yourself on this scale, or haven't you thought much about this?" Responses on a 7-point scale are recoded to range from 0 for "see to it that every person has a job and a good standard of living" to 100 for "just let each person get ahead on his own."

8. "Some people feel that the government in Washington should make every possible effort to improve the social and economic position of blacks. Others feel that the government should not make any special effort to help blacks because they should help themselves. Where would you place yourself on this scale, or haven't you thought much about it?" Responses on a 7-point scale are recoded to range from 0 for "government should help blacks" to 100 for "blacks should help themselves."

9. "Some people believe that we should spend much less money for defense. Others feel that defense spending should be greatly increased. Where would you place yourself on this scale, or haven't you thought much about this?" Responses on a 7-point scale are recoded to range from 0 for "greatly decrease defense spending" to 100 for "greatly increase defense spending."

10. Even for these five issues, the available data are not quite complete. The government spending item was not included in the 1980 ANES survey; and while respondents' own positions on all of the other issues were ascertained in every survey, perceptions of presidential candidates' stances on the issue of aid to blacks were not ascertained in 1992. Thus, for analyses requiring data on candidates' and voters' positions on all five issues, I am limited to focusing on just seven elections: 1984, 1988, 1996, 2000, 2004, 2008, and 2012.

11. These average positions exclude survey respondents who declined to place themselves on the ANES issue scales—16 percent of the eligible sample for government spending, 12 percent for government jobs

and aid to blacks, 15 percent for defense spending, and 27 percent for conservative ideology. They also exclude respondents who were not asked to place themselves, either because they were not reinterviewed after the election or because some questions were only asked of half the sample in some years.

12. Specifically, I estimated each candidate's position on each issue in each election year based on the perceptions of survey respondents rated "very high" or "fairly high" in political information by ANES interviewers. (In most years, there were separate political information ratings in the pre- and postelection interviews, and I included respondents who scored "very high" or "fairly high" in both. In 1988, only the pre-election interviewer provided an information rating.) The proportion of "knowledgeable" respondents by this criterion varied between 17 percent and 36 percent and averaged 27 percent. I used a nonlinear regression analysis to relate these knowledgeable survey respondents' perceptions to candidates' "true" positions and to the respondents' own issue positions, with the weight of their own issue positions allowed to vary with their propensity to support Democratic or Republican candidates. In effect, the model allows respondents to "pull" their perceptions of favored candidates toward their own positions and to "push" their perceptions of disfavored candidates away from their own positions. On the logic of statistical models of misperception of this sort, see Brady and Sniderman (1985). My empirical analysis implies that, on average, someone who was 90 percent likely to vote Republican in a close election underestimated the distance between the Republican candidate's positions and her own by about 19 percent and exaggerated the distance between the Democratic candidate's positions and her own by about 18 percent. Similarly, someone who was 90 percent likely to vote Democratic in a close election exaggerated the distance between the Republican candidate's positions and her own by an average of 16 percent and underesti-mated the distance between the Democratic candidate's positions and her own by about 23 percent. After correcting for these biases, the resulting estimates of candidates' "true" positions reflect the perceptions of knowledgeable, politically neutral observers (equally likely to vote Democrat or Republican in a close election). The average standard error of these estimates is 1.2 (with a range from 0.8 to 2.1) on the 100-point issue scales. Detailed statistical results appear in online supplementary Table D.

13. Relaxing the assumption that the influence of core partisans relative to swing voters is the same for every issue produces quite similar results for most issues. The most important exception is that Republican candidates seem to have attached significant weight (.47, with a standard error of .12) to the views of swing voters on the issue of aid to blacks.

14. A different way of capturing this possibility is to relate the positions of presidential candidates to the positions of their predecessors four years earlier, as well as to the current views of swing voters and core partisans. In analyses of that sort, Republican candidates seem to attach some weight to the positions of their predecessors (.31, with a standard error of .08) but more to the views of the Republican base (.68, with a standard error of .09). Democratic candidates, on the other hand, seem to attach more weight to the positions of their predecessors (.71, with a standard error of .05) than to the views of their base (.43, with a standard error of .06). In both cases, the views of swing voters have no apparent influence on candidates' positions.

15. This anomaly is by no means new. For example, Aldrich (1995, 187), analyzing data from the 1970s and 1980s, noted that "the difference between the two parties' activists are often of the same order of magnitude as those of their presidential candidates." (Aldrich's definition of "activists" was broader than my definition of "core partisans," but similar in spirit.) But in that case, the positions of presidential can-didates could not logically reflect compromises between the views of activists and those of the "median voter" whose preference is supposed to be decisive in formal models of electoral competition.

References

Achen, Christopher H., and Larry M. Bartels. 2016. *Democracy for realists: Why elections do not produce responsive government.* Princeton, NJ: Princeton University Press.

Aldrich, John H. 1983. A Downsian spatial model with party activism. *American Political Science Review* 77:974–90.

Aldrich, John H. 1995. *Why parties? The origin and transformation of political parties in America.* Chicago, IL: University of Chicago Press.

Aranson, Peter H., and Peter C. Ordeshook. 1972. Spatial strategies for sequential elections. In *Probability models of collective decision making,* eds. Richard G. Niemi and Herbert F. Weisberg, 298–331. Columbus, OH: Charles E. Merrill.

Bartels, Larry M. 1998. Where the ducks are: Voting power in a party system. In *Politicians and party politics*, ed. John G. Geer, 43–79. Baltimore, MD: Johns Hopkins University Press.

Bartels, Larry M. 2010. Base appeal: The political attitudes and priorities of core partisans. Paper presented at the annual meeting of the American Political Science Association, Washington, DC. Available from https://my.vanderbilt.edu/larrybartels/files/2011/12/Base_Appeal.pdf.

Brady, Henry E., and Paul M. Sniderman. 1985. Attitude attribution: A group basis for political reasoning. *American Political Science Review* 79:1061–78.

Carmines, Edward G., and James Woods. 2002. The role of party activists in the evolution of the abortion issue. *Political Behavior* 24:361–77.

Clinton, Joshua D., Ira Katznelson, and John S. Lapinski. 2016. Where measures meet history: Party polarization during the New Deal and Fair Deal. In *Governing in a polarized age: Elections, parties, and political representation*, ed. Alan S. Gerber and Eric Schickler. New York, NY: Cambridge University Press.

Cohen, Martin, Mary C. McGrath, Peter Aronow, and John Zaller. 2016. Ideologically Extreme Candidates in U.S. Presidential Elections, 1948–2012. *The ANNALS of the American Academy of Political and Social Science* (this volume).

Cohen, Marty, David Karol, Hans Noel, and John Zaller. 2008. *The party decides: Presidential nomination before and after reform*. Chicago, IL: University of Chicago Press.

Downs, Anthony. 1957. *An economic theory of democracy*. New York, NY: Harper & Row.

Enelow, James M., and Melvin J. Hinich. 1984. *The spatial theory of voting: An introduction*. New York, NY: Cambridge University Press.

Fiorina, Morris P., and Samuel J. Abrams. 2009. *Disconnect: The breakdown of representation in American politics*. Norman, OK: University of Oklahoma Press.

Froomkin, Dan. 6 February 2013. How the mainstream press bungled the single biggest story of the 2012 campaign. *Huffpost Media*.

Hacker, Jacob, and Paul Pierson. 2005. *Off center: The Republican revolution and the erosion of American democracy*. New Haven, CT: Yale University Press.

Hershey, Marjorie Randon. 2009. *Party politics in America*. 13th ed. New York, NY: Pearson Longman.

Holbrook, Thomas M., and Scott D. McClurg. 2005. The mobilization of core supporters: Campaigns, turnout, and electoral composition in United States presidential elections. *American Journal of Political Science* 49:689–703.

Kleefeld, Eric. 18 April 2008. Hillary privately blasted "the activist base of the Democratic Party" for caucus defeats. Available from tpmelectioncentral.talkingpointsmemo.com.

Krugman, Paul. 7 August 2015. From Trump on down, the Republicans can't be serious. *New York Times*.

Layman, Geoffrey. 2001. *The great divide: Religious and cultural conflict in American party politics*. New York, NY: Columbia University Press.

Mann, Thomas E., and Norman J. Ornstein. 2012. *It's even worse than it looks: How the American constitutional system collided with the new politics of extremism*. New York, NY: Basic Books.

Martin, Jonathan, and Patrick Healy. 16 February 2016. Obama's options for a Supreme Court nominee, and the potential fallout. *New York Times*.

Poole, Keith T., and Howard Rosenthal. 2007. *Ideology and Congress*. New Brunswick, NJ: Transaction Publishers.

Riordon, William L. 1905/1963. *Plunkitt of Tammany Hall: A series of very plain talks on very practical politics*. New York, NY: E. P. Dutton.

Stone, Walter J., and Alan I. Abramowitz. 1983. Winning may not be everything, but it's more than we thought: Presidential party activists in 1980. *American Political Science Review* 77:945–56.

Ideological Factions in the Republican and Democratic Parties

By
HANS NOEL

Both the Republican and Democratic parties are internally divided. Each contains a party regular wing, which is interested in winning office and in the compromises necessary to govern. And each contains an ideological wing, which is interested in close adherence to the core coalition of the party. But the nature of the cleavage is very different within the parties. Among Democrats, the cleavage is mild, with most members belonging to the party regular camp, to the chagrin of ideologues, who are for the most part Bernie Sanders supporters. The cleavage among Republicans, though, is so deep that the party could not find a way to bridge it in the so-called invisible primary for 2016, creating an opening for Donald Trump, who is from neither camp.

Keywords: ideology; liberalism; conservatism; party coalitions; realignment; nominations; compromise

It is fashionable to note that both the Republican and Democratic parties are "divided," but it is only trivially true that divisions in the parties exist. Political parties are coalitions of actors who have interests that differ. What is less clear is just how the parties are divided. With diverse parties, there are many and diverse cleavages. Some, however, are more significant than others. In particular, the cleavages that matter are those that present challenges to the party leadership.

Hans Noel is an associate professor of government at Georgetown University. He is the author of Political Ideologies and Political Parties in America *(Cambridge University Press 2013) and a coauthor of* The Party Decides: Presidential Nominations before and after Reform *(University of Chicago Press 2008).*

NOTE: I would like to thank participants at the *ANNALS* workshop at Vanderbilt University for useful comments, especially Larry Bartels, Gary Jacobson, Steve Rogers, John Sides, Michael Tesler, Lynn Vavreck, and John Zaller. Rachel Blum and Justin Rattey provided timely and useful research assistance. Natalie Jackson and Mark Blumenthal were helpful in arranging for and conducting the activist survey.

Correspondence: hcn4@georgetown.edu

DOI: 10.1177/0002716216662433

This article attempts to articulate one important way in which the modern parties are divided, which is different than most previous party cleavages. Whereas past cleavages have divided actors who want very different things from politics, today's parties are divided between actors who mostly want similar things but who differ on how to pursue them.

There are coherent divides in both the more conservative Republican Party and the more liberal Democratic Party. Among conservatives, for instance, there are differences between social traditionalists and free-market libertarians—and within liberalism there are divides between anticapitalists and antiracists. These differences are important—and in many ways very important to the 2016 election cycle—but both parties have largely held together over such divisions. Partly this is because activists in each of the parties tend to agree about issues on both sides of the divides, even as they differ over priorities. What splits parties, though, are rifts between ideologically pure, less compromising members, and more pragmatic, moderate ones. This is a difference not about policy ends but about political means. Not about issues but about strategy. Not about what to do but how we should face the constraints of trying to do it.

Identifying these divides is complicated by the fact that they are not manifest in the same ways in each party. Political parties are complex and mostly disorganized institutions. V. O. Key—who focused on the party in the electorate, the party as an organization, and the party in government—did not know the half of it. An expansive definition of each party would include allied interest groups and activists, who may or may not agree with the formal party organization.

Here, I focus on two groups—elected officials and party activists—and in some cases, I compare them to what we know about the preferences of a third group, voters.

Parties are Coalitions

The prevailing view of political parties, and especially the two major parties in the United States, is that they are coalitions.[1] It can be useful to think of the members of these coalitions in different terms, but following Bawn et al. (2012),[2] I think the most traction comes from viewing them as comprising different social groups. Individual politicians of course represent more than one group, and many groups are divided. But the parties can still be seen as coalitions of, for example, bankers, religious traditionalists, and foreign policy hawks, among others; or of nonwhites, union members and atheists, among others.

But precisely because everyone is a member of more than one group and groups can be divided, it is trickier to nail down empirically what the exact coalitions are. Party platforms do not say "We are for the interests of Latinos," or "We are for Wall Street." The party's agenda in Congress emerges over several bills, and members vary in how much they want their policies to pass and in how much they just want someone else's policies not to pass. Candidates for many offices are often closely related to a single group, rather than representing the entire coalition (Bawn et al. 2015).

We can see the coalition being shaped during presidential nominations. The presidency is uniquely important, but it is also simply unique. In Congress, it is possible for a candidate to represent only a narrow group, and the coalition only emerges when the elected officials assemble in the legislature. Not so with the presidency, which involves players across the entire party. The eventual nominee will, in some respects, stand in for the terms of the party's coalition.

Coalitions are assembled principally by party leaders (Karol 2009), and political activists pressure the leadership to adopt the positions they adopt. Partisan voters may diverge from the coalitions from time to time and force party leaders to react in some way, but the coalitions themselves are shaped by political elites— the party leaders and activists who sort out and articulate the issues around which the parties coalesce. Accordingly, my focus here is on those political elites—the leaders and activists in the upper ends of the parties.

Ideological coalitions in the two major parties

The party coalitions are constantly evolving. The current coalitions can be well described as "liberal" and "conservative," but this was not always the case. Only a half-century ago, the parties each included a significant number of liberals and conservatives.

Party coalitions need not coincide with ideological clusters at all. At the end of the nineteenth century, the Republican Party included protariff businessmen, those with free-silver mining interests, and blacks. These interests were often wildly in conflict with one another, necessitating clever maneuvering by party leaders to hold the party together. In the 1940s and 1950s, the New Deal coalition of the Democrats brought together the northern union members, Catholics, Jews, and ethnic whites, but also southern white segregationists. Republicans included those with business interests as well as Protestants, women's rights groups, and groups on both sides of the emerging conflict over civil rights.

Elsewhere (Noel 2012, 2013), I argue that this development began with the sharpening of a liberal ideological coalition in the early part of the twentieth century followed by a conservative coalition in response. These coalitions brought together the interests, ideas, and policy preferences that we today associate with liberals and conservatives. Liberals favor government economic intervention to encourage equality and labor interests; policies that advantage ethnic, religious, sexual, and racial minorities and disadvantaged groups; women's rights; a multilateral and often less militaristic foreign policy; and a collection of many other positions. Conservatives favor free markets, business interests, a color-blind approach to race and ethnic issues, traditional religious and sexual norms, a foreign policy informed by American exceptionalism, and a number of other positions. I argue that it makes sense to think of these ideological movements as coalitions because they bring together potentially diverse actors, cementing their bonds with appeals to shared principles, values, and even symbols.

These ideological coalitions organized politics in a different way than the existing party coalitions did, and the two kinds of coalition often pulled actors in different directions. For example, most politicians from the South were both

Democrats and conservative—especially, but not only, on racial issues. They would sometimes vote according to their conservative ideological coalition, joining many Republicans, and at other times vote with their party, sticking with Democrats. The New Deal Democratic coalition was held together with an understanding that southern Democrats would back labor legislation they disagreed with in exchange for northern Democrats not pursuing action on civil rights (Feinstein, Schickler, and Pearson 2010; Feinstein and Schickler 2008; Schickler 2016). Some votes were party-line votes. On other votes, a "conservative coalition" of southern Democrats and most Republicans voted against the liberals.

Today, the ideological coalitions are nestled comfortably inside the party coalitions. This transformation is behind most of what we observe as polarization. Scholars who argue that polarization is merely sorting (Fiorina 2005; Levendusky 2009) are right that one of the main things that has happened is that ideologues have sorted into their new parties. However, such sorting has led most actors, especially activists but even many voters, to adopt more ideologically consistent views (Abramowitz 2010; Abramowitz and Saunders 2005).

At the same time, the ideological core of the party is not enough to win elections. This is particularly true because, while voters are more ideologically sorted and more likely to express ideologically consistent beliefs than they used to, most are still not ideological. Even those who self-identity as liberal or conservative do not always hold beliefs associated with that label (Converse 1964; Ellis and Stimson 2012; Kinder and Kalmoe, forthcoming).

Partisan activists and elites, too, sometimes deviate from the ideological coalition for a variety of reasons. For a long time, Democratic Party leaders were hesitant to lead on gay rights, for example, even though this was the liberal position. The electoral needs of the party can override its ideological goals. It is thus wrong to say that the ideological coalitions fully coincide with the party coalitions. Rather, the party coalitions contain the ideological ones.

Ideologues versus regulars

It is common to describe the tensions within each party as between "moderates" and "extremists," but this is not quite correct. "Extremists" are not necessarily further out on an ideological dimension. They are just much more consistent ideologically. Likewise, moderates are usually just less consistently liberal or conservative. They may, in fact, hold more extreme views on the issues that they care about, but do not hold the same views as other liberals or conservatives (Noel 2013, 73; Broockman 2016; Ahler and Broockman 2016). But any two moderates are often not the same. A prochoice, antiwar, anti-affirmative action, antiminimum wage voter is called "moderate," and so is a prolife, prowar, black-lives-matter, fighter for fifteen. Some moderates are truly "in the middle," but unless they hold few policy positions, they are better described as off-dimensional.

Seeing ideologues as simply the core of an ideological coalition and moderates as those who deviate from that core allows us to escape the pervasive ideological spatial model. This model has been very useful for political science, but it is also limiting. As other articles in this volume indicate (Bartels; Cohen, McGrath, Aronow, and Zaller), the most common prediction from the model's application to elections—convergence on the median voter—does not regularly occur.

But a model of a party coalition with an ideological core would not make such a prediction.[3] It is likely that election-seeking politicians may need to deviate from ideological purity in many cases, especially when competing in a national electorate. But politicians in especially homogenous constituencies might do better by appealing to the largest block of ideologically consistent voters—ideologues.

There are four reasons why a politician, activist, or voter might deviate from the ideological core of his/her party. By deviate, I mean actively oppose elements of the coalition. Most people do not care passionately about every part of their party's platform, nor its ideological core. But it is one thing to be indifferent on all but a few issues, something else to outright disagree.

1. They might simply not be ideologically sophisticated. Most voters and even many politicians are like this.
2. They might disagree with the ideology on one or another issue. It is common to hear that someone is "liberal on most things, but not on this." Otherwise conservative business leaders, for instance, may depart from the conservative opposition to more relaxed immigration policy because they see the value in inexpensive labor.
3. They might find that some of the policies advocated by their ideological allies are not politically practical or implementable as policy.

A pair of columns by liberal blogger Matt Yglesias nicely illustrates this phenomenon. Yglesias writes on March 10, 2016, that he is persuaded by Bernie Sanders that universal free education is a good idea. The next week, he writes that he opposes Sanders's plan for the same, not simply because it would be hard politically to implement, but because the current state of higher education in the United States has been built around a different model. The change would require too many other changes to that environment, which the plan has not worked out (Yglesias 2016a, 2016b). In other words, reasonable ideologues can differ about what the best policy is, even while agreeing on goals.

This distinction is similar to the tension often raised in the 2016 Democratic contest between Bernie Sanders's and Hillary Clinton's respective theories of change. Sanders is a revolutionary. Clinton is an incrementalist. It is common to call incrementalists moderates, but that is a function of our commitment to the ideological spatial model, which requires us to array preferences in a space.

4. They might be interested in winning office, and thus need to appeal to activists and voters who are in any of the first three categories.

Liberal ideological activists were ready to expand gay rights much earlier than most of the American public was. Democratic politicians who shared their goals were thus more cautious on the issue. After their loss in 2012, Republicans concluded that they needed to reach out to Latino voters (Barbour et al. 2013). Despite opposition from their conservative base, many Republicans have since looked for a way to reform rather than curtail Latino immigration. However, some election-minded politicians might not face this incentive. If your constituency is Texas or Vermont, you may lose more votes from your ideological core than you gain from those outside it.

All of these deviations from the ideological core could, in theory, create what looks like a thousand fractures, as those compelled to compromise do so on a variety of issues that change from context to context. There are important potential fractures crisscrossing both parties. However, the third and fourth types especially will tend to come from the same people. Some people are simply more inclined to find more workable policy solutions or to expand the coalition.

Thus, Republicans who oppose aggressive attempts to deport undocumented workers are (a) reflecting business conservatives who differ from social conservatives on this issue, (b) acknowledging that these approaches are unworkable, and (c) hoping to avoid alienating Latino voters.

We can call these people "moderates" if we like. But thinking of them instead as deviations from an ideological core allows us to acknowledge that politicians such as Jeb Bush, Paul Ryan, Marco Rubio, and John Kasich have very conservative records on many policy questions, and that politicians such as Barack Obama, Harry Reid, Nancy Pelosi, and Hillary Clinton have pursued very liberal goals. All of these politicians have been described as both moderates and extremists.[4]

In this article, I describe them as party *regulars* or *compromisers*. They are similar to the pragmatists described by Polsby and Wildavsky (1968), but as evidence suggests, such pragmatists are increasingly idealistic as well (Layman et al. 2010). They are also sometimes called *insiders* or *the establishment*, which I discuss below.

Regulars are opposed by *ideologues*. Ideologues may often be more "extreme," but they are also simply less likely to deviate from the ideological core. Politicians such as Ted Cruz, Rand Paul,[5] Rick Santorum, and Bernie Sanders are ideologues.

Ideologues versus outsiders

The regular-ideologue divide is similar to—although theoretically distinct, from—what is termed an insider-outsider conflict. *Insiders* are technically whoever is in power in the party. There are multiple definitions of an *outsider*. Sometimes, an outsider is a politician who is merely not powerful in the party, someone who might be a back-bencher in a parliamentary system. The Tea Party comprises (or claims to comprise) outsiders trying to get in.

But we also sometimes see another group of *ultra outsiders*—people who have held no elective office at all. Herman Cain, Ben Carson, Carly Fiorina, and Donald Trump are such outsiders. This makes the terminology vague. For the sake of clarity, I reserve the term *outsider* for these ultra outsiders.

For disruptive politicians who are still inside the party—people like Ted Cruz— the term *ideologue* is usually accurate. This does not mean that the ideologues have succeeded in taking control of the Republican Party. The House Freedom Caucus members still claim to be the outsiders. And they have to date not been successful in nominating a true ideological conservative for the presidency, nor in selecting one for the top leadership positions in Congress. But they are not outsiders in the same way that Donald Trump is. Trump is not representative of the ideological wing of the Republican Party. But Cruz is. In short, ideologues are often called outsiders, but I try to distinguish between the two concepts.

Measuring Compromise

It is particularly difficult to measure the willingness of politicians to compromise. Often, a compromise will look like "moderation" to most measures of preferences. It can be conceptually difficult to distinguish between compromise and sincere deviation from a pure ideological position.

Here, I focus on three arenas of compromise. First, I look at the action of elected officials, primarily by examining NOMINATE scores of members of Congress. Second, I examine political activists, leveraging a unique survey of politically active citizens. Finally, I consider the cleavages among voters, largely drawing on other analyses of various surveys.

Elected officials and NOMINATE scores

Data on elites at the very top of the party hierarchy can be easy to come by. The familiar NOMINATE scores scale roll call votes to produce a two-dimensional ideological space. The first dimension is typically interpreted as "ideology," while the second dimension has historically been viewed as capturing regional conflict, including the conflict between northerners and southerners during the New Deal coalition era.

The creators of NOMINATE, Keith Poole and Howard Rosenthal, joined by Christopher Hare (2015), argue that the second dimension today captures what they call an insider-outsider divide, which is closer to what I am arguing is compromise:

> The meaning of the second dimension has largely shifted from representing regional differences within the parties (e.g., between northern and southern Democrats) to intra-party divisions that are more subtle and less clear. One of these divisions appears to be an "insider vs. outsider" cleavage that pops up on votes such as raising the debt ceiling, domestic surveillance, and government funding bills.

The issues mentioned are a mix of issues of compromise and issues on which conservatives might disagree. Government funding bills almost certainly include a lot of spending that small-government conservatives would dislike, but such bills are the natural home of logrolls. Domestic surveillance represents another legitimate divide within the conservative ideology. The debt ceiling votes pit party regulars who want to maintain the integrity of the government's past decisions against ideologues who need to take a public stand against government spending.[6]

I have elsewhere argued (Noel 2013, 2014) that both dimensions are a combination of party loyalty and liberal-conservative ideology. The issues that are particularly ideological load on both dimensions, such that having high scores on both dimensions makes one conservative. Votes that involve many issues in a logroll, and especially procedural votes, cut the other way, such that Republicans are high in the first dimension but low on the second. This means that the second dimension captures the degree to which one favors his/her ideology over the procedural demands of the party, which can also be interpreted as the compromise dimension.

Activist survey

Activists are the labor force of political parties. Candidates need votes, but they also need volunteers and donors. Future party leaders often come from the ranks of activists. But the views of activists are often understudied. We have mass surveys for voters, and we can look at the behavior of politicians in office. Activists are a population that must be targeted as well. Surveys of convention delegates provide fruitful insight into activists, but the population is shaped by who is selected to attend the convention in any year.

To avoid these problems, I use a survey of political activists conducted by the Huffington Post via YouGov. In consultation with the author, the Huffington Post conducted three surveys of activists during the lead-up to the 2016 nomination process. The survey interviewed three separate samples of 500 Republicans and 500 Democrats on July 8–12, 2015, September 22–28, 2015, and January 14–20, 2016.

To take the survey, potential respondents cleared a set of filter questions to determine whether they were what I define as *activists*. Survey respondents said they had either done at least two of the following: (1) contributed money to a political candidate, (2) attended a political campaign event such as a fundraiser or rally, (3) done volunteer work for a political campaign, and/or (4) made phone calls to voters asking them to support a political candidate, or they reported having been at least one of the following: (1) a paid staffer for a political campaign or an elected public official, (2) a candidate for or someone who has held elected public office, or (3) an official in a political party (such as a local party chair or a precinct representative).

The activists in this sample thus had to clear a slightly higher bar than is often used to identify activists in mass surveys such as the American National Election Studies. Those who qualify through only the first set of criteria (about 62 percent) report having done much more than wearing a button or placing a yard sign. The second criteria (about 38 percent) are genuine politicians, albeit probably at the very bottom of the hierarchy.

The earlier waves of the survey asked a series of policy questions. They confirm the notion that, broadly speaking, there is considerable consensus on most issues within both parties. Figures 1 and 2 show the preferences of the activists on those issues in July 2015. The figures suggest a great deal of consensus on at least these issues for most of the activists. That is, most activists appear to be part of the ideological coalition at the core of their party.

FIGURE 1
Issue Preferences among Democratic Activists

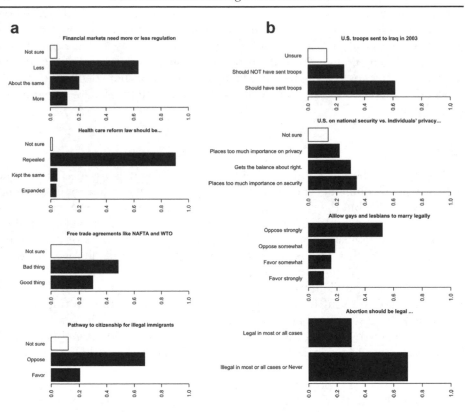

The biggest area of disagreement among Democrats and among Republicans is on trade. Significant proportions of both parties think major trade organizations are a bad thing, while many think they are good. And many in each party are also not sure.

Beyond trade, there are not many major divisions. On financial markets, for instance, there is no disagreement among activists. Neither is there really disagreement between the candidates. Officially, Clinton is just as concerned as Sanders about Wall Street. The claim has been that Clinton is not credible on these issues because of corporate influence. Clinton counters that she wants to be more realistic about the approach. In other words, she would compromise the pure goal of going after banks for a policy that is politically viable and technically workable.

The same is true of other issues that are important in 2016. The Democratic Party is unified on the Iraq War, gay rights, and abortion. On Iraq, Clinton has largely admitted that her support for the war was a mistake, while also claiming that she was motivated by practical considerations. The question for the other issues is not where do the candidates stand, but whether they will pursue the goals in the best way. It is unfortunate that there is no question here on racial issues. The closest is on immigration—here Democrats are very united.

FIGURE 2
Issue Preferences among Republican Activists

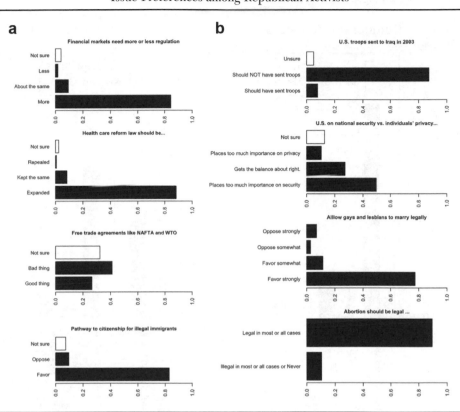

In the July 2015 and January 2016 panels, all respondents were asked whether they thought it was better to have a politician who would: (1) "compromise to get things done," (2) "stick to their principles, no matter what," or (3) "not sure." While this one item cannot capture all of the aspects of the compromise cleavage, it is a useful indicator. For sure, some people who say they value compromise still want the other side to compromise more, and some who say they want to stick to their principles have principles that make them compromise in practice. This is but one measure.

Figure 3 shows the distribution of compromise attitudes. There is very little change in either party between July 2015 and January 2016. Democratic activists are much more likely to want to compromise than are Republican activists.

As we can see from Figure 4, those who value compromise do tend to be less ideologically extreme, in both parties, but only slightly. The activist survey includes very few people who consider themselves moderate, and fewer still who identify with the ideology of the other party. The difference between saying one values compromise versus sticking to principles is similar to the difference between saying "liberal/conservative" and "very liberal/conservative." It may be

FIGURE 3
Valuing Compromise among Democratic and Republican Activists

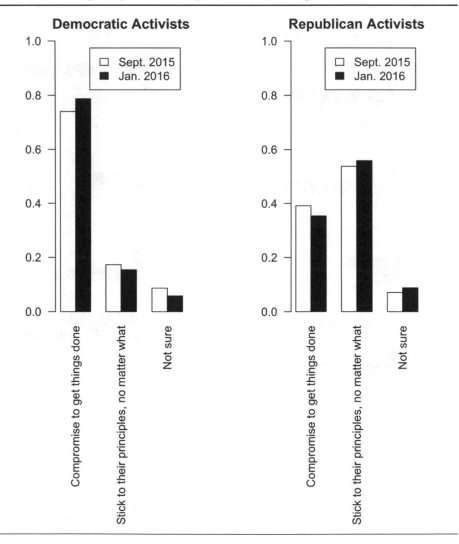

that one's willingness to compromise is even behind whether one includes "very" in their ideology answer. At the same time, a significant number of extremists also value compromise. Almost 40 percent of very liberal Democrats still favor compromise, and about 20 percent of very conservative Republicans do. About 40 percent of merely conservative Republicans want to stick to principles, as do almost 30 percent of merely liberal Democrats. Unwillingness to compromise when you are in fact more moderate (or only "merely" liberal/conservative) could mean being unwilling to compromise with the ideological core. There are not many respondents who seem to fit that description.

FIGURE 4
Valuing Compromise by Ideology

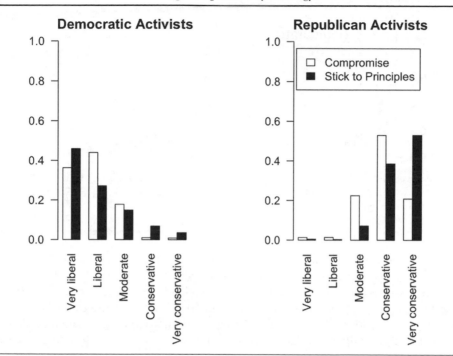

Ideology in the 2016 Presidential Nomination Contests

The presidential nomination is, as noted, an excellent place to look for evidence of partisan divisions, as different elements of the party back different candidates. What we know about the candidates—and what we can understand about why different actors back them—can yield insights into the conflicts within the party.

Both parties face the party regular-ideologue divide. In one party, the pragmatists have won fairly easily, while on the other side, the conflict has set the stage for unpredictable results.

The Republicans

The trouble for Republicans in 2016 is nicely captured by what happened on Capitol Hill in October 2015. While the preprimary phase of the presidential nomination progressed, the Republican Speaker of the House, John Boehner, felt the need to resign midway through his term. Boehner's inability to keep the ideologues in the House in line meant he was unable to do his job.

The House then spent some weeks trying to figure out who could lead it. For a party supposedly united by (or in some accounts fundamentally shaped by) a common ideology, such fracturing is hard to explain. On most policy questions,

FIGURE 5

Distribution of Republican and Democratic Endorsements

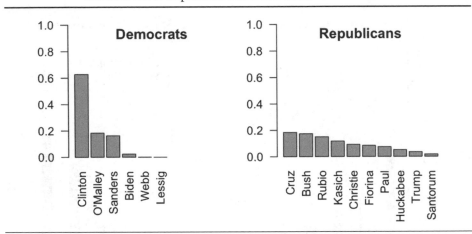

the distance between Boehner and his principle backbenchers in the House Freedom Caucus was not enormous. But the gap could not easily be bridged.

The institutions in the House for selecting a leader are much better than those used to choose a presidential nominee. Paul Ryan, who was the eventual choice, was able to negotiate with the different factions, and party leaders could poll and meet privately with the relatively small number of actors with a stake in the decision.

Out in the country, the Republicans were dealing with the same divide. Cohen et al. (2008) argue that party leaders can and do coordinate around a single presidential candidate, enabling that candidate to win. The Republican Party failed to do that in 2016.

Figure 5 shows the distribution of party leader endorsements in the 2016 campaign in both parties. Following Cohen et al. (2008), I use only endorsements for the candidates that are made before the Iowa caucuses, which met on February 1, 2016. Ted Cruz and Jeb Bush led the pack, followed closely by Marco Rubio, John Kasich, and Chris Christie. The figure shows a deeply fragmented Republican Party. Indeed, this is the most fragmented a party's leaders have been since Cohen and colleagues began collecting these data.

The real lesson from Figure 5, however, is that there was no party favorite at all. Following the accounts of the invisible primary, some of the explanation is clear. While Bush was the top choice of many party regulars, he was despised by the ideologues, who viewed his positions on immigration, Common Core, and other issues as proof that he was not a real conservative. Meanwhile, Cruz, beloved by ideologues, was hated by party regulars, who saw him as a bomb thrower in his time in the Senate. One indication of this fault line is that Cruz drew from those holding offices in the states, mostly due to his many state legislators. Meanwhile, Bush did well among those in Washington. The state-national division reflects the ideologue-regular division. Ideologues have been more

FIGURE 6
NOMINATE Scores of Republican Endorsers

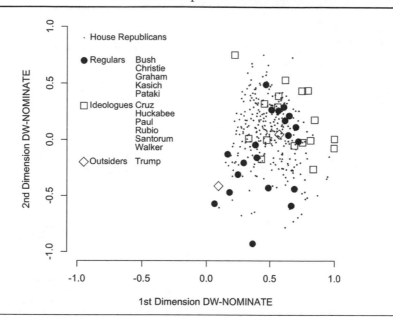

successful at the state level, where Tea Party activists have won local offices as well as a handful of offices in the national legislature. The movement has thus far only begun to crack national office.

If Cruz and Bush are favored by competing factions but unacceptable to the other faction, then Cohen et al. (2008) would expect that the party would find another candidate who could bridge the divide. Some saw Marco Rubio as such a choice. He is almost as ideologically conservative as Cruz, but he had spent a lot of time trying to build connections with party regulars as well.

We know something about the ideological locations of some of the endorsers. Figure 6 shows the NOMINATE scores for the members of the House and Senate who endorsed one of the Republican candidates. I group candidates into three categories: "regulars," "ideologues," and "outsiders." Those not named had not received any endorsements from Congress before the Iowa caucuses.

The behavior of the endorsers is predictable. More ideologically extreme endorsers—and those who are higher on the second dimension, which we saw above may capture the party regulars versus ideologues split—are more likely to endorse ideologues, while more moderate and those low on the second dimension support party regulars. Only two members of Congress endorse an outsider, and notably it is Carly Fiorina, the only outsider to have at least run for office before.

At the same time, there is some overlap between the two groups, suggesting that some members of Congress, mostly neither extreme ideologues nor extreme compromisers, did back a party regular candidate. In most cases, that candidate was Jeb Bush. Bush had a lot of appeal from the middle of the party, at least

FIGURE 7
Support for Candidates among Republican Activists

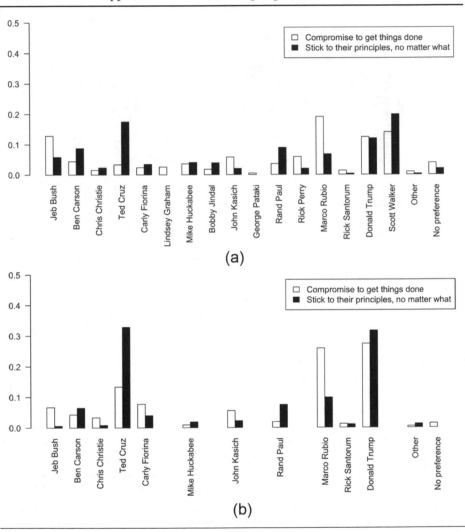

(a)

(b)

nationally. The intense opposition to Bush was not entirely from even the more ideological members of Congress, but these are the most insider of ideologues—those who have won national office. Meanwhile, Rubio had some diverse support, but not very much of it. The support for Cruz was minimal, consistent with the story that the party regulars did not trust him. Figure 6 captures the very top of the party hierarchy—those with elected office in Washington. One might infer from these figures that Bush was well-positioned to win the nomination. But Figure 7 shows the bottom of the party hierarchy, reporting the distribution of first-choice support among the activists in the Huffington Post survey. The top panel shows support in July 2015, before most candidates had dropped out. The bottom panel is from January 2016, right before the Iowa caucuses.

Here, we see some evidence of the Cruz-Bush divide. Ted Cruz had the second-most support among these activists, but it was overwhelmingly from those who favor sticking to principles. Bush had significant support, but it was mostly from the smaller group of Republican activists who favor compromise.

In these data, it appears that Scott Walker was best positioned among the activists, with large degrees of support from both party regulars and ideologues. Marco Rubio's support was only from the party regular wing.

Also notable is the high level of support for Donald Trump from among these activists. This sample is a part of the party, in the Cohen et al. (2008) and Bawn et al. (2012) perspective, albeit the very bottom rungs of power in the party. Trump's support within most of the party is minimal, but he had some support here.

He solidified that support by January. With Walker out of the race, Cruz remained the choice of ideologues, Rubio the choice of compromisers, and Trump actually appeared to be appealing to both kinds of activist. If the only data we had were these activists, Cohen et al. (2008) might infer that the party did decide, and that they decided for Trump. Since we know that the more powerful elements of the party had not backed Trump at this point, and many persisted in opposing Trump until the very end, the inference should be that this is one more dimension on which the party failed to coordinate. Across these data, we find that:

—**Scott Walker** had some early support among low-tier party activists, but almost no support among party leaders.

—**Marco Rubio** had support among some party leaders, and among compromise-oriented activists, but not very much of either, and no support among ideological activists.

—**Ted Cruz** had support among ideological activists and party leaders at the state level, but very minimal support among national party leaders.

—**Jeh Bush** had support among party leaders, and some support among compromise-oriented activists, but very minimal support among ideological activists.

Not one of those four candidates was able to reach more than minimally across the ideological-regulars divide. Cohen et al. (2008) would expect that the party leaders, seeing this situation, would try to find one of these candidates as acceptable. The data suggest that Rubio or Walker might have been such a candidate, but the party failed to coordinate on them.

Why? It is hard to prove, but it seems likely that part of the reason is that the attention given to Donald Trump made it hard to have the public conversation necessary to choose a champion. With Trump dominating the polls, media coverage, and the debates, it was hard to evaluate Rubio, Walker, and the other possibly unifying candidates. Party leaders were confident that Trump would fade in the same way that other outsiders tend to fade. When he did not, it was too late to coordinate.

The Republican Party is divided between regulars and ideologues. Trump is neither. As we saw above, Trump's support among activists comes from those who would compromise and those who want to stick to principles. It is beyond the scope of this article to explain election outcomes, but this outcome has been at odds with the cleavages among the party leadership.

What Trump does indicate is that party cleavages need not be reflected among mass voters. Trump appeals to a group of largely alienated white voters. Many may self-identify as "conservative," but they are not particularly ideological. This is why Trump's ideological apostasies do not bother them.

It has been said[7] that conservatism is identity politics for white people. For more sophisticated conservatives, this identity politics is often expressed in terms of principles such as freedom, religious liberty, and respect for tradition (in the same way that sophisticated liberal ideologues adopt an ideology of egalitarianism and a disdain for hierarchy). But most voters are not sophisticated ideologues. Even most voters who use terms like *liberty* may not consistently apply such terms.

Trump also exploits the internal division on trade, noted in the previous section. He draws especially well among those who oppose trade organizations, as well among those who oppose immigration, although there is less variation on that latter issue. Neither the ideological nor the regular faction has exploited this issue as well as Trump has.

The Democrats

The Democratic Party began the nomination process with a similar cleavage to the Republicans. A group of ideologically uncompromising activists began to insist that more be done to combat Wall Street and the role of money in politics. This group found a champion in Senator Elizabeth Warren, but Warren declined to run.

A large part of Warren's decision may have stemmed from Hillary Clinton's overwhelming support from within the party. Refer back to Figure 5, which also shows the distribution of endorsements for Hillary Clinton on the eve of the Iowa caucus. In summer 2015, before any rivals had entered the race, Clinton's share of support looked even more daunting. If the distribution among the Republicans does not fit the pattern that Cohen et al. (2008) found at all, the distribution among Democrats does. The party had decided for Clinton before anyone else had even thought about running.

Such overwhelming support from the party no doubt scared away a lot of candidates. As many as eighteen candidates were seriously considered among Republicans. Fewer than eight Democrats publicly tested the waters, including several who never had any traction at all.

One candidate undeterred by Clinton was Senator Bernie Sanders, technically not a member of the Democratic Party, but an independent who had caucused with Democratic legislators throughout his career.

Sanders nevertheless garnered minimal support among party leaders, as seen in Figure 5. Clinton's support was exactly the kind of broad party support that

FIGURE 8
NOMINATE Scores of Democratic Endorsers

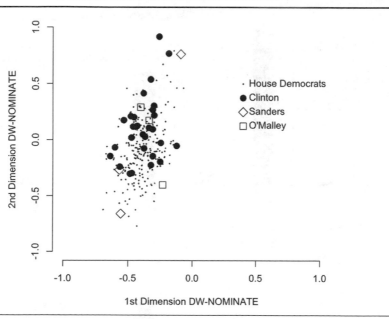

Cohen et al. (2008) predict. In Figure 8, which shows NOMINATE scores for Democratic endorsers, her support ranges over the entire party. The few who back Sanders are from the most ideological wing of the party, but Clinton too has support from among the most liberal. But Sanders did have a lot of backing in the party, just not among the very top of the party. For one thing, he won in the neighborhood of 40 percent of the vote in Democratic primaries (about on par with the percent who supported Donald Trump among Republicans). And Sanders had considerable support among the activists in our survey. Figure 9 shows the activists in July 2015 and January 2016. Interestingly, in July, both candidates appear to have appealed to both compromisers and ideologues. (Recall that among Democrats, most activists are compromisers). Support for Clinton is greater, but the balance is not as lopsided as it is among party leaders.

By January, Clinton's support had not grown much. Clinton supporters are more likely to express their concern for compromise, while Sanders supporters are far more likely to say they wish to stick to their principles. The causal direction in this change is unclear. As the campaign wore on, clashes between the candidates centered on exactly this question. It is more than likely that some of each candidate's supporters changed to reflect the argument being made by their candidate.

But the argument is real. Sanders does have a record of compromising on some issues. This is how he explains his support for gun rights, for instance. But on balance, the rhetoric of the campaign has been Clinton saying that she needs to compromise, sometimes with Wall Street or Republicans or others, to

FIGURE 9
Support for Candidates among Democratic Activists

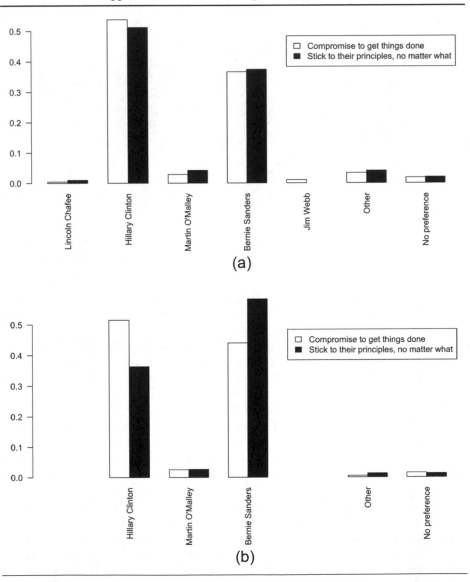

accomplish her goals, and Sanders saying that such compromise threatens a politician's integrity.

There is also evidence that voters divide in this way. Dan Hopkins (2016) has shown that the one thing that best explains support for Clinton over Sanders is support for Barack Obama. Democratic voters who think that Obama betrayed them were in favor of Sanders, whereas those who were happy with Obama's performance prefered Clinton.

This is not to say that the only division between Clinton and Sanders is on compromise. Clinton consistently earned the votes of nonwhites, while Sanders did much better among whites, but especially liberal whites. But from the perspective of policy demanders, the difference on racial issues between Clinton and Sanders was not huge. Sanders had a history with the civil rights movement, and after stumbling in his response to Black Lives Matter activists, he shifted his rhetoric on the issue. Meanwhile, Black Lives Matter has not been uncritical of Clinton—they have tied her to her husband's incarceration policies in the 1990s. Race is an area where the cleavage is much more significant among voters than it is for party leaders. Without question, cleavages other than the compromise divide matter for the Democrats, just as they do for the Republicans.

That the Democrats have better contained their ideological faction does not mean it is not there, or that it does not play a significant role in the party. Sanders forced Clinton to discuss issues that she would not have otherwise. Clinton's voting record is actually not that far from Sanders's, but her campaign would not have been as far to the Left as it is had Sanders not run.

Implications

Conventional wisdom now holds that polarization is asymmetric (Mann and Ornstein 2012). Whatever is happening, it is more severe in the Republican Party. What is less clear is why this is. The lens of ideological coalitions and compromise sheds some light on the pattern. Both parties clearly have ideological cores. The Democratic primaries featured a debate over which candidate was the "real progressive," and Clinton campaigned as a "progressive who likes to get things done." The Republican candidates repeatedly attacked Donald Trump over his ideological heresies.

Both parties also clearly have compromisers. In the national party, regulars such as Paul Ryan and Jeb Bush or Barack Obama and Hillary Clinton are much preferred to ideologues like Ted Cruz or Bernie Sanders. Cruz, a perfect ideologue, struggled to get support from the more powerful party regular wing. Nonideologues Clinton and Trump have prevailed among voters. But the conservative ideological coalition has been much more successful in exerting influence within the Republican Party than the liberal coalition has been among Democrats. The psychological tendency for conservatives to be less likely to embrace complexity or compromise might explain why there are more ideological purists on the Right, but that would not explain the trend.

It is hard to believe that the Democrats are simply better at blocking ideologues. The party led the way in bringing intraparty democracy to presidential nominations. The McGovern-Fraser reforms were introduced after 1968 in direct response to the demands of an ideological wing of the party, and it is hard to see the modern Democratic Party institutions as particularly effective at blocking the participation of some groups.

But Democrats did, in this cycle, succeed at coordinating around a party regular candidate, however. Until recently, the conventional wisdom had been that

Republicans were better at such coordination, with Democrats struggling in 1988, 2004, and 2008. Had they faced a similar problem in 2016, Sanders might look like Donald Trump.

It is possible that liberal ideologues are simply less interested in engaging. Certainly they have not been as active down-ballot as their Tea Party analogue, so far. But Sanders's supporters were just as effective in grassroots warfare in the nomination process as Tea Party favorite Cruz; both candidates dominated the caucuses, which are particularly open to activists.

In short, we see very similar dynamics playing out in both parties, but with much less success among Democrats. None of this is to say that other issue cleavages do not matter. Racial issues, particularly as a matter of emphasis, remain important in the Democratic Party, and Sanders has also exploited the internal disagreement on trade. Republicans differ on trade as well.

One way in which voters on both sides of these or any other cleavage might become more satisfied is if the United States had more than two viable parties. Both the Sanders and Trump camps complained about how both parties' nomination processes were not open to party outsiders, but both were compelled to run in a major party because only those parties have a shot at victory.

Even in multiparty systems, we often observe two major parties or alliances of parties. At the government formation stage, being biggest still has its advantages. These parties are made up of more party-regular type politicians, who take on the responsibilities of governance. Smaller parties pressure the major parties for policy concessions (Bawn and Rosenbluth 2006).

In a two-party system, this pressure comes from within the parties. All parties are about compromise, but parties with broad coalitions must be especially about compromise. One reason the Republicans appear to be more dysfunctional may simply be that they are overrun by ideologues, while our two-party presidential system requires party regulars.

Notes

1. In particular, they are long coalitions, meaning that they are semipermanent logrolls among a subset of political actors. That is, not wide enough to include everyone, but rather long over time or at least over many issues (Aldrich 1995).

2. See also Cohen et al. (2008); Karol (2009); Masket (2009).

3. In this article, I stop short of developing or exploring such a model in a mathematically rigorous way, but there is work in this area, notably models of long coalitions (Schwartz 1989; Aldrich 1995; Bawn 1999; Bawn and Noel 2007).

4. There is especially a tendency for ideological allies to see party regulars as moderates and ideological opponents to see them as extremists. See for example Jacobson (2006).

5. Rand Paul also deviates a great deal from the traditional conservative coalition, but not for reasons three and four above, and not in the way that Bush, Kasich, and others do. Intra-ideological disagreements are still present and very interesting, but given the poor showing of both Paul and his father Ron Paul, it is clear that this cleavage is not especially significant this year.

6. The debt ceiling highlights the degree to which ideologues are just as motivated by electoral concerns. It may not be so much that they think the world is a better place for not having raised the debt ceiling, but that they need to signal that they oppose "politics as usual."

7. By the insightful David Karol (personal communication).

References

Abramowitz, Alan. 2010. *The disappearing center: Engaged citizens, polarization, and American democracy*. New Haven, CT: Yale University Press.

Abramowitz, Alan, and Kyle Saunders. 2005. Why can't we all just get along? The reality of a polarized America. *The Forum* 3 (2). doi:10.2202/1540-8884.1076.

Ahler, Douglas J., and David E. Broockman. 2016. Does elite polarization imply poor representation? *A new perspective on the "disconnect" between politicians and voters*. Working Paper, Stanford University, Stanford, CA.

Aldrich, John. 1995. *Why parties? The origin and transformation of political parties in America*. Chicago, IL: University of Chicago Press.

Barbour, Henry, Sally Bradshaw, Ari Fleischer, Zori Fonalledas, and Glenn McCall. 2013. *Growth and opportunity project*. Available from http://goproject.gop.com/rnc_growth_opportunity_book_2013.pdf.

Bawn, Kathleen. 1999. Constructing "us": Ideology, coalition politics, and false consciousness. *American Journal of Political Science* 43 (2): 303–34.

Bawn, Kathleen, Knox Brown, Angela Ocampo, Shawn Patterson, John Ray, and John Zaller. 2015. Social choice and coordination problems in open house primaries. Paper presented at the annual meeting of the American Political Science Association.

Bawn, Kathleen, and Hans Noel. 2007. Long coalitions under electoral uncertainty: The electoral origins of political parties. Paper presented at the annual meeting of the Midwest Political Science Association. Chicago, IL.

Bawn, Kathleen, and Francis Rosenbluth. 2006. Short versus long coalitions: Electoral accountability and the size of the public sector. *American Journal of Political Science* 50 (2): 251–65.

Bawn, Kathleen, Marty Cohen, David Karol, Seth Masket, Hans Noel, and John R. Zaller. 2012. A theory of political parties: Groups, policy demands and nominations in American politics. *Perspectives on Politics* 10 (3): 571–97.

Broockman, David E. 2016. Approaches to studying representation. *Legislative Studies Quarterly* 41 (1): 181–215.

Cohen, Marty, David Karol, Hans Noel, and John Zaller. 2008. *The party decides: Presidential nominations before and after reform*. Chicago, IL: University of Chicago Press.

Converse, Philip. 1964. The nature of belief systems in mass publics. In *Ideology and discontent*, ed. David Apter, 206–61. New York, NY: Free Press.

Ellis, Christopher, and James A. Stimson. 2012. *Ideology in America*. New York, NY: Cambridge University Press.

Feinstein, Brian, and Eric Schickler. 2008. Platforms and partners: The civil rights realignment reconsidered. *Studies in American Political Development* 22:1–31.

Feinstein, Brian, Eric Schickler, and Kathryn Pearson. 2010. Congressional parties and civil rights politics from 1933 to 1972. *Journal of Politics* 72 (3): 672–89.

Fiorina, Morris P. 2005. *Culture war? The myth of a polarized America*. New York, NY: Pearson Longman.

Hopkins, Dan. 2016. Clinton voters like Obama more than Sanders supporters do. *FiveThirtyEight*. Available from http://fivethirtyeight.com.

Jacobson, Gary. 2006. Disconnected or joined at the hip (Comment on Morris P. Fiorina and Matthew S. Levandusky's "Disconnected: The Political Class vs. the People"). In *Red and blue nation?* vol. 1, eds. Pietro S. Nivola and David W. Brady, 85–95. Washington, DC: The Brookings Institutions.

Karol, David. 2009. *Party position change in American politics: Coalition management*. New York, NY: Cambridge University Press.

Kinder, Donald R., and Nathan P. Kalmoe. Forthcoming. *Neither liberal nor conservative: Ideological innocence in the American public*. Chicago, IL: University of Chicago Press.

Layman, Geoffrey C., Thomas M. Carsey, John C. Green, Richard Herrera, and Rosalyn Cooperman. 2010. Activists and conflict extension in American party politics. *American Political Science Review* 104 (2): 324–46.

Levendusky, Matt. 2009. *The partisan sort: How liberals became Democrats and how conservatives became Republicans*. Chicago, IL: University of Chicago Press.

Mann, Thomas E., and Norman J. Ornstein. 2012. *It's even worse than it looks*. New York, NY: Basic Books.

Masket, Seth. 2009. *No middle ground: How informal party organizations control nominations and polarize legislatures*. Ann Arbor, MI: The University of Michigan Press.

Noel, Hans. 2012. The coalition merchants: The ideological roots of the civil rights realignment. *Journal of Politics* 74 (1): 156–73.

Noel, Hans. 2013. *Political ideologies and political parties in America*. New York, NY: Cambridge University Press.

Noel, Hans. 2014. Separating ideology from party in roll call data. Working Paper, Georgetown University, Washington, DC.

Polsby, Nelson W., and Aaron B. Wildavsky. 1968. *Presidential elections: Strategies of American electoral politics*. 2nd ed. New York, NY: Charles Scribner's Sons.

Poole, Keith, Howard Rosenthal, and Christopher Hare. 2015. House: Vote on clean DHS funding bill. Voteview Blog. Available from https://voteviewblog.wordpress.com.

Schickler, Eric. 2016. *Racial realignment: The transformation of American liberalism, 1932–1965*. Princeton, NJ: Princeton University Press.

Schwartz, Thomas. 1989. *Why parties? Research memorandum*. Department of Political Science, University of California, Los Angeles.

Yglesias, Matthew. 2016a. How Bernie Sanders convinced me about free college. *Vox*. Available from http://www.vox.com.

Yglesias, Matthew. 2016b. There's a big problem with Bernie Sanders's free college plan. *Vox*. Available from http://www.vox.com.

Rise of the *Trumpenvolk*: Populism in the 2016 Election

By
J. ERIC OLIVER
and
WENDY M. RAHN

Despite the wide application of the label "populist" in the 2016 election cycle, there has been little systematic evidence that this election is distinctive in its populist appeal. Looking at historical trends, contemporary rhetoric, and public opinion data, we find that populism is an appropriate descriptor of the 2016 election and that Donald Trump stands out in particular as the populist par excellence. Historical data reveal a large "representation gap" that typically accompanies populist candidates. Content analysis of campaign speeches shows that Trump, more so than any other candidate, employs a rhetoric that is distinctive in its simplicity, anti-elitism, and collectivism. Original survey data show that Trump's supporters are distinctive in their unique combination of anti-expertise, anti-elitism, and pronationalist sentiments. Together, these findings highlight the distinctiveness of populism as a mechanism of political mobilization and the unusual character of the 2016 race.

Keywords: Donald Trump; content analysis; elections; political representation; populism; public opinion

The only antidote to decades of ruinous rule by a small handful of elites is a bold infusion of popular will. On every major issue affecting this country, the people are right and the governing elite are wrong. The elites are wrong on taxes, on the size of government, on trade, on immigration, on foreign policy.

—Donald J. Trump, *The Wall Street Journal*, April 14, 2016

By many accounts, 2016 is the year of the populist. The improbable popularity of Donald Trump and Bernie Sanders has been widely attributed to a massive wave of voter discontent with the governing classes. Many of the 2016 candidates, including Trump, Sanders, Ben Carson, and even Ted Cruz have been tagged

J. Eric Oliver is a professor of political science at the University of Chicago. He is the author of several books and has published numerous articles on local elections, public opinion, and political participation in American politics.

Correspondence: wrahn@umn.edu

DOI: 10.1177/0002716216662639

with the populist label. But while the term populist gets widely applied, its meaning is often unclear. How, for example, can the same term describe both a Jewish, Democratic socialist senator from Vermont whose central concern is the billionaire class and a billionaire New York real estate developer whose central concern is illegal immigration? Can they both be populists? And, more importantly, how can the concept of populism help us to understand this unusual election?

Looking at historical trends, contemporary rhetoric, and public opinion, we suggest that not only is populism an appropriate descriptor of many aspects of the 2016 election but that one candidate stands out in particular as the populist par excellence. Exploiting a large "representation gap," Donald Trump has enjoyed a ripe opportunity to make a strong populist claim to the presidency. Trump capitalized on this by employing a rhetoric that is distinctive in its simplicity, anti-elitism, and high degree of collectivist language. Trump's supporters echo these sentiments, exhibiting a unique combination of anti-expertise, anti-elitism, and pronationalism. Unlike supporters of the other "populist," Bernie Sanders, Trump's supporters are also distinctive in their high levels of conspiratorial thinking, nativism, and economic insecurity. The year 2016 is indeed the year of the populist, and Donald Trump is its apotheosis.

What Is Populism?

Populism is a promiscuous term used to describe a diverse set of political movements around the world. It is applied equally to rightist parties in Europe, leftist movements in Latin America, and anticorruption crusaders in Asia.[1] In the 2016 election cycle, it has been used to characterize candidates as diverse as Sanders on the Left, Ted Cruz on the Right, and Trump somewhere in between. Given this diversity, does the concept of populism still have utility?

A rich body of comparative research suggests that it does. Despite their obvious differences, populist movements share many latent tendencies. At its core, populism is a type of political rhetoric that pits a virtuous "people" against nefarious, parasitic elites who seek to undermine the rightful sovereignty of the common folk. As a style of political communication, populism has several notable traits. Its tone is Manichean, casting politics as a bifurcated struggle between "the people," on one hand, and a self-serving governing class undeserving of its advantaged position, on the other. Its goal is restorative, replacing the existing corruption with a political order that puts the people back in their proper place and that is more faithful to their longings and aspirations. Its worldview is apprehensive, suspicious of any claims to economic, political, or cultural privilege; for populists, the good is found in the common wisdom of the people rather than the pretensions of the expert.[2]

Wendy M. Rahn is a professor of political science at the University of Minnesota. Her research interests include public opinion, political participation, American political history, and food and health politics.

NOTE: We are grateful for the research assistance of Aaron Coggins and Henry Fronk at the University of Minnesota.

But while denigrating economic or political elites is a relatively straightforward maneuver, it is often more challenging to endow the "people" with a real and meaningful existence. Populist politicians do this in a number of ways. They typically start broadly by defining the "people" as anyone who is not an elite. By conjuring the existence of a solidary people who share ill-treatment at the hands of the governing classes, populists seek to transcend cleavages based on class or region (Kazin 1995; Taggart 2000). "Populists in established democracies claim they speak for the 'silent majority' of 'ordinary, decent people' whose interests and opinions are (they claim) regularly overridden by arrogant elites, corrupt politicians, and strident minorities" (Canovan 1999, 5). Populism also defines the "people" by appeals to economic and social nationalism (Gerteis and Goolsby 2005; Jansen 2011). Here, the nation, or "heartland," is the primordial basis for a shared identity (Taggart 2000). This construction of a "we" is facilitated also by the invocation of the people's enemies, both internal and external—the "people" often come to know who they are by who they are not. Consequently, nativism and racism are common in populist appeals, particularly in those European democracies facing immigration pressure. Latin American populism, on the other hand, while more inclusive of a variety of groups (Mudde and Rovira Kaltwasser 2013), frequently draws on the anticolonial ideology of *Americanismo* as a way to draw a circle around the national "we" (Rovira Kaltwasser 2014).

Of course, nearly all democratic politicians seek to align themselves with "the people," which is partly why the populist label gets so widely applied. But populists do more than simply paint themselves on the side of the majority; they make populist rhetoric the center of their campaigns. Anti-elitism and collectivism are the sine qua non of their political existence. Their whole purpose is to challenge the dominant order and give voice to the collective will, goals that are infused with a sense of urgency by proclaiming that a crisis exists (Moffitt 2015; Pappas 2012; Rooduijn 2014b).

Toward this end, populists often employ a distinctive style, one that is simple, direct, emotional, and frequently indelicate (Canovan 1999; Albertazzi and McDonnell 2008; Moffitt and Tormey 2014). By flaunting the usual rules of engagement, the populist's lack of decorum contributes to followers' perceptions of authenticity, distinguishing the populist from the usual "typical politician." Like a "drunken guest" (Arditi 2005) with "bad manners" (Moffit and Tormey 2014), the populist disrupts the normal dinner table, much to the discomfort, even alarm, of the usual patrons.

This transgressive political style signals to the people that the populist politician will go to great lengths to protect her interests, even if it means bending or breaking the rules. To members of the establishment, however, the people-centric and pugnaciousness of the putative populist's rhetoric is demagoguery, successful only because its listeners harbor antidemocratic sympathies (Stanley 2008).[3] But to many lay followers, the populist's distinctive antics provide a focal point to orient themselves, and criticism by established elites only serves to strengthen the bond between the leader and his or her followers (Panizza 2005).[4] A common identity and a sense of linked fate emerge through shared attachment to the populist politician rather than interpersonal attachment to individual group members. By "performing" populism, the psychological distance between populist leaders and their followers is reduced and the bonds among followers solidified.

Despite claiming to represent "the people," the populist's rhetoric is not uniformly embraced across the population. Certain types of people seem to be drawn to populism more than others. According to revisionist historians of the original Populist movement in the late nineteenth century, early American populists were anxious about their status in society, xenophobic, and prone to conspiracy theories (Hofstadter 1955).[5] Less pejoratively, Spruyt, Keppens, and Droogenbroeck (2016) contend that a somewhat similar syndrome is operative in contemporary European populism. They argue that globalization makes certain groups, particularly the less well-educated, insecure both about their labor market prospects and their status in society. Identifying with the "people" becomes a way to cope with the uncertainty and vulnerability of their precarious social position. Populism also allows the individual's problems to become grievances of "people like us," reducing individual responsibility and shifting blame outward. Yet despite the depth of comparative research, there are very few studies about populist sentiment in the United States.[6]

What also remains unclear is why populism is more prevalent at certain times rather than others. Elites, after all, are present in every democracy, yet populist movements are temporal and fleeting. Populist movements can arise in relatively egalitarian countries yet be largely absent from some of the most stratified. We suggest that a populist moment depends on the alignment of a number of key factors: the right political conditions, a charismatic populist leader, and the receptivity of an audience based on their own grievances and psychological predilections. In sum, a *populist moment* requires the right rhetoric spoken by the right person to the right audience at the right time. And, as we look to the data, the 2016 election has all the hallmarks of a populist moment.

Populism in Campaign Communication

The political rhetoric of the 2016 primary campaign was filled with populist rhetoric. This can be empirically demonstrated in a quantitative content analysis of the announcement speeches of the seven top presidential hopefuls (see, e.g., Bonokowski and Gidron 2016; Hawkins 2009; Jagers and Walgrave 2007; Rooduijn and Pauwels 2011; Rooduijn 2014a).[7] To assess the degree of "populist" rhetoric, we used a mix of our own custom content analysis "dictionaries" and the Diction software program. Diction has been used to score quantitatively a wide variety of political texts (Hart 2000; Hart, Childers, and Lind 2013; Hart et al. 2005).[8]

We start with two "dictionaries" that capture anti-establishment rhetoric, one corresponding to political elites and the other, to economic elites.[9] "Political populism" was measured with such words and phrases as politician(s), the government (in Washington), the system, special interests, IRS, lobbyists, donors, and campaign contributions. "Economic populism" includes the terms millionaires, the rich, the wealthy, CEOs, big banks, Wall Street, inequality, and corporations, among others. The word, "elites," was included in both dictionaries. The text of each announcement speech was matched to our anti-establishment dictionaries, and the number of matches was standardized as a percentage of total words. We also included a "blame" dictionary containing terms designating social inappropriateness (e.g., stupid, sloppy) and adjectives describing unfortunate circumstances such as troublesome and discouraging (Hart and Carroll 2013).

The first panel of Table 1 displays the rates of anti-establishment language for the candidates, measured as a percentage of total words. Sanders scores highest in economic populism, invoking business elites twice as often as Clinton. Trump and Carson, the two Republican outsiders, score highest in political populism, invoking political elites twice as often as even Sanders. Blame language is common among all candidates but especially high in both Trump's and Sanders's speeches.

A second feature of populist rhetoric is the creation of a unified people. We developed five scores that measure the candidates' degree of collectivism: references to the American people or Americans; references to "our country/nation;" the use of plural pronouns such as "we, they, our, and ours;" mentions of foreign countries or threats; and appeals to subnational groups. The latter measure is designed to assess the degree to which the candidates internally differentiate "the people" or treat them as a single, homogenous category.

The second panel of Table 1 displays the results of our people-centrism analysis. The two Democratic candidates invoked the collective nationalist terms far more often than the Republicans. Indeed, Donald Trump never referred to Americans or the American people, instead using the locution "our country." On the other hand, Republicans were also less likely to refer to specific groups by name compared with the Democrats.[10] In sharp contrast, candidates like Ben Carson and Donald Trump hardly ever name a specific group; instead, they were far more likely to invoke "we–they" collectivist constructions.[11] These populist candidates conjure a "people" not by amalgamations of specific groups or by even invoking the institutions of state, but by including themselves as part of the group.

Finally, we also used Diction and our own examination to characterize more stylistic and structural characteristics of the candidates' rhetoric to assess its simplicity and "everydayness." The last panel of Table 1 lists different measures of language simplicity including the use of short words and sentences, sentence variety, and appeals to common sense. In terms of simplicity, Carson, Kasich, and Trump stand out from the others. Their sentences are noticeably briefer than the other candidates' and they use shorter words. In addition, there is less variety in their choice of words,[12] and they appeal to common sense.[13] Donald Trump, Ben Carson, and, in most respects, John Kasich seem to speak the language of ordinary people.

In sum, Donald Trump employed the most consistently populist syntax, followed only by Ben Carson. Trump scores high in targeting political elites, blame language, invoking both foreign threats and collective notions of "our" and "they," and the simplicity and repetition of his language. Sanders's language, by contrast,

TABLE 1
Populist Language Scores among Seven Leading Presidential Candidates

	Carson	Clinton	Cruz	Kasich	Rubio	Sanders	Trump
Anti-establishment							
Blame°	2.23	2.63	1.47	2.71	1.37	3.90	3.43
Political %	0.60	0.13	0.21	0.24	0.22	0.23	0.61
Economic %	0.00	0.45	0.04	0.00	0.27	0.99	0.05
People-centrism							
The American people or Americans #	2	23	7	2	9	16	0
Our country or nation #	6	11	0	3	4	5	10
We–they %	5.69	4.45	2.31	5.06	5.63	3.75	6.12
Foreign countries international threats %	0.00	0.13	0.38	0.02	0.22	0.20	1.15
Subnational social categories %	0.34	1.89	0.50	1.02	1.04	0.58	0.10
Language simplicity							
Six-letter words %	14.81	21.33	22.89	11.94	20.63	20.83	13.81
Average words per sentence	12.74	14.91	17.80	13.21	21.00	21.38	9.55
Variety°	0.24	0.28	0.32	0.22	0.34	0.29	0.17
Present concern°	15.48	17.66	12.7	13.26	13.12	13.66	17.81
Appeal to common sense	Yes	No	No	Yes	No	No	Yes

NOTE: °Calculated using Diction.

scores high in economic populism, blame attribution, and invocations of "America" but employs a more complex and sophisticated language. Nor does he score high in the use of "we–they" collectivist rhetoric. Thus while Sanders may be "populist" in a strictly economic sense, his language is not nearly as "of the people" as either Carson's or Trump's.

Why Populism Now?

Our attention now turns to why 2016 is such a ripe time for a populist appeal. Although there is lots of speculation as to what motivates populist movements (economic conditions, class stratification, new media technologies, etc.), we assert that populism originates in a political source, namely, when existing political parties are not responding to the desires of large sections of the electorate. We call such conditions a "representation gap."

FIGURE 1
The Representation Gap

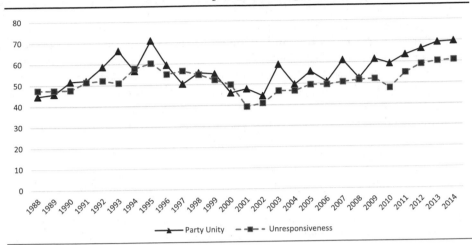

We measure the "representation gap" in two ways. First, we use Congressional Quarterly's party unity votes, votes on which a majority of Democrats opposed a majority of Republicans (we averaged House and Senate party unity votes). We then compare these scores to attitudes of the citizenry toward government responsiveness using different survey questions (e.g., Pew Research Center, American National Election Studies, Gallup) from 1988 to 2014:

—Do you agree or disagree with the following statement: Public officials don't care much about what people like me think.

—People like me don't have any say about what the government does.

—Generally speaking, elected officials in Washington lose touch with the people pretty quickly.

—Do you tend to feel or not feel the people in Washington are out of touch with the rest of the country?

—Voting gives people like me some say about how the government runs things.[14]

As illustrated in Figure 1, there are two points in the last quarter century where the public felt especially unrepresented, the mid-1990s and currently. In looking for explanations for the movement across this time series, we first considered macroeconomic variables such as growth in median household income and unemployment. None proved to be related. Next we examined subjective economic assessments in the form of the familiar Michigan Index of Consumer Sentiment with the same result. There is simply no indication that the economy in 2016 is either objectively weak or subjectively concerning (see also Sides, Tesler, and Vavreck, this volume). Nor is this time series related to rising income inequality.

Instead, the strongest correlation[15] is with the party unity scores. Both party unity and nonresponsiveness rise in the mid-1990s, drop again until 2010, and then rise in tandem in 2016. These findings dovetail nicely with Bartels's (this volume) analysis of "the missing middle." As he shows, the distance between the major parties' core supporters and swing voters is large and has been growing over time. In particular, the Republican base has grown more conservative in its ideology and in its opposition to government spending on services and to government's role in providing jobs, while the Democratic base is out of step from mass opinion on government aid to blacks and the government guarantee of jobs. Also interesting is his finding that swing voters were especially distant from the Republican base in 1996, the year in which party unity votes and the representation gap were equally high in our analysis.

In addition to high levels of partisan conflict, the mid-1990s shares many other interesting parallels with 2016. Both had populist "nonpoliticians" vying for office; in the '90s, it was Pat Buchanan, who worked in the Nixon White House but never held elective office, and H. Ross Perot. Both periods were characterized by expressions of heightened racial tension (the Los Angeles riots and Rodney King in 1992 and the O. J. Simpson trial in 1995; and Black Lives Matter in 2015) and concerns with immigration (California's Proposition 187 in 1994; the border crisis in Texas in 2014). Both periods followed economic recessions and particular catastrophes in the financial sector (the savings and loan crisis and the Great Recession). The national news media in both periods contained many more stories about economic inequality than in previous years.[16] By many measures, the mid-1990s and the mid-2010s look remarkably similar. These results also suggest why Donald Trump's brief presidential candidacy in 2000 never gained traction: by then, the representation gap had declined considerably from its mid-1990s height.

Populism in the People

A strong populism sentiment is also evident in the 2016 American electorate. We find this in a nationally representative Internet survey sample of 1,063 American adult citizens fielded between February 26 and March 3, 2016.[17] To gauge populist attitudes, we asked respondents a battery of fourteen questions about people's feelings toward the political process, experts and common wisdom, and attachment to an American identity. Some of these items were of our own construction while others were adapted from survey studies of populism in other contexts (Akkerman, Mudde, and Zaslove 2014; Elchardus and Spruyt 2016; Hawkins, Riding, and Mudde 2012; Spruyt, Keppens, and Droogenbroeck 2016; Stanley 2011). We then put the responses in a principal component analysis, a statistical method for identifying linearly uncorrelated variables. From this analysis, we find the survey questions load on three, separate dimensions related to populism (see Table 2).

The first dimension, *anti-elitism*, captures feelings of marginalization relative to wealth and political power. The items that load on this dimension include questions like "It doesn't really matter who you vote for because the rich control

TABLE 2
Loadings from Rotated Principle Components Analysis

Question	Anti-elitism	Mistrust experts	National affiliation
People like me don't have much say in what government does (Likert)	0.611		
Politics usually boils down to a struggle between the people and the powerful (Likert)	0.641		0.259
The system is stacked against people like me (Likert)	0.660		
It doesn't really matter who you vote for because the rich control both political parties (Likert)	0.686		
People at the top usually get there (because they have more talent and work harder / from some unfair advantage)	0.495		
I'd rather put my trust in the wisdom of ordinary people than the opinions of experts and intellectuals (Likert)		0.568	
When it comes to really important questions, scientific facts don't help very much (Likert)		0.712	
Ordinary people can really use the help of experts to understand complicated things like science and health (Likert)		0.696	
Politics is ultimately a struggle between good and evil (Likert)	0.386	0.474	
It would be unwise to trust the judgments of the American people for today's complicated political issues / I generally trust the collective judgments of the American people, even for complex political issues			0.614
I generally consider myself to be (different than most Americans / like most other Americans).			0.729
How important is being an American to who you are? (7-point scale)			0.692

both political parties"; "Politics usually boils down to a struggle between the people and the powerful"; "The system is stacked against people like me"; and "People at the top usually get there from some unfair advantage." Together, these questions reflect one of the core elements of populism, the feeling that a small group of wealthy and powerful elites holds all the levers of political power.

FIGURE 2
Partial Correlations of Secondary Variables with Three Dimensions of Populist Attitudes

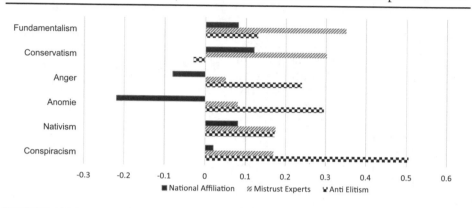

The second dimension, *mistrust of expertise*, indicates a general skepticism of science and expert opinion. It includes responses to the statements: "I'd rather put my trust in the wisdom of ordinary people than the opinions of experts and intellectuals"; "When it comes to really important questions, scientific facts don't help very much"; and "Ordinary people are perfectly capable of deciding for themselves what's true and what's not." Also loading on this dimension is the Manichean notion of politics being a struggle between good and evil. While the first dimension relates to issues of explicit political or economic power, the second dimension items reflect suspicion of knowledge claims and scientific expertise. They also reflect a faith in common wisdom, the idea that folk knowledge is more valid than expert opinion.

The third dimension is what we call *national affiliation*. These are items designed to gauge respondent's affiliation with, and similarity to, the American people and include: "I consider myself to be like ordinary Americans"; "It would be unwise to trust the judgments of the American people"; and "How important is being an American to your sense of self?" Unlike the first two dimensions, which are about opposition to elites, this dimension relates to a collectivist "American" identity.

Although these three dimensions are commonly attributed to populists, they often correspond to different and even contradictory types of attitudes. We can see this by comparing the populism factor scores with other demographic and attitudinal measures.[18] In Figure 2, we depict partial correlation coefficients for six attitudinal factors that are often associated with populism: ideology, anger at the federal government, anomie, nativism, conspiracism, and fundamentalism.[19]

The first two dimensions of populism, anti-elitism and mistrust of experts, share many of the same attitudinal correlates but in different degrees. Anti-elitism's largest correlation is with the conspiracy theory scale. Respondents who think that the system is stacked against them are far more likely to endorse conspiracy theories of all types than not. Conspiracy theories seem to function as a form of populist discourse (Fenster 2008). Not surprising, anti-elitists are less trusting of people in general and are more likely to be angry at the government. Anti-elitists are also more likely to be nativists and hold fundamentalist beliefs.[20]

The second dimension, mistrust of experts, has a slightly different pattern. Here the largest correlation is with fundamentalist Christian beliefs. People who put their faith in the wisdom of "ordinary" people are also more likely to believe in Biblical inerrancy and prophesy. They also score higher in conservatism. And, like anti-elitists, those mistrusting of experts also endorse more conspiracy theories. The mistrust-experts scale also correlates with nativism. This aspect of populism thus looks much more like an ideologically tinged dimension with stronger support among conservatives, particularly those with fundamentalist religious beliefs.

These patterns, however, contrast sharply with the third dimension, national affiliation. Here, we find few significant correlations with any of the attitudinal measures linked to the first two dimensions. Indeed, the only sizable correlations are with anomie and anger, and these are negative. In other words, people who place a lot of value on their American identity are generally more trusting of people and less angry at the American government. We also find that fundamentalists score slightly higher, on average, in their national affiliation scores.

This oppositional pattern between anti-elitism and national affiliation is evident throughout our data and not just with these items. For example, anti-elitists are far more likely to agree that "Congress is no longer an institution that speaks for the people" while nationalists are less likely to agree.[21] Conversely, nationalists are much more likely to agree that "when ordinary Americans come together, they usually prevail."[22]

Together, these findings highlight some of the paradoxes of populism. When the "people" are defined as the "nation" then the people are defined largely by their political and economic institutions; yet allegiance to a nation naturally entails allegiance to institutions and its leaders. This is why we see nationalists as being so much more positive about Congress and business and political elites and optimistic about their own political power. But at the same time, "the people" may also see themselves as also being alienated from the politicians and business leaders who run these institutions. Typically, these paradoxes are often resolved in the persona of the populist politician, often one who portrays himself or herself as against the dominant political establishment. Such leaders are able to rail against systemic inequities and the disenfranchisement of the "true" people while encouraging them to take charge of the situation, particularly by invoking collectivist language as indicated above.

These populist attitudes are most consistently in line among supporters of Donald Trump. Figure 3 shows the average score on each of the three populism dimensions according to responses to the question, "If the general election were held today, which candidate would you support?" The differences that immediately leap out are between supporters of Donald Trump and Ben Carson and the rest of the field. Among the candidates in late February 2016, both Carson and Trump were the only candidates whose supporters score higher, on average, for all three populist dimensions. This is particularly striking for Trump's supporters. They score the highest in mistrust of expertise and national affiliation of the entire sample; they also score second highest in political marginalization.

FIGURE 3
Average Scores on Populism Measures by Candidate

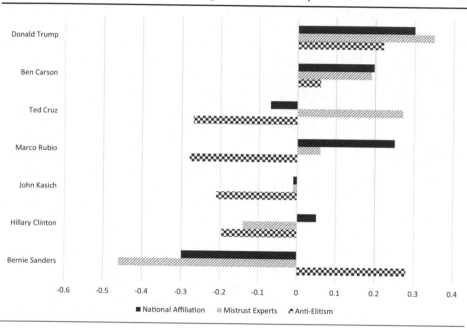

These results contrast with the supporters of Bernie Sanders, the other "populist" in the race. They too score quite high in system marginalization; in fact, they have the highest average score on this dimension in the entire sample. But they are the lowest scorers in both mistrusting experts and national affiliation. The difference with Trump supporters is particularly notable here. Whereas Trump's supporters have the highest averages both on national affiliation and mistrust of experts, Sanders's supporters score the lowest.

The scores for the rest of the candidates' voters also provide an interesting snapshot of their particular political appeal. Cruz's supporters are low in political marginalization but high in mistrust of expertise. The same holds for Rubio's, but they also score quite high in national affiliation. Supporters of Hillary Clinton and John Kasich interestingly have the most similar profiles, being below average in both political marginalization and mistrust of expertise but about average in national affiliation.

The distinctiveness of Trump's supporters is also evident in many of the attitudinal correlates of populism as depicted above. In Figure 4, we list the average scores on the conspiracism, nativism, anomie, and anger items.[23] A three-item financial pessimism scale was also added.[24] Once again, Trump's supporters are different from other voters in that they score above average on all of the attitudes that are related to populism. In the sample, they are the most financially pessimistic and conspiracy minded of all the voters. They also record high levels of mistrust and anger at the federal government. And they score highest on the nativism scale, although Cruz's supporters also score high on the nativist scale as well.

FIGURE 4
Average Attitudinal Measures by Candidate Preference

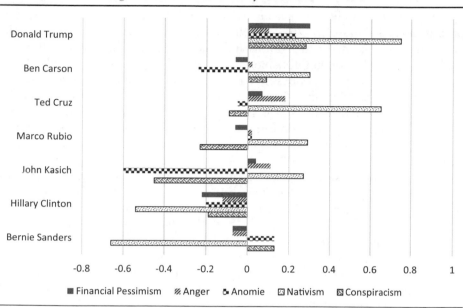

But in most ways, Trump's supporters are highly distinctive from their Republican counterparts. Compared with supporters of fellow populist Carson, for example, Trump's supporters are far more nativistic and socially alienated. Cruz's supporters also express high levels of anger at the government but tend to be more trusting of other people and less enthusiastic about conspiracy theories than Trump's. Kasich's supporters are also far less alienated and conspiracy minded as well.

Looking at all the candidates, the greatest contrasts are between Trump's and Clinton's supporters. On all of these attitudinal scales, Clinton's supporters are the mirror image of Trump's. Clinton voters are far below the sample averages on all the items. Where Trump's supporters see conspiracies, Clinton's do not; where the *Trumpenvolk* fear immigrants, Clinton voters embrace them. And where Trump's supporters express apprehension about their financial future, Clinton voters tend toward optimism.

A similar contrast also exists between Trump and Sanders. Sanders voters, much like Clinton's, are generally the opposite of Trump's supporters. This is especially the case with the nativism scale. The only "secondary" scale where Sanders voters resemble Trump's is in their social alienation. Yet Sanders's supporters are not especially angry at the federal government nor do they feel financially pessimistic. Their anti-elitism is largely based on issues of economic inequality and political marginalization; unlike Trump's supporters, they actively reject both a strong nationalist identity and a denigration of immigrant groups.

Conclusion

Few presidential candidates have invited as much critical scorn or surprising support as Donald Trump. Trump has been accused of being a fascist, an authoritarian, a demagogue, and a dangerous influence on American politics. But our analysis reveals that the improbable emergence of Donald Trump is ultimately rooted in American party politics. Yes, Donald Trump's simple, Manichean rhetoric is quintessentially populist. Yes, his supporters combine the distinct traits of a strong nationalist and ethnocentric identity with a deep suspicion of elites and cultural pretenses. But the opportunity for a Donald Trump presidency is ultimately rooted in a failure of the Republican Party to incorporate a wide range of constituencies.[25]

As with the populist insurgency of Pat Buchanan and Ross Perot in the mid-1990s, the emergence of Donald Trump is reflective of a particularly high level of party enmity as measured by party unity votes. As Bartels (this volume) shows, the distance between "swing voters" and the parties' core constituencies is greater now than it has been in 40 years. Like the original populists, the concerns of these voters are not reflected in either parties' policies. But, unlike their late-nineteenth-century counterparts—who combined nationalism with a strong economic and political reform agenda—today's populist constituency is finding its voice primarily on the Right rather than the Left. Kazin (1995) argues that around 1940, American populism "migrated" rightward as the reform impulse in American politics shifted to causes more important to the liberal intelligentsia than to average voters. Despite this year's attacks on economic elites and Sanders's trade nationalism, the American Left cannot credibly assemble "the people" so essential for a successful populist movement given its dependence on minorities and the more cosmopolitan and well educated. American populism in the twenty-first century has a conservative tinge and is felt most acutely in the political turmoil of the Republican Party.

Notes

1. Examples include Britain's Independence Party, France's National Front, Norway's Progress Party, Hugo Chavez in Venezuela, Lopez Obrador in Mexico, Evo Morales in Bolivia, and South Korea's Roo Moo-hyun.

2. See, e.g., Bonokowski and Gidron (2016), Hawkins (2009), Kazin (1995), Lee (2006), Mudde (2004), Panizza (2005), Stanley (2008), Rooduijn (2014a), Taggart (2000).

3. See Buric (2016), Milbank (2016), and Brooks (2016) on Donald Trump. Earlier populists have faced similar accusations from prominent leaders or commentators. William F. Buckley, for example, branded George Wallace as a would-be dictator (Kazin 1995). During the 2008 election, Sarah Palin earned such monikers as "a demagogue in a skirt" (Hoeller 2008) and "America's lipstick fascist" (Schaeffer 2008) by her critics.

4. In some accounts of populism, the identity of the populist leader is not considered a component of a minimal definition of populism (Mudde and Rovira Kaltwasser 2012). In other perspectives, the leader's charisma plays a more central role. Albertazzi and McDonnell (2008) argue that central to the leader-follower bond is supporters' views that their leader possesses extraordinary qualities while at the same time being one of, and one with, the people.

5. A new generation of historians (e.g., Goodwyn 1978; McNall 1988; Postel 2007) takes strong issue with this reading of the original Populists. The complexity of large-scale social movements like the Populists no doubt permits a variety of interpretations, especially in the absence of survey data on movement activists. Even when analysts agree on one feature, they may construe it in different ways. For Hofstadter (1955), the conspiracism of the Populists was pathological. Ostler (1995), on the other hand, sees conspiracism as a mobilization strategy used by populist leaders to legitimize extraordinary political action.

6. Most of the research on populism among the mass public in the United States is historical or interpretive and not based on public opinion. For exceptions, see Bakker, Rooduijn, and Schumacher (2016), Hawkins, Riding, and Mudde (2012), and Hawkins and Rovira Kaltwasser (2014).

7. Announcement speeches, unlike candidate debates, are not constrained by having to address particular topics. They typically offer a rationale for why the candidate is running, and, as such, are likely to features diagnoses of what ails the body politic and the candidate's proposed solutions to them.

8. See http://www.dictionsoftware.com/published-studies/

9. We follow here the strategy of Bonokowski and Gidron (2016). In their content analysis of presidential speeches, they find sharp differences between the political parties in terms of the content of the populist claims: Republicans were much more likely to critique political targets whereas Democrats concentrated on economic elites.

10. For example, Hillary Clinton's speech mentions specific social categories nearly ninety times, including factory workers, food servers, farmers, firefighters and police officers, Mexican farmworkers, children with disabilities, poor people, single parents, EMTs, construction workers, women of color, immigrant families, and LGBT Americans. In their own overtime analysis of the phrase, *the American people*, Hart et al. (2005) suggest that the token has been used by candidates as *rhetorical compensation* for the increasing diversity of the American public, a political version of "protesting too much."

11. Consider, for example, these lines from Ben Carson's announcement: "That's who we are. We, Americans, we take care of each other. That's why we are called the United States of America." Counterpose a "we" with a "they" and a boundary is created between the people and their antagonists. In Donald Trump's words: "When do we beat Mexico at the border? They're laughing at us, at our stupidity. And now they are beating us economically. They are not our friend, believe me. But they're killing us economically."

12. Defined as the number of different words divided by total words. Calculated by Diction.

13. Our conclusions are similar to those reached by Viser (2015) and Zhong (2016) but using different methods.

14. The survey questions are coded such that the series measures political *un*responsiveness, and so higher values are indicative of a larger representation gap.

15. $r = .73$

16. Leslie McCall's (2013) content analysis of news magazine coverage of inequality themes over the period from 1980 to 2010 finds a sharp spike in 1994 and 1995. Using Factiva, we counted the number of stories in the *New York Times* that mentioned inequality in the headline or lead paragraph. The number more than tripled between 2011 and 2015.

17. The survey took approximately 16 minutes, on average, to complete. The survey was then weighted based on age, education, race, ideology, and gender to best approximate a nationally representative sample.

18. From the rotated factor loadings, we created three factor scores, one for each of the dimensions listed above (anti-elitism, distrust expertise, and national affiliation). The factor scores all have a mean value of zero and a standard deviation of one.

19. Ideology is measured on a five-point scale from very liberal to very conservative. Anger is measured with a five-point scale (pleased, satisfied, indifferent, frustrated, angry) in response to the question, "What are your feelings about the federal government?" Anomie is a scale comprising two questions "Do you think most people would try to (take advantage of you given the chance/be fair)" and "Most people can be trusted/You can't be too careful in dealing with people." Nativism is a scale comprising three items about support for a border (three-point scale), perceptions of whether too many immigrants are criminals (five-point scale), and opinions on whether immigrants are more of a burden or benefit to America. The conspiracism scale was measured by support for five conspiracy theories about the FDA and pharmaceutical companies, public health officials hiding data linking vaccines and autism, whether Wall Street intentionally orchestrated the 2008 recession, whether a secret cabal controls things, and whether the government

helped to plan the attacks of 9/11 (see Oliver and Wood 2014). Fundamentalism is measured with Likert scales on statements about biblical inerrancy, End Times prophesy, the power of prayer, and hidden Bible codes. The correlations with all the attitudinal variables control for education, age, ideology, gender, and race. The correlations with ideology only control for education, age, gender, and race.

20. They also tend to be less educated on average.

21. Respondents were asked how much they agreed with the statement on a five-point Likert scale. Anti-elitism has .32 correlation, national affiliation a –.11 correlation.

22. The full statement was "Although special interests sometimes prevail, when ordinary Americans come together they usually prevail." Responses were on a five-point Likert scale. It had a –.19 correlation with anti-elitism, a .21 correlation with national affiliation.

23. To make them comparable, for each of the scales, the individual items were put in a principle component analysis that generated a factor score with the mean value set to 0 and a standard deviation of 1. The anger item was rescaled so that its lowest value was –1 and highest value was 1.

24. Financial pessimism was measured by responses to three items: "When you think your children are your age, will their standard of living be (better/same/worse) than yours?" "Do you feel anxious about having enough money?" (five-point scale); and "In the coming year, do you think your finances will (get worse/ stay the same/get better)?"

25. David Frum's (2016) analysis is particularly penetrating on this aspect of Trump's appeal.

References

Akkerman, Agnes, Cas Mudde, and Andrej Zaslove. 2014. How populist are the people? Measuring populist attitudes in voters. *Comparative Political Studies* 47 (9): 1324–53.

Albertazzi, Daniele, and Duncan McDonnell. 2008. Introduction: The sceptre and the spectre. In *Twenty-first century populism: The spectre of Western European democracy*, eds. Daniele Albertazzi and Duncan McDonnell, 1–11. New York, NY: Palgrave Macmillan.

Arditi, Benjamin. 2005. Populism as an internal periphery of democratic politics. In *Populism and the mirror of democracy*, ed. Franciso Panizza, 72–117. New York, NY: Verso.

Bakker, Bert N., Matthijs Rooduijn, and Gijs Schumacher. 2016. The psychological roots of populist voting: Evidence from the United States, the Netherlands and Germany. *European Journal of Political Research* 55 (2): 302–20.

Bartels, Larry M. 2016. Failure to converge: Presidential candidates, core partisans, and the missing middle in American electoral politics. *The ANNALS of the American Academy of Political and Social Science* (this volume).

Bonikowski, Bart, and Noam Gidron. 2016. The populist style in American politics: Presidential campaign discourse, 1952–1996. *Social Forces* 94 (4): 1593–621.

Brooks, David. 26 February 2016. The governing cancer of our time. *New York Times*.

Buric, Fedja. 3 March 2016. Trump's not Hilter, he's Mussolini. *Salon*.

Canovan, M. 1999. Trust the people! Populism and the two faces of democracy. *Political Studies* 47 (1): 2–16.

Elchardus, Mark, and Bram Spruyt. 2016. Populism, persistent Republicanism and declinism: An empirical analysis of populism as a thin ideology. *Government and Opposition* 51 (1): 111–33.

Fenster, Mark. 2008. *Conspiracy theories: Secrecy and power in American culture*. Rev. and updated ed. Minneapolis, MN: University of Minnesota Press.

Frum, David. Jan/Feb 2016. The great Republican revolt. *The Atlantic*. Available from http://www.theatlantic.com.

Gerteis, Joseph, and Alyssa Goolsby. 2005. Nationalism in America: The case of the populist movement. *Theory and Society* 34 (2): 197–225.

Goodwyn, Lawrence. 1978. *The populist moment*. Oxford: Oxford University Press.

Hart, Roderick P. 2000. *Campaign talk*. Princeton, NJ: Princeton University Press.

Hart, Roderick P., and Craig Carroll. 2013. *Diction 7: The text analysis program*. Austin, TX: Digitext Inc.

Hart, Roderick P., Jay P. Childers, and Colene J. Lind. 2013. *Political tone: How leaders talk and why*. Chicago, IL: The University of Chicago Press.

Hart, Roderick P., Sharon E. Jarvis, William P. Jennings, and Deborah Smith-Howell. 2005. *Political keywords: Using language that uses us*. New York, NY: Oxford University Press.

Hawkins, K. A. 2009. Is Chavez populist? Measuring populist discourse in comparative perspective. *Comparative Political Studies* 42 (8): 1040–67.

Hawkins, Kirk, and Cristóbal Rovira Kaltwasswer. 2014. The populist specter in contemporary Chile. Paper presented at the Annual Meeting of the Latin American Studies Association.

Hawkins, Kirk, Scott Riding, and Cas Mudde. 2012. Measuring populist attitudes. Political Concepts: Committee on Concepts and Methods, Working Paper Series, Number 55.

Hoeller, Susie. 9 November 2008. A demagogue in a suit. *The Huffington Post*.

Hofstadter, Richard. 1955. *The age of reform*. New York, NY: Knopf.

Jansen, Robert S. 2011. Populist mobilization: A new theoretical approach to populism. *Sociological Theory* 29 (2): 75–96.

Jagers, Jan, and Stefaan Walgrave. 2007. Populism as political communication style: An empirical study of political parties' discourse in Belgium. *European Journal of Political Research* 46 (3): 319–45.

Kazin, Michael. 1995. *The populist persuasion*. New York, NY: Basic Books.

Lee, Michael J. 2006. The populist chameleon: The people's party, Huey Long, George Wallace, and the populist argumentative frame. *Quarterly Journal of Speech* 92 (4): 355–78.

McCall, Leslie. 2013. *The undeserving rich: American beliefs about inequality, opportunity, and redistribution*. Cambridge: Cambridge University Press.

McNall, Scott G. 1988. *The road to rebellion: Class formation and Kansas populism, 1865–1900*. Chicago, IL: University of Chicago Press.

Milbank, Dana. 7 March 2016. Trump's flirtation with fascism. *Washington Post*.

Moffitt, Benjamin. 2015. How to perform crisis: A model for understanding the key role of crisis in contemporary populism. *Government and Opposition* 50 (2): 189–217. doi:10.1017/gov.2014.13.

Moffitt, Benjamin, and Simon Tormey. 2014. Rethinking populism: Politics, mediatisation and political style: Rethinking populism. *Political Studies* 62 (2): 381–97. doi:10.1111/1467-9248.12032.

Mudde, Cas. 2004. The populist zeitgeist. *Government and Opposition* 39 (4): 542–63.

Mudde, Cas, and Cristóbal Rovira Kaltwasser. 2012. Populism and (liberal) democracy: A framework for analysis. In *Populism in Europe and the Americas: Threat or corrective for democracy?* eds. Cas Mudde, and Cristóbal Rovira Kaltwasser, 1–26. New York, NY: Cambridge University Press.

Mudde, Cas, and Cristóbal Rovira Kaltwasser. 2013. Exclusionary vs. inclusionary populism: Comparing contemporary Europe and Latin America. *Government and Opposition* 48 (2): 147–74.

Oliver, J. Eric, and Thomas J. Wood. 2014. Conspiracy theories and the paranoid style(s) of mass opinion. *American Journal of Political Science* 58 (4): 952–66.

Ostler, Jeffrey. 1995. The rhetoric of conspiracy and the formation of Kansas populism. *Agricultural History* 61 (1): 1–27.

Panizza, Francisco. 2005. Populism and the mirror of democracy. In *Populism and the mirror of democracy*, ed. Francisco Panizza, 1–31. New York, NY: Verso.

Pappas, Takis. S. 2012. Populism emergent: A framework for analyzing its contexts, mechanics, and causes. EUI Working Papers RSCAS 2012/01. European University Institute, Florence Italy.

Postel, Charles. 2007. *The populist vision*. Oxford: Oxford University Press.

Rooduijn, Matthijs. 2014a. The mesmerising message: The diffusion of populism in public debates in Western European media. *Political Studies* 62 (4): 726–44.

Rooduijn, Matthijs. 2014b. The nucleus of populism: In search of the lowest common denominator. *Government and Opposition* 49 (4): 573–99. doi:10.1017/gov.2013.30.

Rooduijn, Matthijs, and Teun Pauwels. 2011. Measuring populism: Comparing two methods of content analysis. *West European Politics* 34 (6): 1272–83.

Rovira Kaltwasser, Cristóbal. 2014. Latin American populism: Some conceptual and normative lessons. *Constellations* 21 (4): 494–504.

Schaeffer, Frank. 6 October 2008. Sarah Palin: America's lipstick fascist. *The Huffington Post*.

Sides, John, Michael Tesler, and Lynn Vavreck. 2016. The electoral landscape of 2016. *The ANNALS of the American Academy of Political and Social Science* (this volume).

Spruyt, B., G. Keppens, and F. Van Droogenbroeck. 2016. Who supports populism and what attracts people to it? *Political Research Quarterly* 69 (2): 335–46.

Stanley, Ben. 2008. The thin ideology of populism. *Journal of Political Ideologies* 13 (1): 95–110.

Stanley, Ben. 2011. Populism, nationalism, or national populism? An analysis of Slovak voting behaviour at the 2010 parliamentary election. *Communist and Post-Communist Studies* 44 (4): 257–70.

Taggart, Paul A. 2000. *Populism.* Concepts in the Social Sciences. Philadelphia, PA: Open University Press.

Viser, Matt. 20 October 2015. For presidential hopefuls, simpler language resonates. *Boston Globe.*

Zhong, Weifeng. 2016. *The candidates in their own words: A textual analysis of 2016 presidential debates.* Washington, DC: American Enterprise Institute. Available from www.aei.org.

National Forces in State Legislative Elections

By
STEVEN ROGERS

The race for the White House is at the top of the ticket, but voters will also choose more than 5,000 state legislators in November 2016. While voters elect and hold the president responsible for one job and state legislators for another, the outcomes of their elections are remarkably related. In analyses of elite and voter behavior in state legislative elections, I show that legislators affiliated with the president's party—especially during unpopular presidencies—are the most likely to be challenged, and compared with individual assessments of the state legislature, changes in presidential approval have at least three times the impact on voters' decision-making in state legislative elections. Thus, while state legislatures wield considerable policymaking power, legislators' electoral fates appear to be largely out of their control.

Keywords: elections; state legislatures; presidential elections; state politics; coattails; challenger entry; voter behavior

Presidential elections capture the interest of both voters and political scientists. The average television ratings for the 2016 Republican presidential debates exceeded that for the 2015 World Series, and much of

Steven Rogers is an assistant professor at Saint Louis University, whose research on elections and state politics has appeared in the American Journal of Political Science *and* Legislative Studies Quarterly. *Rogers is currently working on a book manuscript—Accountability in American Legislatures—that addresses whether elections hold state legislators accountable.*

NOTE: I thank Larry Bartels, Brandice Canes-Wrone, Joshua Clinton, and Nolan McCarty for their guidance regarding this project. I am additionally grateful for assistance from Sarah Binder, Nicholas Carnes, Michael Donnelly, and Eric Lawrence, along with feedback from the Princeton Politics American Graduate Research Seminar, 2012 Southern Political Science Association Annual Meeting, State Politics and Policy Conference, and Midwest Political Science Association Annual Meeting.

Correspondence: smrogers@slu.edu

DOI: 10.1177/0002716216662454

FIGURE 1
Democratic Seat Change in State House and U.S. House Elections

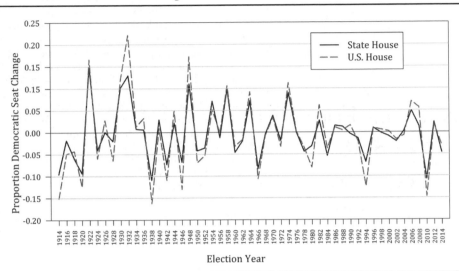

NOTE: Nationwide proportion of seats won or lost by the Democratic Party in state house or U.S. House elections over the last one hundred years.

scholars' attention (e.g., this volume) is focused on the presidential election. Between a Trump presidential candidacy and the potential for the first female president, the interest in presidential politics is not surprising, but what may be surprising is how closely related the race for The White House is to the thousands of state house elections that will also occur this November.

The relationship between national and state politics is suggested by a simple graph. Figure 1 illustrates the nationwide seat change for the Democratic Party in state (black solid line) and U.S. House elections (grey dashed line) over the past 100 years. Legislative seats clearly changed party hands in both federal and state contests each year, but the similarity between federal and state elections is striking. In all but five elections, the party that gained seats in Congress also made net gains in state legislatures. While the correlation (.95) is not definitive, it strongly suggests that there is a common dimension underlying both federal and state elections.

The existence of such a dimension challenges the founders' vision for the American federal system. The founders argued that "the federal constitution forms a happy combination; the great and aggregated interests being referred to the national, the local and particular to the State legislatures" (Madison 1787). Under this conception of government, federal legislators handle national issues; state legislators handle state issues; and voters hold each of these sets of legislators accountable for their respective tasks through elections (Hamilton 1788). Following these expectations, one could look to Figure 1 and explain that

Republicans took control of Congress in 1994 and 2010 because of Democrats' unpopular health care reforms. The explanation, however, is less immediately discerned—at least in regard to accountability—for why Republicans gained hundreds of state legislative seats in each of these elections. Why Republicans made substantial gains in state legislatures in 1994 and 2010 becomes clearer when one disregards the idea that "all politics is local." Tip O'Neil used this famous phrase prior to being elected to the Massachusetts state legislature in 1936, and consistent with theories of electoral accountability (e.g., Ferejohn 1986), this characterization of politics implies that state legislators must consider looming judgments at the ballot box when making decisions regarding state workers' rights, education polices, or raising taxes (e.g., Hamilton 1788; Key and Cummings 1966; Arnold 1992). Otherwise, they will lose their jobs.

Figure 1 suggests and the analyses here provide more systematic evidence that Tip O'Neil's characterization of politics is wrong. Instead of being local affairs, state legislative elections are dominated by national politics. To demonstrate this, I study the behavior of political elites and voters in state legislative elections. I find legislators affiliated with the president's party—especially during unpopular presidencies—are the most likely to face major party challengers, and compared with individuals' assessments of the state legislature, changes in presidential approval have at least three times the impact on voters' decision-making in state legislative elections. With both elites and voters responding to national instead of state legislative politics, state legislators' electoral fates appear largely out of their own control.

Presidential Politics in Legislative Elections

Political scientists have long documented the relationship between presidential politics and the behavior of both elites and voters in lower level elections. Jacobson (1989) and Lublin (1994), for example, argue that challengers to sitting members of Congress strategically account for presidential politics before deciding to contest an incumbent for their seat. Additionally, there is a rich literature on voter behavior in congressional elections focusing on presidential coattails (e.g., Campbell 1960), congressional elections serving as a referendum on the president (e.g., Tufte 1975), and midterm elections "balancing" the congressional and executive branches of government (e.g., Erikson 1988). Each of these studies provides evidence of a relationship between the executive and legislative politics in federal elections.

The Constitution prescribes that members of Congress work with the president to establish federal policies, so it is perhaps unsurprising that there is a relationship between presidential politics and congressional elections. If voters want to better ensure the president's proposals become law, they can vote the president's copartisans into Congress. State legislators also have some role in federal politics, such as in redistricting or recent Medicaid expansions, but their primary responsibility is state lawmaking. Recent state laws have curbed collective bargaining in Ohio and automatically registered voters in Oregon. These specific policies are in addition to the decisions state legislators across the country make when appropriating their $800 billion in state tax revenue each year. To promote representative policymaking, theories of electoral accountability suggest voters will assess these policies and determine whether the policy-makers should keep their jobs (Ferejohn 1986; but see also Fearon 1999).

Despite state legislators' important policymaking responsibilities, there are repeated indicators that "the American people are not boiling with concern about the workings of their state government" (Key 1956, 3). A 2009 Yale University poll found that fewer than half as many voters closely followed news about state politics as did national politics (Leiserowitz, Maibach, and Roser-Renouf 2009). In turn, less than 20 percent of voters can identify their state legislator (Vanderbilt University poll 2013), and many have undefined views of their legislature. Approximately 21 percent of respondents to the 2008 Cooperative Congressional Election Study were "not sure" whether they approved of their state legislature as compared to the 2 percent of respondents who had a similar lack of opinion regarding President Bush. These disparities may not be surprising considering the meager amount of media attention state legislative politics receives, even at the local level. When monitoring news coverage of political campaigns leading up to the 2004 presidential election, the Lear Center found that only 1 percent of local news coverage was devoted to state legislative elections compared with 61 percent of coverage devoted to the presidential election (Kaplan, Goldstein, and Hale 2005).

With little attention given to the legislature, voters in need of an assessment of state political actors could heuristically turn to their more accessible evaluation of the president (Tversky and Kahneman 1974; Kahneman and Frederick 2002; see also Gabaix and Laibson 2005).[1] This behavior by voters is a by-product of parties "[imposing] great political simplicity on the most complex governmental system of the world" (Schattschneider 1942, 53). A shared party label between the president and state legislators, however, may oversimplify the electoral process. State legislative elections could become "second-order" elections analogous to European Parliament elections, in which votes are cast "on the basis of factors in the main political arena of the nation" (Reif and Schmitt 1980, 9). Second-order elections are unlikely to serve what is presumably elections' first-order purpose: to hold state legislators accountable for their own performance.

At least two conditions must be satisfied for state legislative elections to serve their first-order purpose. Voters must have a fair opportunity to cast a ballot against the policy-makers, and votes must be meaningfully connected to what policy-makers are doing themselves (Powell 2000, 51). To satisfy the former condition, voters need a candidate to emerge to challenge the incumbent, and to satisfy the latter condition, there needs to be a strong relationship between how an elected official performs in office and in elections. The next sections illustrate how national politics affects the extent to which both these conditions are satisfied through analyses of challenger entry and voter decision-making in state legislative elections.

Presidential Politics and Challenger Entry in State Legislative Elections

The first condition for accountability requires that voters have an alternative choice to the incumbent in an election. Alternative choices in state legislative elections, however, are relatively rare compared with congressional elections. Figure 2 illustrates the proportion of U.S. House and state incumbents who faced major party challengers in presidential election years since the 1970s.[2] On average, 20 percent more U.S. House incumbents face challengers compared with state house incumbents. In more recent elections, a third of state legislative incumbents did not face a challenger in either the primary or general elections from 1992 to 2010 (Rogers 2015). Otherwise stated, a third of state legislative incumbents won reelection just by signing up.

The low levels of challenger entry in state legislative elections illustrated by Figure 2 are not promising for those who hope state legislative elections provide accountability. Levels of competition in state legislatures are partly explained by institutional features of state legislatures, such as professionalism (Hogan 2004; Squire 2000) and campaign finance laws (Mayer and Wood 1995; Werner and Mayer 2007; Hamm and Hogan 2008; Malhotra 2008), but it is also important to consider candidates' decisions regarding when to run for office. Jacobson (1989), for example, argues that congressional candidates strategically run for office to take advantage of a president's popularity and shows that presidential approval correlates with the percentage of quality challengers in U.S. House elections (Jacobson 1989, Table 3). This relationship suggests that during an unpopular Democratic presidency, Republican congressional challengers will take advantage of the antipresident sentiment and be more likely to run, giving voters more opportunities to electorally sanction Democrats who perform poorly.

The first election following the Watergate investigation provides a prime example of candidates adopting this type of strategy. Most candidates had to determine when to run while Nixon was still in office, and likely recognizing the president's unpopularity, Democrats challenged 163 of the 164 Republican U.S. House incumbents seeking reelection. State legislative Democratic candidates, however, also appeared to make similar strategic decisions. Every Republican state legislator was challenged by a Democrat in more than fifty state legislative chambers (Tidmarch, Lonergan, and Sciortino 1986). Democrats did well at both the federal and state levels in 1974 (Figure 1), and this success would not have been possible if Democrats had not decided to run for office.

One can see comparable patterns in more recent state legislative elections. Following an unpopular Iraq War and Hurricane Katrina during the George W. Bush administration, 63 percent of state legislative Republicans faced a major party opponent compared with 52 percent of Democrats in 2006. Following unpopular health care reforms of the Obama administration, more than 68 percent of state legislative Democrats faced opponents in 2010 when the comparable figure for Republicans was 55 percent. And in 2012 in Tennessee—a state where 55 percent of voters disapproved of Obama's performance as

FIGURE 2
Challenge Rates to Incumbents in the State House and U.S. House

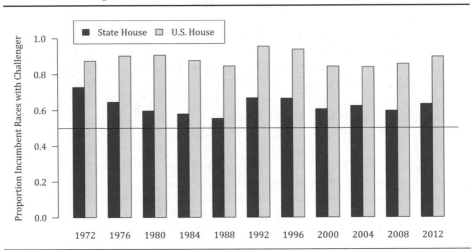

NOTE: Dark and light grey bars illustrate the proportion of State House and U.S. House incumbents who faced a major party challenger in presidential election years since 1972. On average, the difference in rates in challenger entry is greater than 20 percent.

president—Democrats chose not to challenge Republicans in thirty-seven of ninety-nine state house districts, meaning Republicans had to win only thirteen of forty-five contested elections to retain their majority in the Tennessee state house. When asked why this was the case, Tennessee Republican Glen Casada responded that "President Obama and the anti-president attitude" was "the biggest thing working for us" (Cass 2012).

To investigate the extent to which the "antipresident attitude" matters for state-level elites' decision-making and more specifically whether Jacobson's theory of strategic entry—where candidates take advantage of national political conditions—translates to the state legislative level, I examine challenger entry in state legislative elections from 1991 through 2010 in forty-four states.[3] The dependent variable is whether a sitting state legislator, who survived the primary, from a single-member district received a major party opponent (Klarner et al. 2013).

Similar to Jacobson, my independent variable of interest is the president's average approval rating in the Gallup poll from April through June of the election year. My focus on the second quarter of the election year aims to capture political conditions for the approximate time period when many candidates decide to challenge an incumbent. If state legislative challengers take advantage of national political conditions, incumbent state legislators of the president's party should be more likely to face an opponent when the president is unpopular. Similarly, state legislators unaffiliated with the president's party should more often face competition when the president is popular. State legislative challengers may also anticipate riding presidential coattails in presidential elections or fear being swept up in "midterm loss." I therefore estimate the relationship between presidential approval and challenger entry for all elections, as well as separately for presidential and midterm elections.

Following previous studies of state legislative challenger entry, my analyses account for more local political conditions, such as those within the state or district. Since a candidate likely does not want to be part of a meaningless minority party, face an unfriendly district, or challenge a particularly strong incumbent, I control for the preelection seat share of the minority party (Dubin 2007; State Partisan Composition 2016), district's partisanship, incumbent's previous vote share, and the number of terms served by the incumbent.[4] I additionally account for institutional variation across states and elections, such as the state's annual income growth, legislature's level of professionalism (Squire 2012), and whether a state has term limits. Prior work also finds legislative competition is greater immediately following redistricting (Pritchard 1992) or in non-Southern elections (Squire 1989). Each estimation, therefore, accounts for whether an election took place under these conditions. Given the dichotomous dependent variable, I use probit regressions to estimate the relationship between challenger entry and my independent variables of interest, and for clarity in presentation, I convert probit estimates to average predicted probabilities in text and figures.

Analyses in Table 1 present statistical relationships between the independent variables and state legislative challenger entry for all elections (first two columns), presidential elections (middle two columns), and midterm elections (last two columns). Providing evidence that state or local conditions influence state legislative competition, challengers more often emerge in states with narrower legislative majorities, but state legislative incumbents face fewer challengers if the district partisanship is favorable to the incumbent party. Estimates in Table 1 furthermore suggest that incumbents who oversaw stronger state economies are less likely to face competition. Income growth of 2 percent in the second quarter of an election year reduces the likelihood of a general election challenger by approximately 2 percent.

While state or local conditions appear to influence whether an incumbent state legislator receives a challenger, statistical analyses in Table 1 also suggest that the levels of competition largely depend on an incumbent's affiliation with national political actors. State legislators affiliated with the president's party are 4.5 percent more likely to face opposition than those unaffiliated with the president's party (see Table 1, columns 1 and 2). Challengers from both sides of the aisle, furthermore, appear to recognize that the president's party does poorly in midterm elections. Members of the president's party are 1.4 percent more likely to face a challenger in a midterm rather than presidential election (see Table 1, columns 3 and 5). Meanwhile incumbents unaffiliated with the president's party are 1.8 percent less likely to face a challenger in the midterm (see Table 1, columns 4 and 6).

The president's legislative copartisans are additionally more likely to be challenged when the president is unpopular. Using estimates from the first two columns of Table 1, Figure 3 illustrates the disparity in the probabilities of incumbents facing a challenger—separated by their affiliation with the

TABLE 1

Challenger Entry as a Function of Political Contexts Subset by Incumbents' Party and Type of Election

Variable	President's party incumbents all elections	Not president's party incumbents all elections	President's party incumbents presidential elections	Not president's party incumbents presidential elections	President's party incumbents midterm elections	Not president's party incumbents midterm elections
Average Q2 presidential approval	-0.012*	-0.001	-0.008*	0.006*	-0.013*	0.002
	(0.001)	(0.001)	(0.002)	(0.002)	(0.002)	(0.002)
Change annual log Q2 state personal inc.	-4.206*	-1.947*	-2.947*	-4.455*	-5.161*	-2.08*
	(0.490)	(0.506)	(0.793)	(0.838)	(0.710)	(0.760)
Minority party seat share	0.942*	1.008*	0.946*	1.048*	0.951*	0.883*
	(0.109)	(0.107)	(0.165)	(0.146)	(0.148)	(0.158)
Professionalism	-0.123	0.050	-0.484*	0.365*	0.273	-0.283
	(0.110)	(0.107)	(0.158)	(0.152)	(0.155)	(0.153)
Southern dummy	-0.625*	-0.647*	-0.657*	-0.695*	-0.59*	-0.596*
	(0.028)	(0.028)	(0.041)	(0.039)	(0.040)	(0.040)
Logged district size	0.140*	0.104*	0.133*	0.059*	0.138*	0.157*
	(0.016)	(0.016)	(0.023)	(0.022)	(0.022)	(0.023)
Term limits enacted	0.015	-0.108*	0.024	-0.027	-0.002	-0.160*
	(0.024)	(0.023)	(0.035)	(0.033)	(0.032)	(0.033)
First election after redistricting dummy	0.107*	0.157*	0.131*	0.249*	0.043	-0.024
	(0.034)	(0.031)	(0.041)	(0.036)	(0.074)	(0.089)
Freshman dummy	-0.103*	-0.003	-0.128*	-0.008	-0.086*	-0.003
	(0.028)	(0.027)	(0.040)	(0.039)	(0.038)	(0.039)

(continued)

TABLE 1 (CONTINUED)

Variable	President's party incumbents all elections	Not president's party incumbents all elections	President's party incumbents presidential elections	Not president's party incumbents presidential elections	President's party incumbents midterm elections	Not president's party incumbents midterm elections
Terms served	-0.011°	-0.010°	-0.012°	-0.004	-0.011°	-0.016°
	(0.004)	(0.004)	(0.006)	(0.005)	(0.005)	(0.005)
Incumbent party presidential vote	-1.615°	-1.258°	-1.660°	-1.297°	-1.628°	-1.211°
	(0.081)	(0.078)	(0.119)	(0.106)	(0.112)	(0.117)
Incumbent previous vote share	-2.694°	-2.588°	-2.843°	-2.671°	-2.616°	-2.688°
	(0.129)	(0.124)	(0.187)	(0.170)	(0.179)	(0.185)
Incumbent previously contested dummy	-0.178°	-0.155°	-0.232°	-0.173°	-0.145°	-0.188°
	(0.048)	(0.046)	(0.071)	(0.062)	(0.066)	(0.070)
Member of the Democratic Party	0.241°	0.002	0.156°	-0.035	0.203°	0.115°
	(0.026)	(0.027)	(0.045)	(0.045)	(0.041)	(0.046)
Constant	2.376°	1.754°	2.491°	2.062°	2.378°	1.166°
	(0.193)	(0.191)	(0.282)	(0.273)	(0.274)	(0.284)
Log-likelihood	-10520.47	-10862.58	-5064.301	-5551.188	-5427.688	-5239.959
N	18895	18660	9053	9754	9842	8906

NOTE: Probit estimates of the likelihood of a major party challenger contesting an incumbent state legislator from 1991 to 2010. Columns are divided by type of incumbent (member of the president's party or not member of the president's party) and type of election (presidential or midterm). Standard errors in parentheses.

°$p \leq .05$.

215

FIGURE 3
Predicted Probabilities of State Legislators Facing a Major Party Challenger under
Different Levels of Presidential Approval

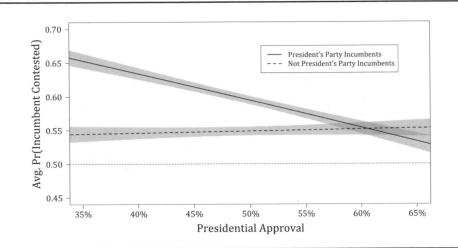

NOTE: Using estimates from the first column of Table 1, the solid line represents the predicted probability of an incumbent state legislator of the president's party being challenged
under different levels of presidential approval. Grey regions represent 95 percent boot-
strapped confidence intervals. Only under popular presidencies is a member of the president's
party less likely to be challenged than state legislators not affiliated with the president.

president's party—under different levels of presidential approval. A 10 percent
decrease in presidential approval increases the average predicted probability of a
member of the president's party facing an opponent by approximately .04.
During unpopular presidencies, the president's state legislative copartisans are
much more likely to face competition. When the president's approval rating is 35
percent, the estimated probability of a member of the president's party being
challenged is .65 (solid line), but the comparable probability for state legislators
unaffiliated with the president's party is only .54 (dashed line).

The third and fifth columns of Table 1 suggest that the relationship between
presidential approval and challenger entry is stronger in the midterm election. A
10 percent decrease in presidential approval increases the probability of a member of the president's party facing a challenger in a presidential election by .026,
but the impact of the same change in presidential approval increases the probability of a challenger by .039 in the midterm. With more than 5,000 state legislative elections each election year, these changes in probabilities translate into
whether hundreds of state legislators face competition in the general election.

Presidential Politics and Voter Behavior

The findings in Table 1 and Figure 3 suggest that state legislative challengers are
strategic like their federal counterparts and partly base their decisions to

challenge an incumbent on the popularity of the president. The underlying assumption of this strategy is that voters displeased with the president will also be more likely to vote against a member of the president's party in a state legislative contest, but there is relatively little existing evidence that individual evaluations of the president relate to vote choice in state legislative elections.[5]

To investigate the extent to which this relationship exists, I employ two sets of surveys. I first rely on the 2008, 2010, and 2012 Cooperative Congressional Election Study (CCES). YouGov Polimetrix conducted these online surveys in two waves, interviewing the same respondents in October and November of those years. In the first wave, individuals were asked whether they approved of the president, governor, and state legislature; and in the second wave, respondents stated how they voted in their state legislative elections. To complement these recent nationwide surveys and examine elections since the 1970s, I use New Jersey state polls conducted by the Eagleton Institute of Politics. New Jersey state elections occur in the "off-year" (e.g., 2007 or 2009), separate from federal elections and presumably should be less sensitive to national political influences.

For the first set of survey analyses using the CCES, I estimate how vote choice relates to voters' approval ratings of the president, governor, and state legislature while controlling for a respondent's party identification.[6] My dependent variable is whether a voter supported the state house majority party in an election. My approval ratings of political actors are on a five-point scale ranging from "strongly disapprove" to "strongly approve," and I code these responses to be consistent with my dependent variable.[7] To examine the relationship between a voter's evaluations of political actors and vote choice, I use a weighted probit analysis using sample weights provided by the CCES.[8] To simplify interpretations, I convert probit estimates to predicted probabilities in text and figures. For differences in predicted probabilities, I adjust the variable of interest and hold other variables at their weighted sample means.

Providing evidence that local politics matters in state legislative elections, statistical analyses in Table 2 suggest that when voters strongly approve of their state legislature instead of strongly disapprove, the probability they vote for a candidate of the state house majority party increases by up to .12. Similarly, strongly approving instead of strongly disapproving of the governor changes the predicted probability of a state house vote by at least .18. Punishing an unpopular governor's legislative party can stall the governor's legislative agenda, and the relationship between vote choice and gubernatorial approval could reflect this tactic by voters.

Assessments of state-level actors' performance play some role in state legislative elections, but findings presented in Table 2 provide evidence that state legislative politics are more national than local. Shifts in presidential approval from strongly disapproving to strongly approving can change predicted probabilities of voting for the president's copartisans by at least .38. The relative impact of presidential to state legislative approval is remarkable. Figure 4 summarizes the predicted probabilities of voting for candidates of the state house majority or president's party using estimates from the 2012 election. The solid line represents the probability of voting for the state house majority party under different levels of state legislative approval, and the dotted line plots the probabilities of

TABLE 2
State House Vote Choice as a Function of Approval Ratings and Party ID

Election year	2008	2010	2012
Presidential approval	.205°	.413°	.433°
	(.011)	(.014)	(.014)
Governor approval	.131°	.077°	.087°
	(.013)	(.013)	(.016)
State legislative approval	.096°	.090°	.059°
	(.015)	(.017)	(.018)
Party ID (7 pt.)	.561°	.492°	.477°
	(.010)	(.013)	(.013)
Constant	.037°	.112°	.050°
	(.018)	(.024)	(.020)
Log-pseudolikelihood	−5165.3	−5844.5	−6719
N	18815	30757	28443

NOTE: Probit estimates of state house vote choice as a function of voters' assessments of the political actors and partisan identification. These data from the Cooperative Congressional Elections Studies are weighted to make them representative of registered voters in the 2008, 2010, and 2012 elections. Standard errors in parentheses.
°$p \leq .05$.

voting for a legislative candidate of the president's party for given levels of presidential approval. With growing approval, predicted probabilities of voting for these parties' candidates increase, but changes in presidential approval have at least three times the impact of comparable shifts in state legislative approval.

The relationship between presidential approval and state legislative vote choice is robust. Levels of voter political knowledge or divided state government have no attenuating effect, and the relationship persists among wealthy, educated, or politically interested voters. The correlation between state legislative vote choice and presidential approval also consistently emerges when estimating the model on data subset by state. Therefore in state legislative elections across the country, changes in presidential approval clearly matter more than shifts in state legislative approval even though legislative parties control the legislature's performance more than the president's.[9]

The findings from the CCES surveys provide persuasive evidence that national politics influences voters' decisions in state legislative elections. These analyses, however, only examine recent state elections that coincide with federal contests. Some state elections, such as those in New Jersey or Virginia, occur in the "off-year" separate from presidential or congressional elections. When advocating off-year elections, New Jersey Governor Alfred Driscoll asserted that "the election for a Governor and for Assemblymen should not coincide with a Presidential election. The importance of a gubernatorial election merits an election that will not be overshadowed by a national contest for the Presidency" (New Jersey Constitutional Convention 1947).[10] While the focus of this study is assembly

FIGURE 4
Voter Behavior in State Legislative Elections under Different Levels of State Legislative
and Presidential Approval

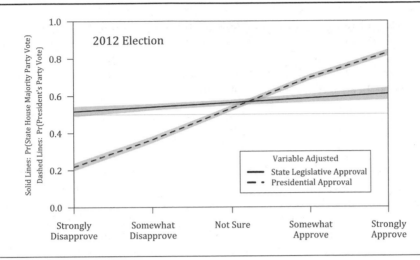

NOTE: Comparisons of the relationships between an individual's assessments of the president or state legislature and their state house voting decisions in the 2012 elections. The solid line represents the predicted probability of voting for a candidate of the state house majority party under different levels of state legislative approval, and the dashed line represents the probability of voting for a member of the president's party under different levels of presidential approval. The relative influence of presidential approval is at least three times that of state legislative approval.

rather than gubernatorial elections, Driscoll's overarching point regarding state elections still applies. By being held separate from federal contests, off-year elections should be less likely to be "overshadowed," and New Jersey provides an excellent opportunity to evaluate the influence of presidential politics in state legislative elections under electoral conditions presumably less sensitive to national politics.

I, therefore, examine New Jersey voters' state legislative voting behavior using polls from the Eagleton Institute of Politics. This investigation tests the robustness of findings regarding the impact of national conditions on voter behavior in state legislative elections in two key respects. First, it analyzes elections that occur in the off-year. Second, it examines polls from each of the five presidential administrations since the 1970s instead of only more recent elections. Similar to the CCES analysis, I estimate the relationship between vote choice and a voter's approval rating of the president, governor, and state legislature while controlling for an individual's party identification.[11] To account for New Jersey's multimember districts and options to vote for two Democrats, split the ticket, or vote for two Republicans, I estimate this relationship with an ordered probit regression.

Table 3 presents evidence that presidential influences in state legislative elections are not solely a result of federal election coattails nor a recent phenomenon.

In each Eagleton poll, approving instead of disapproving of the president can change the probability of a state legislative vote for the president's party by at least .27. While gubernatorial politics matters more in some elections than others, assessments of the New Jersey state legislature's performance never have a meaningful relationship with vote choice. The final column of Table 3 indicates that these off-year election findings are not confined to New Jersey, as national influences have similar effects in Virginia legislative elections, which also occur in odd-numbered years.[12] National politics, therefore, appears to permeate elections, even when there are no federal candidates on the ballot.

Discussion

My analyses suggest an unpopular presidency is bad news for the president's state legislative copartisans on multiple fronts. Not only will a member of the president's party be more likely to face a challenger in the general election, but when voters go to polls, many will likely vote for the state legislative challenger instead of the member of the president's party because they are displeased with the president. These complementary behaviors by elites and voters in state legislative elections help to explain the striking pattern of election outcomes illustrated by Figure 1 and provide evidence that there is a common dimension underlying both federal and state legislative elections: national politics.

Applying these findings to the upcoming 2016 election, a popular Barack Obama may help state legislative Democrats to regain seats lost in 2014. Meanwhile an unpopular Obama may mean more defeats for state-level Democrats. It, however, may be difficult for Obama's party to suffer many more losses. Following the 2014 election, Democrats held fewer state legislative seats than they had at any time since before the Great Depression, prompting members of the national media such as Chris Cillizza, Matt Yglesias, and Chuck Todd to call Democrat losses in state legislatures "the single most overlooked and underappreciated story line of President Obama's time in office" (Cillizza 2015; Yglesias 2015; Todd 2015).

Cillizza, Yglesias, and Todd bring attention to the underappreciated relationship between presidential and state legislative politics; my contribution to this volume provides evidence of the remarkable strength of this relationship. But another underappreciated point is that the influence of national forces in state legislative politics makes contests for the state legislature "second-order elections" where state legislators' own performance has relatively little to do with their own electoral success. Recall Figure 3, which suggests that being a member of the president's party increases the likelihood that a state legislator faces a challenger by more than 4 percent. By means of comparison, state legislators would have to oversee more than 4 percent growth in the state economy to offset this increased competition. Similarly, Figure 4 shows that compared with individual assessments of the state legislature, changes in presidential approval have at least three times the impact on voters' decision-making in state legislative elections. These analyses are just a portion of findings regarding the dim prospects for

TABLE 3

New Jersey and Virginia Off-Year State Legislative Voting as a Function of Approval Ratings and Party ID

State and Election Year	NJ 1973	NJ 1975	NJ 1979	NJ 1983	NJ 1985	NJ 1987	NJ 1995	NJ 2007	VA 2007
Presidential approval	.216*	.218*	.252*	.210*	.323*	.179*	.423*	.228*	.296*
	(.060)	(.050)	(.074)	(.064)	(.082)	(.059)	(.078)	(.063)	(.023)
Governor approval	.015	.202*	.088	.094	-.012	.146*	.228*	.074	.18*
	(.068)	(.064)	(.067)	(.066)	(.102)	(.068)	(.085)	(.055)	(.043)
State legislative approval	.005	.013	.080	-.033	.151	.022	-.017	.092	.186*
	(.078)	(.063)	(.069)	(.075)	(.099)	(.069)	(.095)	(.058)	(.039)
Party ID	.746*	.707*	.902*	.711*	.860*	.665*	.758*	.684*	.613*
	(.055)	(.050)	(.056)	(.059)	(.084)	(.053)	(.069)	(.051)	(.043)
Intercept: R votes | split votes	-.232*	-.498*	-.292*	-.048	-.052	-.098	-.267*	-.051	.185*
	(.099)	(.082)	(.106)	(.088)	(.134)	(.095)	(.103)	(.094)	(.070)
Intercept: split votes | D votes	.141	-.262*	-.215*	.109	.043	-.057	-.182	.282*	.573*
	(.098)	(.080)	(.105)	(.088)	(.134)	(.095)	(.102)	(.096)	(.072)
Log-likelihood	-211.444	-353.944	-220.603	-192.25	-92.577	-195.878	-127.763	-251.3	-452.272
N	446	654	638	415	323	509	461	523	1052

NOTE: Ordered probit estimates of state house vote choices as a function of voters' assessments of the president, governor, and state legislature along with party identification. Column headings indicate the state and year of the poll. The Eagleton Institute of Politics conducted the New Jersey polls, and the *Washington Post* conducted the Virginia poll. In these off-year election states, presidential approval consistently correlates with state house vote choice.

accountability in state legislatures. I show elsewhere that there is little evidence that state legislators are held accountable for worsening crime, education, or economic policy outcomes, and few individual legislators pay an electoral price for extreme ideological representation or unpopular roll-call votes (Rogers 2013).

Taken together these findings suggest that state legislators have relatively little control over their own elections. State legislators control what happens at the state house, not the White House, and if national forces dominate state legislative elections, it undermines theories' of accountability claim that there should be a meaningful relationship between how state legislators perform in office and elections. Tip O'Neil's characterization of politics, therefore, does not seem to apply to state legislatures. Instead of being local affairs, state legislative elections are dominated by national politics.

Notes

1. Voters may also use state legislative elections to signal displeasure with (Piketty 2000; Kellerman 2008) or repudiate an unpopular president, similar to how federal midterm elections can be considered presidential referendums (e.g., Tufte 1975). In a related literature on gubernatorial elections, Arceneaux (2006) finds that voters distinguish between presidential and gubernatorial responsibilities, but Carsey and Wright (1998) discover national forces such as presidential approval influence gubernatorial contests. Similarly, work on federalism finds that national conditions influence regional elections (Anderson and Ward 1996; Leigh and Mcleish 2009; Rodden and Wibbels 2011; see also Erikson and Filippov 2001; Kedar 2006; Leon 2012; Martins and Veiga 2013).

2. For a more thorough review of the determinants of state legislative challenger entry, see Rogers (2015).

3. I exclude states with "off-year" voting (e.g., 2007 and 2009) to make comparisons between midterm and presidential elections. Main results are similar when including off-year states. I also exclude Nebraska due to their nonpartisan legislature.

4. I measure partisanship using district-level presidential vote for the incumbent state legislator's party. For the 1991–2000 elections, I use Gore-Bush vote, and for the 2001–10 elections, I use averaged Bush-Kerry and McCain-Obama vote. My analysis is missing Gore-Bush vote for the New Mexico Senate and the Arkansas, Colorado, and Mississippi state legislatures and Kerry-Bush vote for Florida and Mississippi.

5. Prior work provides evidence of a relationship between the national economy and state legislative elections, focusing on seat or chamber changes (Berry, Berkman, and Schneiderman 2000; Campbell 1986; Chubb 1988; see also Klarner 2010; Simon, Ostrom, and Marra 1991; Fiorina 1994). This statistical association potentially reflects a relationship between voters' evaluations of the president and their decisions in state legislative elections, but the relationship between seat changes and the national economy could also be the result of other factors, such as challenger entry decisions and voter turnout. Objective measures of economic performance furthermore do not necessarily translate into subjective assessments of the government at the individual level (De Boef and Kellstedt 2004; Krause 1997), limiting inferences regarding how evaluations of the president shape voters' decisions in state legislative contests.

6. The 2008 and 2010 surveys asked, "For whom did you vote for in the state legislative elections" in the respondent's lower chamber. In 2008, individuals could select a "not sure" response, but in 2010, this option was unavailable. To simplify my presentation, I focus on registered voters who gave a definitive Democrat or Republican response. Findings are similar when including "not sure" responses in a multinomial probit estimation. Estimates available upon request.

7. For example, strongly approving a Democratic state legislature receives a similar coding to strongly approving a Democratic president. Substantive findings are similar when either using dummy variables for approval levels instead of a cardinal measure or substituting voters' assessments of the economy for their approval ratings of political actors. There are a considerable number of "not sure" responses to the governor and state legislative approval questions, and I code these responses as a middle category to reflect

uncertainty regarding whether the respondent disapproves or approves of these political actors. "Not sure" respondents may have answered correctly if given different closed item responses (Mondak 1999, 72). Main conclusions do not change when omitting "not sure" respondents. All estimates available upon request.

8. CCES samples are wealthier, better educated, and more politically interested than the general population. Main findings are not sensitive to including controls for these demographic differences.

9. All estimates available upon request.

10. This quote was found thanks to Bishop and Hatch (2012).

11. Over the past 40 years, the Eagleton Institute at times changed the wordings of the vote choice, approval, and party identification questions. To maintain comparability to CCES estimates in Table 2, I code response categories similar to the CCES analysis. Results from an alternative model specification without these adjustments are similar.

12. Of the New Jersey elections examined, only 1973 and 1985 had a gubernatorial election. Virginia results use a 2007 *Washington Post* poll. Instead of a vote choice question, this survey asked "regardless of your local contest, which party would you like to see in control of the Virginia state legislature after the November elections, the (Democrats) or the (Republicans)?" I code "divided" responses as the middle category.

References

Anderson, Christopher J., and Daniel S Ward. 1996. Barometer elections in comparative perspective. *Electoral Studies* 15 (4): 447–60.

Arceneaux, Kevin. 2006. The federal face of voting: Are elected officials held accountable for the functions relevant to their office? *Political Psychology* 27 (5): 731–54.

Arnold, R. Douglas. 1992. *The logic of congressional action.* New Haven, CT: Yale University Press.

Berry, William D., Michael B. Berkman, and Stuart Schneiderman. 2000. Legislative professionalism and incumbent reelection: The development of institutional boundaries. *The American Political Science Review* 94 (4): 859–74.

Bishop, Bradford, and Rebecca Hatch. 2012. Perception of state parties and voting in subnational elections. Unpublished manuscript. Durham, NC: Duke University.

Campbell, Angus. 1960. Surge and decline: A study of electoral change. *The Public Opinion Quarterly* 24 (3): 397–418.

Campbell, James E. 1986. Presidential coattails and midterm losses in state legislative elections. *The American Political Science Review* 80 (1): 45–63.

Carsey, Thomas M., and Gerald C. Wright. 1998. State and national factors in gubernatorial and senatorial elections. *American Journal of Political Science* 42 (3): 994–1002.

Cass, Michael. 22 April 2012. GOP expects to increase majorities in TN House, Senate. *The Tennessean.*

Chubb, John E. 1988. Institutions, the economy, and the dynamics of state elections. *The American Political Science Review* 82 (1): 133–54.

Cillizza, Chris. 4 November 2015. The 2015 election tightened the Republican stranglehold on state government. *The Washington Post.* Available from https://www.washingtonpost.com.

De Boef, Suzanna, and Paul M. Kellstedt. 2004. The political (and economic) origins of consumer confidence. *American Journal of Political Science* 48 (4): 633–49.

Dubin, Michael J. 2007. *Party affiliations in the state legislatures: A year by year summary, 1796–2006.* Jefferson, NC: McFarland.

Erikson, Robert S. 1988. The puzzle of midterm loss. *The Journal of Politics* 50 (4): 1011–29.

Erikson, Robert S., and Mikhail G. Filippov. 2001. Electoral balancing in federal and sub-national elections: The case of Canada. *Constitutional Political Economy* 12 (4): 313–31.

Fearon, James. 1999. Electoral Accountability and the control of politicians: Selecting good types versus sanctioning poor performance. In *Democracy, Accountability, and Representation*, eds. Adam Przeworski, Susan C. Stokes, and Bernard Manin. New York, NY: Cambridge University Press.

Ferejohn, John. 1986. Incumbent performance and electoral control. *Public Choice* 50 (1): 5–25.

Fiorina, Morris P. 1994. Divided government in the American states: A byproduct of legislative profes-
     sionalism? *American Political Science Review* 88 (2): 304–16.
Gabaix, Xavier, and David Laibson. 2005. *Bounded rationality and directed cognition*. New York, NY: New
     York University. Available from http://pages.stern.nyu.edu/~xgabaix/papers/boundedRationality.pdf.
Hamilton, Alexander or James Madison. 8 February 1788. Federalist No. 52: The House of Representatives.
     New York Daily Packet.
Hamm, Keith E., and Robert E Hogan. 2008. Campaign finance laws and candidacy decisions in state
     legislative elections. *Political Research Quarterly* 61 (3): 458–67.
Hogan, Robert E. 2004. Challenger emergence, incumbent success, and electoral accountability in state
     legislative elections. *The Journal of Politics* 66 (4): 1283–303.
Jacobson, Gary C. 1989. Strategic politicians and the dynamics of U.S. House elections, 1946–86. *The
     American Political Science Review* 83 (3): 773–93.
Kahneman, Daniel, and Shane Frederick. 2002. Representativeness revisited: Attribute substitution in
     intuitive judgment. In *Heuristics and biases: The psychology of intuitive judgment*. New York, NY:
     Cambridge University Press.
Kaplan, M., K. R. Goldstein, and M. Hale. 2005. *Local news coverage of the 2004 campaigns*. Los Angeles,
     CA: USC Annenberg School and University of Wisconsin.
Kedar, Orit. 2006. How voters work around institutions: Policy balancing in staggered elections. *Electoral
     Studies* 3:509–27.
Kellerman, Michael. 2008. Balancing or signaling? Electoral punishment in sub-national elections.
     Unpublished manuscript. Cambridge, MA: Harvard University.
Key, V. O. 1956. *American state politics: An introduction*. 1st ed. New York, NY: Knopf.
Key, V. O., and Milton C. Cummings. 1966. *The responsible electorate: Rationality in presidential voting,
     1936–1960*. Cambridge, MA: Belknap Press.
Klarner, Carl. 2010. Forecasting the 2010 state legislative elections. *PS: Political Science & Politics* 43 (4):
     643–48.
Klarner, Carl, William Berry, Thomas Carsey, Malcolm Jewell, Richard Niemi, Lynda Powell, and James
     Snyder. 2013. State Legislative Election Returns (1967–2010). ICPSR34297-v1. Ann Arbor, MI: Inter-
     University Consortium for Political and Social Research [distributor].
Krause, George A. 1997. Voters, information heterogeneity, and the dynamics of aggregate economic
     expectations. *American Journal of Political Science* 41 (4): 1170–200.
Leigh, Andrew, and Mark Mcleish. 2009. Are state elections affected by the national economy? Evidence
     from Australia. *Economic Record* 85 (269): 210–22.
Leiserowitz, Anthony., Edward Maibach, and Connie Roser-Renouf. 2009. *Global warming's six Americas
     2009: An audience segmentation analysis*. New Haven, CT: Yale Program on Climate Change
     Communication.
Leon, Sandra. 2012. How does decentralization affect electoral competition of state-wide parties?
     Evidence from Spain. *Party Politics* 3 (20): 391–402.
Lublin, David Ian. 1994. Quality, not quantity: Strategic politicians in U.S. Senate elections, 1952–1990.
     The Journal of Politics 56 (1): 228–41.
Madison, James. 22 November 1787. Federalist No. 10: The same subject continued: The union as a
     safeguard against domestic faction and insurrection. *New York Daily Advertiser*.
Malhotra, Neil. 2008. The impact of public financing on electoral competition: Evidence from Arizona and
     Maine. *State Politics & Policy Quarterly* 8 (3): 263–81.
Martins, Rodrigo, and Francisco José Veiga. 2013. Economic voting in Portuguese municipal elections.
     Public Choice 155 (3–4): 317–34.
Mayer, Kenneth R., and John M. Wood. 1995. The impact of public financing on electoral competitiveness:
     Evidence from Wisconsin, 1964–1990. *Legislative Studies Quarterly* 20 (1): 69–88.
Mondak, Jeffery J. 1999. Reconsidering the measurement of political knowledge. *Political Analysis* 8 (1):
     57–81.
New Jersey Constitutional Convention. 24 June 1947. vol. 5. Trenton, NJ. Available from http://www.
     njstatelib.org/slic_files/searchable_publications/constitution/constitutionv5/NJConst5n30.html.
Piketty, Thomas. 2000. Voting as communicating. *The Review of Economic Studies* 67 (1): 169–91.
Powell, G. Bingham. 2000. *Elections as instruments of democracy: Majoritarian and proportional visions*.
     New Haven, CT: Yale University Press.

Pritchard, Anita. 1992. Strategic considerations in the decision to challenge a state legislative incumbent. *Legislative Studies Quarterly* 17 (3): 381–93.

Reif, Karlheinz, and Hermann Schmitt. 1980. Nine second-order national elections - A conceptual framework for the analysis of European election results. *European Journal of Political Research* 8 (1): 3–44.

Rodden, Jonathan, and Erik Wibbels. 2011. Dual accountability and the nationalization of party competition: Evidence from four federations. *Party Politics* 17 (5): 629–53.

Rogers, Steven. 2013. Accountability in a federal system. Ph.D. diss., Princeton University. Available from http://www.stevenmrogers.com/Dissertation/Rogers-Dissertation.pdf.

Rogers, Steven. 2015. Strategic challenger entry in a federal system: The role of economic and political conditions in state legislative competition. *Legislative Studies Quarterly* 40 (4): 539–70.

Schattschneider, Elmer Eric. 1942. *Party government*. New York, NY: Praeger.

Simon, Dennis M., Charles W. Ostrom, and Robin F. Marra. 1991. The president, referendum voting, and subnational elections in the United States. *The American Political Science Review* 85 (4): 1177–92.

Squire, Peverill. 1989. Competition and uncontested seats in U. S. House elections. *Legislative Studies Quarterly* 14 (May): 281–95.

Squire, Peverill. 2000. Uncontested seats in state legislative elections. *Legislative Studies Quarterly* 25 (1): 131–46.

Squire, Peverill. 2012. *The evolution of American Legislatures: Colonies, territories, and states, 1619–2009*. Ann Arbor, MI: University of Michigan Press.

State Partisan Composition. 20 April 2016. National Conference of State Legislature.

Tidmarch, Charles M., Edward Lonergan, and John Sciortino. 1986. Interparty competition in the U.S. states: Legislative elections, 1970–1978. *Legislative Studies Quarterly* 11 (3): 353–74.

Todd, Chuck. 2015. Meet the Press Transcript: November 8, 2015. *NBC News*. Available from http://www.nbcnews.com.

Tufte, Edward R. 1975. Determinants of the outcomes of midterm congressional elections. *The American Political Science Review* 69 (3): 812–26.

Tversky, Amos, and Daniel Kahneman. 1974. Judgment under uncertainty: Heuristics and biases. *Science* 185 (4157): 1124–31.

Werner, Timothy, and Kenneth R. Mayer. 2007. Public election funding, competition, and candidate gender. *PS: Political Science and Politics* 40 (October): 661–67.

Vanderbilt University poll. November 2013. Center for the Study of Democratic Institutions, Vanderbilt University. Available from http://www.vanderbilt.edu/csdi/Nov2013.pdf.

Yglesias, Matt. 2015. Democrats are in denial. Their party is actually in deep trouble. *Vox*. Available from http://www.vox.com.

Polarization, Gridlock, and Presidential Campaign Politics in 2016

By
GARY C. JACOBSON

The American electorate has grown increasingly divided along party lines in recent decades, by political attitudes, social values, basic demography, and even beliefs about reality. Deepening partisan divisions have inspired high levels of party-line voting and low levels of ticket splitting, resulting in thoroughly nationalized, president- and party-centered federal elections. Because of the way the electoral system aggregates votes, however, historically high levels of electoral coherence have delivered incoherent, divided government and policy stalemate. The 2016 nomination campaigns have exposed deep fissures within as well as between the parties, and their results threaten to shake up electoral patterns that have prevailed so far during this century, with uncertain and perhaps unpredictable consequences for national politics. The 2016 election is certain to polarize the electorate, but the axis of polarization may not fall so neatly along party lines as it has in recent years.

Keywords: partisanship; polarization; gridlock; 2016 election

The American electorate, poised to choose the next president and Congress, has over the past several decades grown increasingly divided along party lines, by political attitudes, social values, basic demography, and even beliefs about reality. Deepening partisan divisions have inspired high levels of party-line voting and low levels of ticket splitting, resulting in thoroughly nationalized, president- and party-centered federal elections (Jacobson 2015a). As the battles for the 2016 nominations made abundantly clear, however, the Democratic and Republican coalitions are far from monolithic. Donald Trump's rise to the top

Gary C. Jacobson is Distinguished Professor of Political Science Emeritus at the University of California, San Diego. He specializes in the study of U.S. elections, parties, interest groups, public opinion, and Congress. His most recent book is A Divider, Not a Uniter: George W. Bush and the American People *(Longman 2007).*

Correspondence: gjacobson@ucsd.edu

DOI: 10.1177/0002716216658921

in the face of nearly unanimous opposition from Republican leaders, donors, and pundits not only exposed deep fissures within the party, but also threatened to disrupt and perhaps reshape the current national party alliance. The 2016 election ends the recent string of presidential contests featuring mainstream candidates from both parties who have inspired cohesively partisan voting patterns. It has the potential to shake up electoral patterns that have prevailed during this century, with uncertain and perhaps unpredictable consequences for national politics.

In this article, I review the electoral trends that have set the stage for 2016 and then consider the potential for the nomination contests, their surprising result, and the ensuing general election matchup between Donald Trump and Hillary Clinton to reconfigure the inherited political landscape. The looming question of whether the 2016 election will constitute a historic turning point or merely a temporary disruption of long-term electoral trends gives the election unusual interest—in addition, of course, to the enormous implications it holds for the future of the country. The election will surely polarize the electorate, although the axis of polarization may not fall so neatly along party lines as it has in recent years. Departures from party loyalty are not guaranteed, however, for the divisions within the parties are overshadowed by the even wider divisions between them on most national issues and leaders. How these divisions play out in House and Senate elections as well as the presidential contest will determine whether gridlock in Washington—which has made no small contribution to the popular anger and frustration fueling the intraparty insurgencies of Trump and, on the Democratic side, Bernie Sanders—has any chance of being broken.

Gridlock will not be broken easily if at all. The historically high level of electoral coherence observed in recent years has delivered incoherent, divided government and policy stalemate, not because voters have been ambivalent, but because of the way the electoral system aggregates its votes for different federal offices. The Constitution gives presidents, senators, and representatives distinct electoral bases and calendars to complement the division of authority among national institutions—part of its successful design, famously articulated by James Madison in Federalist 51—to thwart simple majority rule. This electoral system, combined with the peculiarities of current partisan divisions, has left American national politics stalemated. In its present configuration, it gives Republicans a major structural advantage, allowing them to win a majority of House seats with a minority of votes. Republican House majorities have been unable to fulfill their campaign vows to undo Barack Obama's policies and alter the direction of national politics, however, because a national Democratic majority renewed Obama's lease on the White House in 2012. Whether this form of divided government continues after the 2016 election will be determined largely by voters' responses to Trump's divisive and disruptive candidacy.

The Contemporary Electorate

Party leaders and partisan voters alike have by almost every measure grown increasingly polarized along party lines during the past several decades. Polarization is most visible at the elite level in the incessant public clashes among partisan warriors in

Washington over matters large and small and in record levels of ideological polariza-tion as measured by roll-call votes cast in Congress during Obama's presidency (Poole, Rosenthal, and Hare 2016). But ordinary Americans have also become increasingly polarized by party, and the more active they are politically, the more their divisions echo those of elected leaders. Over the past four decades, largely in response to the more sharply differentiated alternatives presented by the national parties and their candidates, voters have sorted themselves into increasingly distinct and discordant political camps (Abramowitz 2010; Jacobson 2013; Levendusky 2009; Baumer and Gold 2010; Abrams and Fiorina 2015). Their partisan identities, ideo-logical leanings, and policy opinions have become more consistent internally and more divergent from those of rival partisans (Jacobson 2013; Pew Research Center 2014). The political cleavages that once divided up the public in diverse ways now tend to coincide, leaving ordinary Democrats and Republicans in disagreement on a growing range of issues. Traditional partisan divisions over the role and size of gov-ernment (with a focus on taxes, regulation, and health care) have widened, as have differences over social issues such as abortion, same-sex marriage, immigration, race, and gun control (Abramowitz 2015; Pew 2014). Partisans differ in beliefs about sci-entific realities as well as in values and opinions; most Democrats, for example, believe humans are heating up the planet, with potentially dire consequences; most Republicans do not (Dugan 2015; Pew 2013).

Polarization also has an affective component, with expressed feelings about the rival party and its leaders growing increasingly negative (Abramowitz 2015; Abramowitz and Webster 2016; Jacobson 2011). Such sentiments are reinforced by growing differences among partisans in their fundamental psychological makeup (Graham, Haidt, and Nosek 2009; Hetherington and Weiler 2015). Attitudinal, affec-tive, and psychological differences between Republicans and Democrats reflect in part the divergent demographic bases of the parties. The Democratic coalition has a larger proportion of young, single, female, secular, urban, ethnic minority, LGBT, unarmed, and highly educated voters; it is weakest in the South. The Republican coalition is overwhelmingly white as well as disproportionately older, married, reli-giously observant, male, of middling education, suburban or rural, gun owning, and southern (CNN 2012; Pew 2014; Gallup 2016). Crucial for 2016 and beyond, the Democratic coalition comprises growing segments of the population, including Latinos, the fastest growing category; the current Republican coalition is made up largely of shrinking demographic groups. As people have sorted themselves into separate coalitions, they have, by their choices about where to live and work, also sorted themselves into distinctive electoral units, which have consequently become increasingly homogeneous politically and lopsidedly partisan (Bishop 2008; Stonecash, Brewer, and Mariani 2003; Levendusky 2009; Jacobson 2013; Abramowitz 2015).

The Obama Factor

The divisions between ordinary Democrats and Republicans have been growing steadily wider for several decades for multiple reasons, but it is no coincidence that they peaked during Obama's presidency. Presidents always shape their party's popular image and attractiveness as an object of identification, but Obama has been an exceptionally powerful focal point for the organization of political attitudes (Jacobson 2012a, 2015a). The partisan split in evaluations of his job performance is the widest on record. During the first half of 2016, an average of 86 percent of Democrats, but only 11 percent of Republicans, approved of how he was handling his job.[1]

Republican disdain for Obama is not a recent development. Most Republican partisans, especially the conservative majority sympathetic to the Tea Party movement, have regarded Obama as a dishonest radical with a socialist agenda ever since the 2008 John McCain–Sarah Palin campaign portrayed him as one (Jacobson 2012b; Bradberry and Jacobson 2013). To a great many ordinary Republicans, Obama is not merely a conventionally objectionable Democrat but a person whose name, race, upbringing, associations, alleged objectives, and presumed values put him outside the boundaries of what is acceptable in an American leader. The widespread acceptance among Republicans of bogus claims about his birthplace and religion reflects this mindset. As recently as September 2015, 30 percent of Republicans responding to a CNN poll said that Obama was foreign-born (and thus ineligible to be president), and 43 percent said that he was a Muslim (Agiesta 2015). A portion of this is simply opportunistic Obama bashing invited by the survey questions, but even as such it underlines the intensity of so many Republicans' antipathy toward the president and their eagerness to deny his legitimacy. This antipathy has a racial component; numerous studies confirm that racial animus has shaped reactions to Obama since his emergence as a presidential contender and throughout his presidency (e.g., Weisberg and Divine 2009; Piston 2010; Tesler and Sears 2010; Tesler 2013, 2016; Kam and Kinder 2012; Pasek, Krosnick, and Thompson 2012; Tien, Nadeau, and Lewis-Beck 2012).

Disdain for Obama and everything he has done, as well as specious beliefs about his religion and birthplace, are especially prevalent among Trump's supporters,[2] feeding their enthusiasm for a candidate in almost every conceivable way the polar opposite of the president (Axelrod 2016). Catering to sentiments prevalent in the Republican primary electorate, not only Trump but every Republican candidate in 2016 vowed to undo virtually everything Obama has achieved in domestic and foreign affairs.

Ordinary Democrats, in contrast, have from the beginning viewed Obama as a mainstream Democrat pursuing policies regarding health care, economic regulation, race relations, the environment, immigration, abortion, same-sex marriage, gun control, and foreign affairs that largely reflect their party's traditional priorities and current preferences.[3] Even when they have been unhappy with his handling of some specific issues, they have continued to approve of his overall job performance; his average overall job rating among Democrats (86 percent in the first half of 2016) has been higher than his ratings for handling any specific policy domain, including the economy (81 percent), health care (74 percent), foreign policy (71 percent), and terrorism (73 percent).[4] Their inclination to back Obama generally despite some unhappiness with various aspects of his performance is probably reinforced by strongly negative opinions of his Republican and

FIGURE 1
Party Loyalty and Ticket Splitting in Contested Elections, 1952–2014

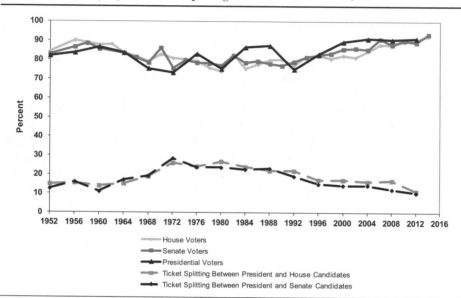

SOURCE: American National Election Studies Cumulative Data File, 1995–2012; for 2014, the Cooperative Congressional Election Study.

conservative media antagonists; Democrats' approval of his performance rose to its highest level since early 2013 as he came under withering attack from the entire Republican field during the 2016 primary debates.

Electoral Consequences

The emergence of polarized partisanship has had profound electoral consequences. Extending a long-term trend, party loyalty in voting for all federal offices reached a postwar high in the two most recent elections (see Figure 1). In the 1970s, an average of 22 percent of self-identified partisans defected to the other party's candidates; since 2008, fewer than 10 percent have done so. In 2012, 91 percent of partisans voted for their party's presidential nominee; in 2014, 93 percent voted for their party's House and Senate candidates. Ticket splitting—voting for a presidential candidate of one party, a House or Senate candidate of the other—has consequently become increasingly rare. In the 1970s, about a quarter voted split tickets; in 2012, only 11 percent did so.

Voting congruence at the individual level produces congruent aggregate outcomes at the district and state levels. The correlation between the district-level vote shares of House and presidential candidates has risen from an average of .62 in the 1970s to .95 in 2012; the square of this correlation specifies the proportion of variance shared by the vote across these offices, which reached a remarkable

FIGURE 2
Presidential Voting and District Level Results, 1956–2012

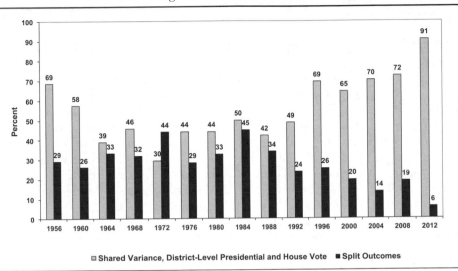

SOURCE: Compiled by author.

91 percent in 2012 (see Figure 2). Meanwhile, the proportion of districts delivering split verdicts—majorities for presidential candidate of one party, House candidates of the other—fell to a postwar low in 2012; only 26 of the 435 House districts produced split outcomes. House candidates now find it exceedingly difficult to win districts that lean even slightly toward the other party at the presidential level. In both 2012 and 2014, only twelve candidates won districts where their party's 2012 presidential candidate ran more than two points behind his national vote percentage. This represents a dramatic change from the 1970s, during which an average of more than fifty House candidates succeeded in winning districts against the partisan grain (Jacobson 2015b).

A similar, if less pronounced, trend appears in Senate elections; the state-level correlations between presidential and Senate voting in 2012 of .80 was exceeded only in 1956 in the postwar era (.82), and the state-level correlation between the 2012 presidential and 2014 Senate vote reached .87, the highest for any midterm on record. The incidence of split state-level outcomes has also declined steadily, and going into the 2016 election, 84 of the 100 senators were serving states won by their party's presidential candidate in the most recent election, another postwar record (Jacobson 2015b).

Electoral Coherence Produces Divided Government

The trends depicted in the previous section raise an obvious question: How did the electorate's extraordinary coherence during the two most recent elections nonetheless perpetuate divided government, with a Democratic president facing a solidly Republican House and, after 2014, Senate? The explanation for this apparent paradox lies in the distribution of partisans across electoral units; for the divided government in place today is not the result of ambivalent loyalties and preferences among voters, but of the way votes are aggregated by the electoral system.

In presidential elections, high rates of party-line voting favor whichever candidate represents the larger party in the electorate—always, according to American National Election Studies (ANES; 2010) data from 1952 through 2012, the Democrats (although sometimes by a tiny margin). The ANES and other major surveys found a clear Democratic advantage among party identifiers in 2012, and the distribution of partisans across the states also favored Democrats in the Electoral College (Jacobson 2015a). Extreme levels of party-line voting on both sides were thus a net plus for Obama, and demographic trends favoring the Democrats nationally suggest the same will generally be true for future Democratic candidates (Jacobson 2016a).

In congressional elections, however, party-line voting and electoral coherence strongly favor Republicans because they enjoy a major structural advantage in the distribution of partisans across congressional districts. Although Republican gerrymanders reinforced this advantage after the 2000 and 2010 censuses, it has existed for decades as a product of coalition demographics. Democrats win the lion's share of ethnic minority, single, young, secular, and LBGT voters who are concentrated in urban districts that deliver lopsided Democratic majorities. Regular Republican voters are spread more evenly across suburbs, smaller cities, and rural areas, so fewer Republican votes are "wasted" in highly skewed districts.

The result is illustrated by Figure 3, which shows that, except after 1964, substantially more House seats have leaned Republican than have leaned Democrat (leaning estimated here as having a district vote for their party's presidential candidate at least 2 percentage points above the national average) for at least six decades. This imbalance was as great in the 1970s as it is today, but with the rise of party-line voting and decline in ticket splitting, it has become much more consequential. Thus, although Obama won by nearly five million votes in 2012, Romney outpolled Obama in 226 districts, while Obama ran ahead in only 209. Democrats actually won a majority of the major-party vote cast nationally for House candidates that year, their share rising from 46.6 percent in 2010 to 50.7 percent in 2012; but with party loyalty so prevalent and split outcomes so rare, their share of seats grew only from 44.4 percent to 46.2 percent. Under the current configuration, Democrats would have to win all of the Democratic-leaning and balanced districts plus eight Republican-leaning districts to reach a majority in the House (218 seats).

The Republicans enjoy a similar if more modest structural advantage in Senate elections. Although Al Gore won (very slightly) more popular votes nationally than George W. Bush in 2000, Bush won more votes in thirty of the fifty states. In 2012, Obama, with five million more votes than Romney, won barely more than half the states (twenty-six). Notice that the proportion of closely balanced House districts in Figure 3 (those delivering presidential results within 2 percentage points of the national vote) has shrunk by nearly two-thirds since the 1980s

FIGURE 3
District Partisan Advantage, 1952–2014

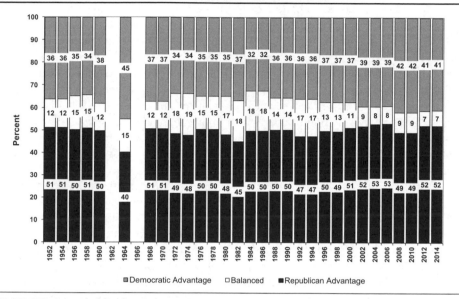

■ Democratic Advantage   □ Balanced   ■ Republican Advantage

SOURCE: Compiled by the author.

and after 2012 was below 7 percent. Although critics blame partisan gerrymandering for the trend, its main source is changes in voting behavior and residential
sorting, for it is equally evident at the state level (Abramowitz, Alexander, and
Gunning 2006; Jacobson 2016b). In 1976, twenty states, accounting for a total of
299 electoral votes, were won by less than 5 percentage points. In 2012, only four
states, with a total of 75 electoral votes, fell into this category (Abramowitz 2015,
22). The presidential "battleground" has become much smaller even as closely
contested presidential elections have become the norm.

Party Factions and Polarization in 2016

The pattern of highly competitive, partisan, polarized, and president-centered
national elections characteristic of twenty-first-century America has been challenged in 2016 by the emergence during the nominating campaigns of fissures
within the parties, much deeper on the Republican side but also visible among
Democrats. Hillary Clinton's anticipated coronation was turned into long slog by
Bernie Sanders's challenge from the Left. Sanders's growing appeal to young
white liberals cut Clinton's lead in national polls from an average of 25 points in
December to single digits in April. Clinton barely eked out a win in Iowa and lost
badly to Sanders in New Hampshire, states where liberal whites populate the
Democratic coalition. She ran much stronger than Sanders among older and

minority voters, and their numbers in subsequent primaries allowed her to survive these and later setbacks to take an insurmountable lead in votes and delegates, even as the Sanders challenge continued through the final primary in June.

For better or worse, Clinton was seen as the heir to Barack Obama, someone who had served in his administration and would defend or extend his major accomplishments on health care, economic regulation, diplomacy, the environment, and immigration. Although she made gestures to the Left in response to Sanders's progress, Clinton's long career was as a moderate Democrat whose orthodox positions placed her at the median of the Democrats' center-left coalition, just like Obama (RAND 2016). Her problems within the party were more about character than ideology; her responses to investigations into her use of a private email account while secretary of state and her Wall Street links fed the perception among many voters—including Democrats—that she was not trustworthy.[5]

Clinton's candidacy is not, then, by itself potentially disruptive of recent electoral configurations. She is nearly as polarizing as Obama, heir to that aspect of his presidency as well. Republicans have never warmed to Clinton, and they have been especially negative when she is running for president. By spring 2016, a 68-point gap in opinions of Clinton had opened up between partisans, with averages of 77 percent of Democrats but only 9 percent of Republicans viewing her favorably. With Republicans expressing such uniformly negative opinions of Clinton, she could not under normal circumstances be expected to win many cross-party votes. And despite some reservations, she would be an easy choice for the vast majority of Democratic partisans against any conventional Republican nominee. Such a matchup would have almost certainly extended the pattern of polarized partisanship characteristic of the Obama years.

Circumstances were anything but normal in 2016, however. Billionaire developer and entertainer Donald Trump executed a hostile takeover of the Republican Party that exposed its national leaders' impotence and disconnect from a large segment of the party's base. Trump rose to dominate the field by mobilizing and exploiting the anti-immigrant, anti-Mexican, anti-Muslim, anti-Obama, and anti-globalization sentiments simmering in a substantial subset of ordinary Republicans and not a few independents (e.g. Lee et al. 2016; Tesler 2016). His bullying, vulgar, hyperbolic trash talk, unleashed against detractors in both parties and the media, tapped into a rich vein of right-wing populist disdain for cultural, corporate, and political elites. That much of what he said was self-contradictory, wildly misinformed, or flatly untrue, and that his fantastic promises were untethered to any discernible reality, did not seem to faze his supporters in the least (Kessler 2016). Trump's approach invited comparisons with earlier American exploiters of populist bigotry, xenophobia, and fear, such as George Wallace and Pat Buchanan, as well as with current leaders of the nativist Right in European countries. The style and substance of Trump's campaign had even conservatives pondering the extent to which he should be considered a fascist (Douthat 2015; Lee 2015).[6]

Trump exposed a fault line in the Republican coalition that cut across ideology. He found backers in all of the party's ideological factions, but with support concentrated among less educated blue-collar Republicans, especially men, resentful of their eroding economic prospects and declining cultural centrality. Given

Trump's disdain for "losers," a label he applies liberally to his detractors, it was ironic though not surprising that his appeal was largely confined to Americans who felt like losers themselves (Pew 2016). Most of his supporters shared Trump's rejection of Republican economic orthodoxy, opposing changes in Social Security and Medicare, free trade, and deference to Wall Street and the U.S. Chamber of Commerce; they did not accept the conventional Republican dogma that the road to prosperity lies in tax cuts for the wealthy, deregulation, and open trade (Tesler 2016). The most powerful draw, however, was his promise of an immigration policy consisting of a wall on the Mexican border, mass expulsions, and exclusion of Muslims. For this, even many conservative Christians gave him a pass for his self-celebrated philandering, multiple marriages, questionable faith, and dubious commitment to their social issue agenda. When Trump vowed to "make American great again," many of his followers (and detractors) heard "make America white again."[7]

Trump's sustained lead in national polls appalled mainstream Republican leaders not only because of his unorthodox positions on economic issues, but even more so because of his potential effect on both the short- and long-term fortunes of their party. He excited a substantial and enthusiastic portion of the Republican base, but his appeal did not extend much beyond it. Overall opinions of Trump during the early primary season were the least favorable of any of the leading candidates among partisans in all categories; in polls taken in March and early April of 2016, an average 31 percent expressed a favorable opinion of him, 65 percent, an unfavorable one.[8] He had little crossover appeal; the incidence of unfavorable opinions among Democrats began high (typically more than 80 percent) and grew higher as the campaigns progressed, reaching an average of 87 percent in May and June. Trump's white, male, blue-collar constituency formed a smaller portion of the electorate than the minority groups he insulted and alienated.[9] The very characteristics that attracted his supporters repelled an even larger group of voters—white women and minorities.

Republican congressional leaders worried that Trump's nomination would bring disaster to the Republican ticket, threatening their control of the Senate and even the House (Kamisar 2015; Gerson 2015; Bernstein 2015; Cornwell 2016). They also rightly worried about its long-term implications for their party's future. As I note in my companion piece earlier in this volume, a party's choice of nominee (and platform) updates its popular image and thus attractiveness as an object of identification (Jacobson 2016c; 2016d). Trump's command of the Republican stage for so long in 2016 threatened to redefine who and what the Republican Party stands for in ways that would erode its long-term viability. The Republican autopsy of Romney's 2012 loss had recommended expanding the party's appeal to blacks, Asians, Latinos, women, gays, and young people (Walshe 2013). Trump's nomination had the exact opposite effect, but even if he had fallen short, the nomination contest's damage to the party's standing among these growing segments of the population would have continued to register.

Aside from Trump's danger to their party's electoral future, many mainstream Republican leaders and pundits were genuinely appalled by his character (Goldberg 2015; Will 2015b; Linker 2015). Columnist Peter Wehner, who had served in the Reagan and both Bush administrations, offered this critique: "Mr. Trump's virulent combination of ignorance, emotional instability, demagogy, solipsism and vindictiveness would do more than result in a failed presidency; it could very well lead to a national catastrophe. The prospect of Donald Trump as commander in chief should send a chill down the spine of every American. . . . If Mr. Trump heads the Republican Party, it will no longer be a conservative party, it will be an angry, bigoted, populist one" (Wehner 2016). No fewer than twenty-two "movement" conservative luminaries, including Glenn Beck, L. Brent Bozell III, Mona Charen, Erick Erikson, William Kristol, Yuval Levin, Edwin Meese III, John Podhoretz, and Thomas Sowell contributed to a *National Review* symposium denouncing Trump's candidacy (Conservatives against Trump 2016). Every living former Republican presidential candidate—both Bushes, Bob Dole, John McCain, and most vocally Mitt Romney—opposed his nomination as well.

Failing to derail Trump's nomination, the losing Republican candidates and other party leaders faced an agonizing choice: they could support a nominee many of them thought would be disastrous for the party (and, if he somehow won, for the country), or they could advocate an option that could only help Clinton: abstaining, voting for a conservative third-party candidate, or voting, however unhappily, for Clinton herself. Their dilemma was sharpened by the fact that Republican leaders, like ordinary Republican voters, disliked and distrusted Clinton and loathed the prospect of enduring what they envisioned as a third Obama term. Remarkably, even someone as scathing in his critique of Trump as Wehner said that even if Trump were the nominee, he would never vote for Hillary Clinton; absent an acceptable third party option, he would skip the presidential ballot (Wehner 2016). That Wehner found a vote for Clinton to be inconceivable despite his opinion of Trump serves as eloquent testimony to how polarized American political elites have become.

Ordinary Republicans not in the Trump camp faced the same unwelcome choices: vote loyally for their party's nominee, abstain from a presidential vote, stay home entirely, defect to a third party (should one be available), or defect to Clinton. Their decisions will determine how far the extraordinary partisan coherence observed in recent elections will recede. Democrats will be united behind Clinton by their desire to protect Obama's legacy and to keep a Republican they detest out of the White House. Clinton's main challenge will be to bring the younger white liberals who formed Sanders's main constituency and reliably Democratic minority voters to the polls.[10] Republican voters are, like their leaders, more divided. Whether they will stay that way is uncertain, but early in the election year they seemed much readier to desert Trump than Democrats were to desert Clinton. In polls taken in March, an average of 87 percent of Democrats said that they would vote for Clinton, whereas only 77 percent of Republicans said that they would vote for Trump.[11] It was numbers like this—and the fact that Clinton was beating Trump by a wider margin than any of the other Republican prospects in horse-race polls—that had Republican leaders so concerned.

A prime worry was that a Trump candidacy would cost them the Senate and perhaps even the House. Their concern was not unfounded in light of the low levels of ticket splitting in recent elections, but party loyalty has also been very high in House and Senate elections, so these two tendencies would be in tension. Whether Republicans and independents who reject Trump will also desert Republican congressional candidates is another crucial question that only the election can answer. Historical experience offers a mixed picture when party-splitting insurgents win nominations. In 1964, according to the ANES, 27 percent of Republicans voted for Lyndon Johnson rather than Barry Goldwater. Of these presidential defectors, 61 percent also defected to the Democratic House candidate, and Republicans lost 47 of the 158 seats they defended in districts won by Johnson. In 1972, 41 percent of Democrats voted for Richard Nixon rather than George McGovern; but only 27 percent of the defectors also voted for the Republican House candidate, and Democrats lost only 15 of the 191 seats they defended in districts won by Nixon. The Goldwater precedent is of course what worries Republican leaders the most, as it should; for the 1964 election took place in an era when, as now, ticket splitting was relatively uncommon, whereas by 1972 split-ticket voting had become much more prevalent (see Figure 1).

Still, in light of the Republicans' formidable structural advantage in the House, it would take a truly disastrous performance by the Republican presidential candidate to cost them control. The Democrats would have to pick up at least thirty seats, which would require, as noted earlier, winning all of the Democratic-leaning and balanced districts plus eight Republican-leaning districts. Based on the 2014 vote, it would take an across-the-board swing of about 7 percentage points to put the Republican's vote share below 50 percent in a majority of the districts. In June 2016, the authoritative *Cook Political Report*, which classifies all House districts according to their competitiveness, listed thirty-three Republican seats at some risk—two rated likely Democrat, three leaning Democrat, seventeen toss-ups, and eleven leaning Republican—so that Democrats would have to sweep all but three of these seats to reach thirty (*Cook Political Report* 2016). The more of the at-risk Republican seats Democrats failed to take, the more of the likely or solidly Republican seats they would have to win. It is not impossible for the House to change hands in 2016, but it would take a huge pro-Democratic tsunami to make it happen. A Trump candidacy holds the potential to generate one—if he remains as unpopular as he was during the first half of 2016 and especially if disaffected Republicans stay home in droves—but it is by no means a sure thing.

The Senate is a different story. In 1964, Republicans netted a loss of only two Senate seats during the Goldwater rout, but twenty-six of the thirty-five contested seats were already held by Democrats. In 1972, amid rampant ticket splitting, Democrats actually won two additional Senate seats. This year's Senate lineup is the inverse of 1964, with twenty-four Republican but only ten Democratic seats in play. Seven of the Republican seats are in states won by Obama in 2012, comprising six of the seven Republican seats Cook listed in June as being at risk (six toss up, one leaning Republican). Two Democratic seats were also deemed competitive (one toss up, one leaning Democratic). Thus even with only a modest wind at their backs, the Democrats have a reasonable chance of gaining the four additional seats they would need to control the Senate (assuming they also win the White House and their vice president can break ties). With a real blowout, they could reach a solid majority. Whatever happens in the presidential election, the contest for control of the Senate will be, if recent experience is any guide, extraordinarily intense and wildly expensive, with the many millions of dollars spent independently by outside groups dwarfing the already ample spending by the candidates in states where the outcome is in any doubt (Jacobson and Carson 2016, 91–96).[12] It will be fascinating to see how, and how effectively, the Republican Senate campaigns conducted by candidates and their independent allies in blue and purple states deal with the crosscurrents generated by the Trump insurgency.

Trump's most serious rival among the other sixteen original aspirants turned out to be Texas senator Ted Cruz, another highly polarizing figure with very few friends among national Republican elites, but for somewhat different reasons (Jacobson 2016a). His candidacy, though unsuccessful, is worth reviewing, because should Trump lose, Cruz is almost certain to pursue nomination again in 2020 and, based on his showing in 2016, would be a leading prospect. As with Trump, Republicans worried that Cruz's candidacy would hurt the party's down-ticket candidates. Cruz began his campaign with very few friends among national Republican leaders, earning the title of "most hated man in the Senate" (Grieder 2013), through demagoguery and personal insults to members on both sides; no senator endorsed him during the preprimary season. Cruz's avowed strategy for winning the general election was to adopt radically conservative positions on virtually every issue and to use apocalyptic, fear-mongering rhetoric to mobilize white middle- and working-class social, religious, and anti-government conservatives who, his campaign claimed, have stayed home in past presidential elections out of indifference to mainstream Republican candidates such as Bob Dole, John McCain, and Mitt Romney. This strategy's drawback for Republicans with long memories was that the last time the party tested the "missing conservative voter" hypothesis, with Barry Goldwater in 1964, the result was the worst Republican electoral debacle since 1936 (Will 2015a). Its premises are, as Republican campaign professionals are unhappily aware (Rove 2015), extremely shaky and would remain so in 2020, for its target constituency already turns out at comparatively high rates.

Cruz's approach was deliberately polarizing, adopting positions placing him further to the Right than any serious Republican candidate in the postwar era, including Goldwater. He would abolish the Departments of Education, Energy, Commerce, and Housing and Urban Development and the Internal Revenue Service. He would eliminate the estate tax and impose a flat 10 percent income tax and the equivalent of a 16 percent value added tax, providing a huge windfall to the wealthiest Americans while sharply reducing federal revenues; the ensuing deficit would be addressed by cuts in social programs for low-income people. He would ban abortion with no exception for rape and incest and work to overturn the right of same-sex couples to marry. He denies human-caused climate change and would roll back any environmental regulation that interfered with energy development. His policy on immigration echoed Trump's, building a wall along the border and denying legal status to any of the eleven million undocumented immigrants already in the country.[13] He would rescind Obama's protection of immigrants brought to the United States as children and eliminate birthright citizenship.

Cruz's rhetoric was as extreme as his program. Its theme was that America is in horrible shape and only a radical return to an imagined pre–New Deal world of small government and state sovereignty would reverse its downward trajectory. The government is not just the problem (Reagan's formulation) but the tyrannical enemy. After one Democratic debate in late 2015, Cruz said, "We're seeing our freedoms taken away every day, and last night was an audition for who would wear the jackboot most vigorously" (Cohen 2015). Cruz also sought support from conservative Christians, promising to defend them against the onslaught of seculars, Muslims, and gays, the last of whom he accused of waging "jihad" against opponents of same-sex marriage (Kutner 2015). There was, in short, nothing in Cruz's campaign suggesting any inclination or capacity to expand his or his party's appeal beyond its most conservative segments.

Cruz's emergence as Trump's strongest rival disconcerted national Republican leaders (and many but not all prominent conservative pundits) as much as Trump's rise to first place, their joint success regarded by some as a threat not only to the party's electoral fortunes in 2016 but to its very soul. Michael Gerson concluded that "for Republicans, the only good outcome of Trump vs. Cruz is for both to lose. The future of the party as a carrier of a humane, inclusive conservatism now depends on some viable choice beyond them" (Gerson 2016). Other prominent Republicans concurred (Rubin 2016; Kim and O'Brien 2016; see also Raju 2016). For David Brooks, "The worst is the prospect that one of them might somehow win. Very few presidents are so terrible that they genuinely endanger their own nation, but Trump and Cruz would go there and beyond" (Brooks 2016, A27).

A Cruz-Clinton contest would have generated somewhat more orthodox partisan divisions than a Trump-Clinton contest, but Cruz's extreme positions and rhetoric would still have been a burden to Republican congressional candidates because it promised to drive away moderate Republicans and independents without attracting a compensating share of Democrats. The Coldwater precedent would be even more apropos than for Trump, for Cruz split his party more along ideological than class lines. Republican denouncers of Trump and Cruz debated who would be the bigger drag on the Republican ticket (Martin 2016; Sherman and Bresnahan 2016), but both were viewed as posing major problems for Republican congressional candidates. Still, establishment Republicans and conservative pundits appeared to find it easier to reconcile a Cruz than a Trump nomination because the former did not challenge conservative economic dogmas and positions on social issues (except by taking them to further extremes) and, compared with Trump, seemed less dangerously ignorant and impulsive. Losing with Cruz would do less long-term damage to the party than losing with Trump.

As the chances of candidates more acceptable to the Republican establishment faded—only John Kasich's candidacy remained alive after Rubio's humiliating defeat in Florida on March 15—the looming prospect of a Trump nomination generated talk among some Republican leaders and conservative commentators of creating a third party option for Republicans repulsed by Trump but unable to stomach voting for Clinton. That this would hand the election to Clinton was acknowledged, but the hope was that it would protect Republican congressional candidates by giving Republicans refusing to vote for Trump a reason to come to the polls. It would also provide a spokesperson for the party's conventionally conservative positions that congressional candidates could point to while rejecting association with a candidate whose persona or agenda would be poison locally (Burns 2016; Friedersdorf 2016). An alternative strategy was to somehow prevent Trump from winning a delegate majority, producing a brokered convention that could pick a candidate more acceptable than Trump or Cruz. Trump's string of victories after he lost Wisconsin on April 5 rendered that strategy moot. Even if deals at the convention succeeded in denying Trump the nomination despite his plurality of delegates, many of his supporters, already disdainful of the party establishment, would certainly have revolted, either staying home or supporting an independent Trump candidacy, again with fatal consequences for the Republican nominee. Cruz, with the second most delegates, would have demanded the nomination were it denied to Trump, and any other choice would anger his supporters as well. Considering their likely consequences, that such scenarios received serious contemplation underlines how badly Trump's ascendancy fractured the Republican coalition.

A Divisive General Election

An election pitting Clinton against Trump promises to be nasty and highly divisive. As they clinched their nominations, Clinton and Trump were underwater on favorability, more so than any previous nominees (Wright 2016). In polls taken in May and early June, net favorability averaged –25 for Trump and –12 for Clinton. When an ABC News/*Washington Post* survey asked in early March whether respondents could see themselves supporting any of then-remaining candidates, the collective response was effectively "none of the above" (see Figure 4). Among partisans, 17 percent of Democrats said they could not see themselves supporting Clinton; among Republicans, 33 percent could not see themselves supporting Cruz, and a remarkable 42 percent could not see themselves supporting Trump. That Trump nonetheless steamrolled his way to the nomination despite these numbers is truly astonishing.

With most voters expressing negative views of both nominees, the obvious general election strategy for both sides will be to do everything possible to drive up their rival's negatives even further. To win, Trump will have to induce a majority of voters to dislike and distrust Clinton even more than they dislike and distrust him. The Republican campaign and its independent allies will try to whip up fear and persuade the fearful that they and the country would be in mortal danger from ISIS and other enemies if Clinton were to become president. We will hear much about unprotected emails and Benghazi as vehicles to attack Clinton's honesty and judgment.

Clinton's obvious campaign strategy against Trump is also personal, dwelling on what offends people (including many Republicans) about him already: his

FIGURE 4
Potential Support for Candidates in the General Election

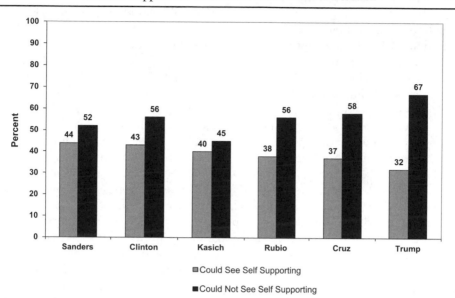

SOURCE: ABC News/*Washington Post* Poll, March 3–6, 2016.

narcissism, instability, ignorance, bigotry, misogyny, authoritarian instincts, checkered business record, and brazen indifference to truth. On policy, expect a spirited defense of Obama's achievements against Republican pledges to destroy them root and branch, particularly if Obama's approval ratings remain in positive territory. The goal will be to mobilize women, younger voters, religious and ethnic minorities, and moderates against the dire threat posed to their values and interests by Trump in the White House.

Is There an End to Stalemate and Gridlock?

As it is shaping up, the 2016 election has no prospect of reducing national divisions, although a Trump candidacy may shift the axis of polarization within the electorate away from the strict party lines that has been the norm during this century. What are the election's chances of ending gridlock in Washington? The current stalemate could be broken in several ways. A Clinton victory combined with a Democratic takeover of the House and Senate is one scenario. It would replicate the configurations of the 103rd (1993–94) and 111th (2009–10) Congresses, which enabled Democrats to advance their traditional agenda, particularly in the 111th, with the Affordable Care Act and reforms of the financial system. But these precedents suggest that a unified Democratic government, although capable of important legislative achievements, would be short lived. Given the Republicans' structural advantage, Democrats can only win a House majority by taking a significant number of Republican-leaning House districts, which would be difficult to retain in the 2018 midterm when a flawed Republican presidential candidate no longer heads the ticket and the electorate is predictably older, whiter, and more Republican.

Another possibility is a Republican presidential victory, which would almost certainly be accompanied by the party's retention of the House and Senate. It is entirely unclear how a Trump presidency would affect gridlock, partly because his policy proposals are vague and undeveloped, partly because he would face opposition within his own party's congressional ranks as well as from Democrats to many of his stated objectives. How conventional conservatives such as House Speaker Paul Ryan, Senate Majority Leader Mitch McConnell, and most of the members they lead would respond to Trump's specific proposals for undoing the Affordable Care Act, imposing tariffs, banning Muslim immigrants, and funding a national roundup of undocumented immigrants and the construction of a massive wall on the Mexican border is impossible to predict with any confidence. Trump's ability to rally the public behind any of these proposals would be limited by the fact that a majority of Americans do not support them. An ostensibly unified Republican government would probably be anything but unified in practice, continuing the bitter intraparty conflicts displayed in the 113th Congress, costing John Boehner his speakership, and in the contest for the nomination. If Trump were to nonetheless prevail with Congress, national policy would undergo some truly radical and extraordinarily divisive changes.

Ironically, however, the most likely outcome is that despite all the discontent, anger, and disdain for politics and politicians roiling the electorate in 2016, something close to the status quo will prevail: a Democratic president with politics nearly identical to Obama's facing Republican House and perhaps Senate majorities adamantly opposed to the president but hamstrung by internal divisions over policy and tactics. Hillary Clinton should be the favorite to win, but even if she does, the Republicans' structural advantage is likely to keep at least the House in Republican hands, with most of the familiar players and problems returning once again when the new Congress convenes in 2017. The same configuration that fueled the Trump and Sanders insurgencies would be back in place.

Notes

1. Based on thirty-six Gallup, CBS News/*New York Times*, Pew, and CNN polls.

2. According to the January 4–10, 2016, NBC News/Survey Monkey poll, 85 percent of Trump supporters strongly disapproved of Obama's performance, second only to Ted Cruz's supporters (90 percent; Clinton, Englehardt, and Lapinski 2016). Trump supporters were especially prone to delusions about Obama's religion and birthplace; a September 2015 Public Policy Polling survey reported that among Republican Trump supporters (29 percent in this poll), 66 percent said Obama was a Muslim, and 61 percent said he was foreign-born. Among all Republicans, the respective figures were 54 percent and 44 percent.

3. For example, Democratic respondents place themselves, Obama, and the Democratic Party at very similar locations on the American National Election Studies 7-point liberal-conservative and issues scales (ANES 2010).

4. Averages from Gallup, CBS/*New York Times*, Quinnipiac, and ABC News/*Washington Post* polls from January through June 2016, compiled by author.

5. In the CBS New/*New York Times* poll taken February 12–16, 2016, 60 percent of Democrats deemed Clinton "honest and trustworthy," but 35 percent said she was not; the comparable figures for Bernie Sanders were 77 and 13; see http://www.cbsnews.com/news/cbs-news-national-poll-hillary-clinton-holds-lead-over-bernie-sanders/.

6. The general verdict was that he is more of a "proto-fascist," because despite similarities in style and approach with the likes of Mussolini, he has not formed a paramilitary wing to support his movement and has not proposed abolishing American democracy (although he appears ignorant or disdainful of its institutional checks).

7. Prominent white supremacists were among Trump's most enthusiastic supporters (Mahler 2016).

8. Average is from eleven ABC News/*Washington Post*, Bloomberg, Gallup, NBC News/*Wall Street Journal*, Quinnipiac, YouGov, and Associated Press GfK polls.

9. The share of white voters with no more than a high school education and anti-immigrant views (defined as falling below the median of .57 on the immigration scale from Table 1) in the 2014 Cooperative Congressional Election Study (Ansolabehere 2015) was 17 percent (9 percent if confined to males); the proportion of nonwhites was 21 percent, a share certain to be higher in 2016.

10. Younger voters are not Trump fans; their average ratio of favorable to unfavorable opinions of Trump in the January and February YouGov polls was 21:71, and this includes all voters under 30, not just Democrats; but younger voters are also notoriously harder to get to the polls than older voters.

11. Averages are from ABC News/*Washington Post*, CBS News/*New York Times*, CNN, Quinnipiac, and YouGov surveys taken in March 2016.

12. More than 59 percent of the astonishing $667 million spent in the nine most competitive Senate races in 2014 were not under the candidate's control.

13. He did not, however, endorse Trump's police-state proposal to organize a force of federal agents to round up and quickly expel every man, woman, and child among them.

References

Abrams, Samuel J., and Morris P. Fiorina. 2015. Party sorting: The foundation of polarized politics. In *American gridlock: the sources, character, and impact of polarization*, eds. James A. Thurber and Antoine Yoshinaka, 113–29. New York, NY: Cambridge University Press.

Abramowitz, Alan I. 2010. *The disappearing center: Engaged citizens, polarization, and American democracy*. New Haven, CT: Yale University Press.

Abramowitz, Alan I. 2015. The new American electorate: Partisan, sorted, and polarized. In *American gridlock: the sources, character, and impact of polarization*, eds. James A. Thurber and Antoine Yoshinaka, 19–44. New York, NY: Cambridge University Press.

Abramowitz, Alan I., Brad Alexander, and Matthew Gunning. 2006. Incumbency, redistricting, and the decline of competition in U.S. House elections. *Journal of Politics* 68 (1): 75–88.

Abramowitz, Alan I., and Steven W. Webster. 2016. The rise of negative partisanship and the nationalization of U.S. elections in the 21st century. *Electoral Studies* 41 (1): 12–22.

Agiesta, Jennifer. 14 September 2015. Misperceptions persist about Obama's faith, but aren't so widespread. CNN.

American National Election Studies. 2010. Time series cumulative data file [dataset]. Stanford University and the University of Michigan [producers and distributors]. Available from www.electionstudies.org.

Ansolabehere, Stephen. 2015. Cooperative congressional election study, 2014: Common content. [Computer file] Release 1: April 15, 2015. Cambridge, MA: Harvard University [producer] Available from http://cces.gov.harvard.edu.

Axelrod, David. 25 January 2016. The Obama theory of Trump. *New York Times*, A21.

Baumer, Donald C., and Howard J. Gold. 2010. *Parties, polarization, and democracy in the United States*. Boulder, CO: Paradigm Publishers.

Bernstein, Jonathan. 2015. The Trump effect begins to hit Congress. *Bloomberg Politics*. Available from http://www.bloombergview.com.

Bishop, Bill. 2008. *The big sort: Why the clustering of like-minded America is tearing us apart*. Boston MA: Houghton Mifflin.

Bradberry, Leigh, and Gary C. Jacobson. 2013. The Tea Party and the 2012 presidential election. *Electoral Studies* 40 (4): 500–508.

Brooks, David. 12 January 2016. The brutalism of Ted Cruz. *New York Times*, A27.

Burns, Alexander. 2 March 2016. Anti-Trump Republicans call for a third-party option. *New York Times*.

Clinton, Josh, Drew Englehardt, and John Lapinski. 12 January 2016. Poll: Obama approval depends on voter characteristics. Available from http://www.msnbc.com/msnbc/poll-obama-approval-depends-voter-characteristics.

CNN. 10 December 2012. *President: Full results: Exit polls*. Available from http://www.cnn.com.

Cohen, Michael A. 15 October 2015. Ted Cruz hits low point in Republican rhetoric. *Boston Globe*.

Conservatives against Trump. 21 January 2016. *National Review Online*. Available from http://c7.nrostatic .com.

Cook Political Report. 2016. House race ratings for 17 June 2016; Senate race ratings for 10 June 2016. Washington, DC.

Cornwell, Susan. 15 January 2016. Republican lawmakers worry about running on Trump's coattails. *Yahoo News*. Available from news.yahoo.com.

Douthat, Ross. 3 December 2015. Is Donald Trump a fascist? *New York Times*.

Dugan, Andrew. 2015. *Conservative Republicans alone on global warming timing*. Gallup. Available from http://www.gallup.com.

Friedersdorf, Conor. 24 February 2016. Will U.S. conservatives mount a third-party challenge if Trump is the nominee? *The Atlantic*. Available from http://www.theatlantic.com.

Gallup. 2016. *Election polls – Presidential vote by groups*. Available from http://www.gallup.com/poll/139880/Election-Polls-Presidential-Vote-Groups.aspx.

Gerson, Michael. 13 August 2015. Trump declares war on America's demography. *Washington Post*. Available from https://www.washingtonpost.com.

Gerson, Michael. 18 January 2016. For the sake of the Republican Party, both Trump and Cruz must lose. *Washington Post*.

Goldberg, Jonah. 15 September 2015. No movement that embraces Trump can call itself conservative. *National Review*. Available from http://www.nationalreview.com.

Graham, Jesse, Jonathan Haidt, and Brian A. Nosek. 2009. Liberals and conservatives rely on different sets of moral foundations. *Journal of Personality and Social Psychology* 96 (5): 1029–46.

Grieder, Erica. 1 April 2013. The most hated man in the Senate. *Foreign Policy*. Available from http://foreignpolicy.com.

Hetherington, Marc J., and Jonathan D. Weiler. 2015. Authoritarianism and polarization in American politics, still? In *American gridlock: The sources, character, and impact of polarization*, eds. James A. Thurber and Antoine Yoshinaka, 86–112. New York, NY: Cambridge University Press.

Jacobson, Gary C. 2011. *A divider, not a uniter: George W. Bush and the American people*. 2nd ed. New York, NY: Longman.

Jacobson, Gary C. 2012a. The president's effect on partisan attitudes. *Presidential Studies Quarterly* 42 (4): 683–718.

Jacobson, Gary C. 2012b. Polarization, public opinion and the presidency: The Obama and anti-Obama coalitions. In *The Obama presidency: Appraisals and prospects*, eds. Bert A. Rockman, Andrew Rudalevige, and Colin Campbell, 94–121. Washington, DC: CQ Press.

Jacobson, Gary C. 2013. Partisan polarization in American politics: A background paper. *Presidential Studies Quarterly* 43 (4): 688–708.

Jacobson, Gary C. 2015a. Barack Obama and the nationalization of electoral politics in 2012. *Electoral Studies* 40 (4): 471–81.

Jacobson, Gary C. 2015b. Obama and nationalized electoral politics in the 2014 midterm. *Political Science Quarterly* 130 (1): 1–26.

Jacobson, Gary C. 2016a. Age, race, party, and ideology: Generational imprinting during the Obama presidency. Paper presented at the annual meeting of the Midwest Political Science Association, April 7–10, Chicago, IL.

Jacobson, Gary C. 2016b. Partisanship, money, and competition: Elections and the transformation of congress since the 1970s. In *Congress Reconsidered*. 11th ed., eds. Lawrence C. Dodd and Bruce I. Oppenheimer. Thousand Oaks CA: Sage Publications.

Jacobson, Gary C. 2016c. The coevolution of affect toward presidents and their parties. *Presidential Studies Quarterly* 46 (2): 1–29.

Jacobson, Gary C. 2016d. The Obama legacy and the future of partisan conflict: Demographic change and generational imprinting. *The ANNALS of the American Academy of Political and Social Science* (this volume).

Jacobson, Gary C., and Jamie L. Carson. 2016. *The politics of congressional elections*. 9th ed. New York, NY: Rowman & Littlefield.

Kam, Cindy D., and Donald R. Kinder. 2012. Ethnocentrism as a short-term force in the 2008 American presidential election. *American Journal of Political Science* 56 (1): 326–40.

Kamisar, Ben. 2 December 2015. GOP memo says what to do if Trump is nominee. *The Hill*.

Kessler, Glenn. 15 January 2016. Fact checking the 2016 presidential hopefuls. *Washington Post*. Available from https://www.washingtonpost.com.

Kim, Seung Min, and Connor O'Brien. 21 January 2016. Graham: Choice between Trump, Cruz like "being shot or poisoned." *Politico*. Available from http://www.politico.com.

Kutner, Jenny. 10 April 2015. Ted Cruz: Gay community is waging a "jihad" against people of faith. *Salon*. Available from http://www.salon.com.

Lee, M. J. 25 November 2015. Why some conservatives say Trump talk is fascist. CNN. Available from http://www.cnn.com.

Lee, M. J., Sara Murray, Jeremy Diamond, Noah Gray, and Tal Kopan. 27 January 2016. Why I'm voting for Trump. CNN. Available from http://www.cnn.com.

Levendusky, Matthew. 2009. *The partisan sort: How liberals became Democrats and conservatives became Republicans*. Chicago, IL: University of Chicago Press.

Linker, Damon. 9 December 2015. Why conservative pundits hate Donald Trump. *The Week*. Available from http://theweek.com.

Mahler, Jonathan. 29 February 2016. Donald Trump's message resonates with white supremacists. *New York Times*.

Martin, Jonathan. 16 January 2016. Donald Trump or Ted Cruz? Republicans argue over who is the greater threat. *New York Times*.

Pasek, Josh, Jon A. Krosnick, and Trevor Thompson. 2012. The impact of anti-black racism on approval of Barack Obama's job performance and on voting in the 2012 presidential election. Unpublished manuscript, Stanford University.

Pew Research Center. 2013. *GOP deeply divided about climate change*. Research report. Washington, DC: Pew Research Center.

Pew Research Center. 2014. *Political polarization in the American public*. Research report. Washington, DC: Pew Research Center.

Pew Research Center. 2016. *Campaign exposes fissures over issues, values and how life has changed in the U.S.* Research report. Washington, DC: Pew Research Center.

Piston, Spencer. 2010. How explicit racial prejudice hurt Obama in the 2008 election. *Political Behavior* 33 (4): 432–51.

Poole, Keith T., Howard Rosenthal, and Christopher Hare. 16 January 2016. More on polarization through the 114th. Voteviewblog.

Raju, Manu. 12 January 2016. The Ted Cruz pile on: GOP senators warn of revolt should he win the nomination. CNN.

RAND. 27 January 2016. Despite "outsider" popularity, voters see little difference between candidates on ideology. Available from http://www.rand.org/news/press.

Rove, Karl. 1 April 2015. The myth of the stay-at-home Republicans. *Wall Street Journal*.

Rubin, Jennifer. 19 January 2016. Does the GOP want a hater as president? *Washington Post*.

Sherman, Jake, and John Bresnahan. 13 January 2016. Pollster: Cruz would hurt Republican House hopefuls most. *Politico*. Available from http://www.politico.com.

Stonecash, Jeffrey M., Mark D. Brewer, and Mack D. Mariani. 2003. *Diverging parties: Social change, realignment, and party polarization*. Boulder CO: Westview Press.

Tesler, Michael. 2013. The return of old-fashioned racism to white Americans' partisan preferences in the early Obama era. *Journal of Politics* 75 (1): 110–23.

Tesler, Michael. 27 January 2016. A newly released poll shows the populist power of Donald Trump. The Monkey Cage, *Washington Post*.

Tesler, Michael, and David O. Sears. 2010. *The 2008 election and the dream of a post-racial America*. Chicago IL: University of Chicago Press.

Tien, Charles, Richard Nadeau, and Michael S. Lewis-Beck. 2012. Obama and 2012: Still a racial cost to pay? *PS: Political Science and Politics* 45 (4): 591–5.

Walshe, Shushanna. 13 March 2013. RNC completes "autopsy" on 2012 loss, calls for inclusion not policy change. *ABC News*.

Wehner, Peter. 14 January 2016. Why I will never vote for Donald Trump. *New York Times*.

Weisberg, Herbert F., and Christopher Divine. 2009. Racial attitude effects on voting in the 2008 presidential election: Examining the unconventional factors shaping vote choice in a most unconventional election. Paper presented at the Mershon Conference on the Transformative Election of 2008, October 1–4, Columbus, OH.

Will, George. 1 April 2015 (2015a) Cruz's electoral theory doesn't add up. *National Review*.

Will, George. 12 August 2015 (2015b). Donald Trump is a counterfeit Republican. *Washington Post*.

Wright, David. 22 March 2016. Poll: Trump, Clinton score historic unfavorable ratings. *CNN Politics*. Available from http://www.cnn.com.

SAGE Deep Backfile Package

Content ownership is becoming increasingly important in hard budgetary times. Investing in the SAGE Deep Backfile Package means owning access to over 400 SAGE journal backfiles.

5 good reasons to own the deep archive from SAGE...

1. Breadth

SAGE has collected over 400 journal backfiles, including over 500,000 articles of historical content covering interdisciplinary subjects in business, humanities, socials science, and science, technology and medicine.

2. Depth

SAGE's deep backfile coverage goes to volume 1, issue 1; through the last issue of 1998 (content from January 1999 to the present is included in the current subscription). You will own content spanning over a century of research. Our oldest article is from 1879 in **Perspectives in Public Health** (formerly *The Journal of the Royal Society for the Promotion of Health*).

3. Quality

We pride ourselves on high-quality content, meeting our markets' need for interdisciplinary, peer-reviewed, journal backfiles to provide your library. Close to 50% of the journals in the entire **SAGE Deep Backfile Package** are ranked in the Thomson Reuters Journal Citation Reports®.

4. Award-winning *SAGE Journals* online delivery platform

Materials are easy to find on *SAGE Journals* (SJ), hosted on the prestigious HighWire Press platform.

5. Pricing

We offer **flexible backfile purchase and lease options** to accommodate library budgets of all sizes. This package option offers the most value for your money, including great savings off list price for individual journal backfile purchases.

Need something more specific?

Titles included in the **SAGE Deep Backfile Package** are also available in smaller, discipline-specific packages:

- **Humanities and Social Science (HSS) Backfile Package**

- **Scientific, Technical, and Medical (STM) Backfile Package**

- **Health Sciences Backfile Package**

- **Clinical Medicine Backfile Package**

For more information, contact
librarysales@sagepub.com